Cases in Clinical Forensic Psychology

MARGO C. WATT

UNIVERSITY OF TORONTO PRESS
Toronto Buffalo London

Toronto Buffalo London
utorontopress.com

ISBN 978-1-4875-4277-1 (cloth) ISBN 978-1-4875-4279-5 (EPUB)
ISBN 978-1-4875-4278-8 (paper) ISBN 978-1-4875-4280-1 (PDF)

Library and Archives Canada Cataloguing in Publication

Title: Cases in clinical forensic psychology / Margo C. Watt.
Names: Watt, Margo C., author.
Description: Includes bibliographical references and index.
Identifiers: Canadiana (print) 20230478999 | Canadiana (ebook) 20230479049 | ISBN 9781487542771 (cloth) | ISBN 9781487542788 (paper) | ISBN 9781487542795 (EPUB) | ISBN 9781487542801 (PDF)
Subjects: LCSH: Forensic psychology – Canada – Case studies. | LCSH: Clinical psychology – Canada – Case studies. | LCSH: Criminal justice, Administration of – Canada – Case studies. | LCGFT: Case studies.
Classification: LCC RA1148.W38 2024 | DDC 614/.15–dc23

Cover design: Lind Design
Cover image: iStock.com/agsandrew

We welcome comments and suggestions regarding any aspect of our publications – please feel free to contact us at news@utorontopress.com or visit us at utorontopress.com.

Every effort has been made to contact copyright holders; in the event of an error or omission, please notify the publisher.

We wish to acknowledge the land on which the University of Toronto Press operates. This land is the traditional territory of the Wendat, the Anishnaabeg, the Haudenosaunee, the Métis, and the Mississaugas of the Credit First Nation.

University of Toronto Press acknowledges the financial support of the Government of Canada and the Ontario Arts Council, an agency of the Government of Ontario, for its publishing activities.

ONTARIO ARTS COUNCIL
CONSEIL DES ARTS DE L'ONTARIO
an Ontario government agency
un organisme du gouvernement de l'Ontario

Funded by the Government of Canada
Financé par le gouvernement du Canada
Canada

CASES IN CLINICAL FORENSIC PSYCHOLOGY

For Noah and Nipsy

Contents

Introduction: A Brief History of Clinical Forensic Psychology in Canada

With Preet Banga

Professor T. is a Belgian TV drama about an eccentric professor of criminal psychology at the University of Antwerp. Professor Jasper Teerlinck is a consultant for the local police. While assisting with a difficult rape case, a homicide investigator (one of his former students) tells Professor T that "Quinsey, Rice, and Harris claim that only 23% of sex offenders reoffend." Professor T retorts: "Quinsey, Rice, and Harris are idiots. They only take reported offences into account." Of course, TV is not real and Quinsey, Rice, and Harris (1995) are not idiots. Being referenced in such a popular series, however, might be the equivalent of celebrity status for Canadian clinical forensic psychologists.

Clinical forensic psychology refers to the application of clinical psychology research and practice (assessment, diagnosis, treatment, consultation) in the criminal justice context. The term captures the integration of clinical psychology as an applied professional discipline (scientist-practitioner model) and forensic psychology as an experimental discipline. According to Nesca (2022), the subdiscipline of clinical forensic psychology formally emerged in 2001 following APA's certification of forensic psychology as a specialized application of clinical psychology (see https://www.apa.org/ed/graduate/specialize). The term is intended to include correctional psychology, police psychology, and legal psychology, all of which are represented in cases throughout this book. Illustrative of the evolution of the term and the integration of the two fields, some chapters in this book have a greater focus on clinical psychology, while others lean more heavily on legal and correctional psychology. This book assumes a broad definition of clinical forensic psychology that is intended to include all those who conduct research and/or practise with criminal justice–involved populations or individuals at risk for involvement with any sphere of the legal system – criminal, civil, or correctional.

The rapidly increasing usage of the term clinical forensic psychology is evidenced by a cursory APA PsycInfo search. Whereas there were 63 entries between 1950 and 2000, there are 588 entries between 1950 and 2022 – 525 entries since 2000 alone. While the vast majority of these entries are *clinical AND forensic*, *forensic AND clinical*, or *forensic clinical*, clinical forensic psychology is emerging as the preferred term.

A recent article by Hill and Demetrioff (2019) titled "Clinical Forensic Psychology in Canada" describes the findings of a survey of 110 Canadian clinical forensic psychologists. Most were working in correctional facilities, independent practice, forensic hospitals, and outpatient forensic clinics. Within these settings, the most frequently performed types of psychological evaluations were violence risk assessments (70%), general risk assessments (54%), and presentence assessments (30%). Clinical forensic psychologists conduct other types of assessments, such as dangerous offender assessments (Criminal Code, 1992, Section 760; see chapter 7) and youth forensic assessments (Youth Criminal Justice Act, 2002). Unlike their counterparts in the United States and elsewhere (see Pouls et al., 2022), however, Canadian practitioners have been largely excluded from conducting fitness to stand trial and criminal responsibility assessments. Although the Criminal Code of Canada (CCC; Section 672) allows for these to be done by "a medical practitioner or any other person who has been designated by the Attorney General," historically, this has been interpreted to mean "medical practitioner." A recent Canadian Psychology Association Task Force (see Roesch et al., 2019) petitioned the federal government to change Section 672 to allow these assessments to be conducted by a "qualified mental health professional," which would include clinical forensic psychologists. This change would bring consistency with other sections of the CCC, and would improve access of accused persons and the courts to qualified assessors – including trained clinical forensic psychologists, some of whom have been instrumental in developing measures that comprise part of these assessments (e.g., Fitness Interview Test-Revised; Roesch et al., 2006).

While Canada may lag behind other countries with respect to certain clinical forensic practices, it has always punched well above its weight with its number of influential clinical forensic psychology researchers and practitioners. In an invited address to the 2013 convention of the Canadian Psychological Association, J. Thomas Dalby (Athabasca University) traced the genesis of forensic psychology (including in Canada) to Hugo Münsterberg and his seminal work, *On the Witness Stand* (1909a) – a collection of magazine articles that champions the application of psychology to the law. Of course, Münsterberg's contributions extended to correctional, clinical, and industrial-organizational psychology with books such as *Psychology and Crime* (1909b), *Psychotherapy* (1909c), and *Psychology and Industrial Efficiency* (1913). In a published article based on the speech, Dalby (2014) included a list of Canadian affiliated contributors to the science of forensic psychology (see table 0.1).

Throughout the present book are references to many of the giants whose names are included in Dalby's (2014) list, such as Steve Porter and Robert Hare (Psychopathy Checklist; see chapter 9), Donald Dutton (paranoia and violence; see chapter 10), and Ron Roesch (criminal responsibility; see chapter 6). Also included are references to names not on Dalby's list but who advance and promote the field of clinical forensic psychology through their various research and practice activities. These individuals include Mary Ann Campbell (University of New Brunswick); Veronica Stinson, Meg Ternes, and Marc Patry (Saint Mary's University; see chapter 1); Jane Barker (Nipissing University; see chapter 7); and Chris Mushquash (Lakehead University; see chapter 2). Contributors to many of the chapters in this book include current and former undergraduate and graduate students who represent the bright future for the discipline. These students include Jessica Doyle (University of New Brunswick); Marie-Claire Leclerc (University of Ottawa); Claire Keenan (Saint Mary's University); Tamara Speth and Angelina MacLellan (Dalhousie University); Juliana Khoury (University of Regina); Ethan Draper, Elle Lévesque,

Table 0.1. Canadian affiliated contributors to the science of forensic psychology

Andrews	Hart	Paulhus
Barbaree	Helmus	Porter
Bennell	Hemphill	Pozzulo
Boer	Jaffe	Quinsey
Bonta	Kingston	Read
Book	Koch	Rice
Brown	Kroner	Roesch
Bruck	Kropp	Schneider
Camilleri	Langevin	Schuller
Coles	Laws	Serin
Connolly	Leschied	Serran
Cotton	Lindsay	Seto
Cupchik	Looman	Spidel
Cutler	Marshall	Tombaugh
Dalby	Mills	Viljoen
Douglas	Moore	Webster
Dutton	Motiuk	Wells
Evans	Nesca	Williams
Firestone	Nicholaichuk	Wong
Forth	Nicholls	Woodworth
Gendreau	Nunes	Wormith
Gordon	Nussbaum	Yarmey
Hanson	Ogloff	Yuille
Hare	Olver	Zamble
Harris	Patrick	Zapf

Source: Dalby (2014).

Preet Banga, and Ryanne Chisholm (St. Francis Xavier University); and Christopher Lively (Memorial University of Newfoundland).

This book assumes an evidence-based approach and highlights how the science of clinical forensic psychology informs all aspects of criminal justice cases: police investigative techniques, eyewitness testimony, pretrial publicity, jury selection and decision-making, forensic evaluations and psychological autopsies, and mental health in corrections. Each chapter focuses on one or two cases that prompt the questions "How did this happen?" "Why did this happen?" and "What can we learn from what happened?" Case studies draw the reader up close and personal with the crime, the criminal, and the criminal justice system, providing an opportunity to examine the particulars of an event, an individual, a legal construct, a psychological phenomenon, and so forth in a more personally meaningful way. This approach is intended to challenge the reader to consider the various antecedents and consequences of events, and clinical and legal processes.

The cases in this book are exclusively Canadian and have been selected to illustrate issues that cannot always be adequately covered in textbooks. The chapters are ordered to align with the three components of the criminal justice system: police (front door), courts, and corrections (back door). The cases have been chosen because they typify a phenomenon of interest or because they are uniquely informative in some way. Interestingly, although not by design, some of the cases overlap in time or place. For example, Anthony Hanemaayer (chapter 2) was wrongfully convicted for an offence committed by Paul Bernardo, who was Karla Homolka's partner in crime (chapter 7); Paul Bernardo and Russell Williams (chapter 9) would have crossed paths at Kingston Penitentiary before it closed in 2013. Both Ashley Smith (chapter 8) and Melissa Shephard (chapter 9) resided at the Nova Institution for Women in Truro, NS, albeit at different times; and a correctional manager who worked at the Nova Institution, Alanna Jenkins, was a victim of Gabriel Wortman (chapter 10). Detective Jim Smyth interviewed both Russell Williams (chapter 9) and Michael Rafferty (chapter 5). This book includes cases that have transformed Canadian laws and criminal justice practices (e.g., Ashley Smith's death in custody; spree killing in Nova Scotia; Mr. Big operations; wrongful convictions; juror stress and well-being). A number of cases in this book attest to the racism that pervades our criminal justice system (e.g., Colten Boushie, Cindy Gladue, Donald Marshall Jr.). The cases run the gamut from false confessions to wrongful convictions to acts of unspeakable horror to deaths in custody and to those who, ultimately, may have eluded justice.

REFERENCES

Criminal Code, R. S. C., c. C-46, as amended 1992.

Dalby, J. T. (2014). Forensic psychology in Canada a century after Münsterberg. *Canadian Psychology*, *55*(1), 27–33. https://doi.org/10.1037/a0035526

Hill, D., & Demetrioff, S. (2019). Clinical-forensic psychology in Canada: A survey of practitioner characteristics, attitudes, and psychological assessment practices. *Canadian Psychology/Psychologie canadienne, 60*(1), 55–63. https://doi.org/10.1037/cap0000152

Münsterberg, H. (1909a). *On the witness stand: Essays on psychology and crime.* Doubleday.

Münsterberg, H. (1909b). *Psychology and crime.* T. F. Unwin.

Münsterberg, H. (1909c). *Psychotherapy.* T. F. Unwin.

Münsterberg, H. (1913). *Psychology and industrial efficiency.* Mifflin.

Nesca, M. (2022). *Clinical forensic psychology: An introduction.* Cognella Academic Publishing.

Pouls, C., Jeandarme, I., Al-Taiar, H., Bradford, J., Canton, W., Kristiansson, M., Thibaut, F., Verreyt, V., & Konrad, N. (2022). Criminal responsibility evaluations: Benchmarking in different countries. *International Journal of Law and Psychiatry, 81*(4). https://doi.org/10.1016/j.ijlp.2022.101775

Quinsey, V. L., Rice, M. E., & Harris, G. T. (1995). Actuarial prediction of sexual recidivism. *Journal of Interpersonal Violence, 10*(1), 85–105. https://doi.org/10.1177/088626095010001006

Roesch, R., Kayfitz, J. H., Watt, M. C., Cooper, B. S., Guy, L. S., Hill, D., Haag, A. M., Pomichalek, M., & Kolton, D. J. C. (2019). Fitness to stand trial and criminal responsibility assessments: Advocating for changes to the Canadian criminal code. *Canadian Psychology/Psychologie canadienne, 60*(3), 148–54. https://doi.org/10.1037/cap0000173

Roesch, R., Zapf, P. A., & Eaves, D. (2006). FIT-R: Fitness Interview Test-Revised. A structured interview for assessing competency to stand trial. Professional Resource Press/Professional Resource Exchange.

Youth Criminal Justice Act. (2002). SC 2002, c. 1.

CHAPTER ONE

What's Wrong with Mr. Big? False Confessions

The Case of Nelson Hart

With Christopher J. Lively and Ethan Draper

On 4 August 2002, Nelson Hart and his wife, Jennifer, were preparing to celebrate "Gander Day" with their three-year-old twin daughters – Krista and Karen. While waiting for Jennifer to get ready, Nelson drove the twins to a secluded beach just west of Gander, NL. Typically, Hart avoided being alone with the twins due to his risk for severe epileptic seizures. Indeed, after removing the girls from the car, Hart suffered a massive seizure and, when he came to, saw Krista "into the water" (*R. v. Hart*, 2014). Confused and unable to swim, Hart drove to get his wife, dropped her at the beach, and went to call authorities. Although paramedics were able to retrieve both twins from the water, Karen was deceased, and Krista died the following day. Hart suffered a second seizure in the police car while being taken for questioning. The RCMP launched a criminal investigation and, although Hart was an early suspect, it would be three years before he was arrested and charged with two counts of first-degree murder. What happened in those intervening three years would change Canadian law.

In many ways, Nelson Hart was a logical suspect in the death of his daughters. At 33 years of age, Nelson Lloyd Hart was a man with a troubled past (e.g., rumoured mental health problems; poor work record) and had some additional current challenges (e.g., gambling problem). The eldest of three sons, he had suffered from epilepsy since nine months of age, apparently a patrilineal inheritance. It seems his seizures repelled his schoolmates and "prevented him from being normal" (Köhler, 2013). After repeating Grade 5 three times, Hart left school at age 12. While he managed to obtain a driver's licence, he lost it several times due to his epilepsy. In his 20s, his seizures worsened under the stress of trying to live on his own following an altercation with his mother's new partner. In a 2006 interview with *Maclean's* magazine, his mother claimed: "He was sort of a child in a man's body" (Köhler, 2013). In 1997, Hart was approved to receive live-in care, which is how he met his wife, Jennifer Hicks – the live-in care nurse hired to help with Hart's needs. Before long, the two became a couple and, in 1999, the twins were born. Hart was frightened by the prospect of having children and struggled under the responsibility. He was chronically poor. A $25,000 settlement for a neck injury sustained in a 1998 car accident vanished quickly and, by August 2002, he was a slave to gambling machines. The situation was so dire that Social Services had threatened to take the twins into care. According to Jennifer, she had to choose between Nelson and the girls (see Köhler, 2013).

It seems Nelson Hart was not entirely honest with police about what happened that day at the beach. He did not tell them that he had suffered a massive seizure until a week after the drownings. Moreover, he told a somewhat different story of how events unfolded to his new friend, Steph Sauve. Sauve's arrival into Nelson Hart's life in the winter of 2005 was serendipitous and quite auspicious. After the drownings, Nelson and Jennifer had separated for a while but now were back together and living in poverty (no bed, no food) in Grand Falls, NL, about an hour east of Gander. One day, Sauve stopped to ask directions from Hart, explaining that he was looking for his sister, a drug addict and gambler, because their mother was dying in Montreal. Sauve offered Hart $50 to help him locate his sister. When Hart's efforts to find the woman in Grand Falls failed, Sauve gave him another $50 and a carton of cigarettes to search a nearby town. Hart never did find the woman but the dole-outs of money continued. When Sauve offered him money to collect and deliver a package, Hart grew suspicious – thinking it might be drugs. He consulted with his mother, and they called the local RCMP. Apparently, the RCMP's response was "If he's foolish enough to pay you, then let him" (Köhler,

2013). Before long, Sauve was paying Hart to do a range of odd jobs, such as transporting vehicles around the province and running errands to the mainland. Jennifer often accompanied Nelson, and the two enjoyed free dinners and hotel rooms. With his earnings, Hart bought a $4,000 headstone for Krista and Karen.

Hart soon discovered that he had been recruited by an organized crime group, a group from which he felt helpless to escape. "When I got into it," says Hart, "I couldn't back out" (Köhler, 2013). While Hart enjoyed the money, he declined the offers of strippers, saying: "I'm married, I love my wife, I thinks the world of her." Over the course of time, Hart was exposed to implicit and explicit acts of violence, and he felt increasingly vulnerable. When challenged by the "crime boss" to "[t]ell me how you done away with your daughters," Hart protested. "Never, sir, never, I never hurt my daughters," he said. "I'm epileptic, sir." The boss was displeased. "Oh, no, no, no — don't go lying to the boss," he said. "Don't lie to the boss." Eventually, Hart relented and confessed that "I drowned my daughters, I pushed them over the wharf." He even reenacted the scene with Sauve at Little Harbour. On 13 June 2005, the RCMP arrested Hart at the airport in Gander. As Hart hastened to call his friend Sauve, police told him: "No point in calling Steph. He's with us." Thus, Nelson Hart learned the truth that "his friend" Sauve and the many other characters he had met over the past six months, including the "crime boss," were not who they claimed to be. These people were not organized crime figures, but undercover RCMP officers engaged in an elaborate ruse known as a "Mr. Big" operation.

A BRIEF HISTORY OF THE "MR. BIG" TECHNIQUE

"Mr. Big" is a covert investigative operation used by police to elicit confessions from suspects in cold cases or cases with little forensic evidence, especially murder. Typically, the operation includes a four-stage process: intelligence probe, introduction (i.e., "the bump"), relationship/credibility-building, and evidence-gathering (Keenan & Brockman, 2010; Lutes, 2020). The intelligence probe stage involves police officers gathering information about the target (e.g., their usual whereabouts, lifestyle, and typical associates). The introduction stage involves an undercover officer "bumping" into the target, befriending them in some way, and recruiting them for seemingly small tasks (as was done by Steph Sauve to Nelson Hart). The relationship/credibility-building stage involves introducing/recruiting the target into a powerful, fictitious criminal organization whose boss ("Mr. Big") can offer safety and protection if the target can prove themselves and show their commitment to the organization; the price of admission, however, is that the boss requires all members of the organization to confess to all previous criminal activity as a means to establish trust. The evidence-gathering stage is essentially getting the target to confess to the crime under investigation by police (see Luther & Snook, 2016, for a summary of all stages and an in-depth explanation of how various social influence factors challenge the admissibility of Mr. Big confessions in court).

The RCMP (2015) refer to the Mr. Big operation as a "major crime homicide technique"; sometimes, it is called the "Canadian technique," having originated and been popularized in Canada (Moore et al., 2009). While legal in Australia and New Zealand (where it is called the "Crime Scenario Undercover Technique"; see East, 2017), Mr. Big is banned in the United States, the United Kingdom, and Germany because of its potential to violate people's rights (see Smith et al., 2009, 2010). In Canada, it has drawn criticism for preying on suspects' vulnerabilities and eliciting false (coerced) confessions (to be discussed later).

The first recorded use of a Mr. Big-like operation was in Manitoba in the *R. v. Todd* (1901) case. Todd was suspected of the murder of a Mr. Gordon. The chief of police recruited two men, neither of whom was a peace officer, to act as detectives in procuring evidence against Todd. The two "detectives" approached Todd pretending to be members of an organized crime gang with the promise of large profits to be made if he joined. Of course, to join, Todd would have to affirm that he had committed some serious crime. In this way, Todd was induced to confess to the murder of Gordon. Although the trial judge deemed the evidence-gathering operation to be "vile," "base," and "contemptible," he concluded that "it does not seem to be a sufficient ground for excluding the evidence" (*R. v. Todd*, 1901; see Coughlan, 2015). Concerns about the manner by which Todd's confession was elicited presaged the controversy that would revolve around such operations for the next 100+ years.

The first real Mr. Big operation may have been the *R. v. Beaulac* (1999) case (see Keenan & Brockman, 2010). Here, an undercover officer posed as a gangster and got Beaulac to confess to the brutal murder of a young woman in 1981. At trial, Beaulac claimed that his confession was false and that he had been merely boasting in order to be accepted into the "gang." Most credit two RCMP detectives from British Columbia – Al Haslett and Peter Marsh – as being the architects of Mr. Big. Haslett is portrayed in two episodes (S1E01, S2E06) of *The Detectives* (Duszara et al., 2018). In a CBC The Fifth Estate interview in 2015, Haslett (now retired) defended Mr. Big: "[We] seek the truth. We don't go there, we don't wake up in the morning and say 'we're going to get confessions.' This is not a bunch of cowboy cops going out and doing this. This is planned, the scenarios are planned, thought out, and we go to seek the truth" (Bridges & Dinh, 2019).

PREVALENCE OF "MR. BIG" AND CHALLENGES AGAINST ITS USE IN CASE LAW

According to self-reported RCMP statistics in 2008, Mr. Big operations had been used in over 350 cases across Canada (Dawson, 2011). Reportedly, the operation was successful in clearing or charging the person of interest in 75 per cent of cases; the other 25 per cent remained unresolved and/or required further investigation. Of cases referred for prosecution, an estimated 95 per cent resulted in a conviction (see Bridges & Dinh, 2019). An academic study has found an 88 per cent conviction rate with 81 Mr. Big confessions (e.g., Keenan & Brockman, 2010) and another found a 91.5 per cent conviction rate with 153 Mr. Big confessions (e.g., Puddister & Riddell, 2012; see Lutes, 2020; Sukkau & Brockman, 2015). While police champion this record of success, especially given the alternative of not pursuing suspects, others (e.g., lawyers, legal scholars, and psychologists) consider the risks associated with Mr. Big to be too many and too consequential. These risks include tunnel vision (i.e., police becoming too fixated on one suspect; FPT Heads of Prosecution Committee, 2018), "the Lucifer effect" (e.g., inducing an innocent suspect to commit crimes; see Zimbardo, 2007), elicitation of false confessions (Smith et al., 2010), and influencing jurors' moral prejudice (Connors et al., 2019). These staggering statistics and their implications for wrongful convictions have been the impetus for limits being imposed on Mr. Big. These limits have evolved over a number of cases: *R. v. Rose* (1983), *United States v. Burns* (2001), *R. v. Hart* (2002), and *R. v. Mack* (2014). The latter two, in particular, have been instrumental in the Supreme Court of Canada (SCC) tightening the reins on the Mr. Big operation.

The *R. v. Hart* (2002) case represented the first time that the SCC ruled on the general admissibility of Mr. Big confessions. The court cited three main concerns: (a) reliability of a confession elicited by threats and inducements, (b) potential for prejudice against the accused for their willingness to participate in crimes they believed to be real, and (c) "risk that the police will resort to unacceptable tactics in their pursuit of a confession" (Lutes, 2020, p. 222). Prior to the Hart case, police had fewer restrictions on how they investigated a suspect (outside of custody). Undercover confessions took place in something of a "legal vacuum," where an individual's right to remain silent (Canadian Charter of Rights and Freedoms [CCRF], Section 7, 1982) and the voluntary confession rule did not apply (see Lutes, 2020).

Since the 2002 Hart case, Mr. Big confessions are considered presumptively inadmissible and subject to *voir dire* ("see say"). A *voir dire* is a trial within a trial where the admissibility of evidence is assessed. A two-prong test is applied to determine the reliability of the confession. First, the Crown needs to demonstrate that the *probative* value (i.e., evidence that tends to prove) of the Mr. Big evidence outweighs its *prejudicial* effect (i.e., evidence that may unfairly bias, such as bad character evidence and moral prejudice). For example, Hart's actions (i.e., delivering stolen goods for a crime organization) could be seen to reflect poorly on his character and thereby be prejudicial. In reality, of course, what he was delivering was not contraband so, at worst, he was guilty of attempting to commit the offence (see Coughlan, 2015). Second, the accused needs to demonstrate that police misconduct (e.g., use of coercion to elicit a confession) resulted in an abuse of process. Protections against abuse of process are included in common law and Section 7 of the CCRF. These protections are intended "to guard against state conduct that society finds unacceptable and which threatens the integrity of the justice system" (Government of Canada, 2019). While there is no precise formula for determining if a particular Mr. Big operation was abusive, it is imperative that police not "overcome the will" (*R. v. Hart*, 2014) of the accused and coerce a confession. Unacceptable police tactics include actual or threatened physical violence against the accused; providing coercive inducements; or preying on an accused's vulnerabilities such as mental health problems, addictions, or youthfulness (*R. v. Hart*, 2014).

FALSE CONFESSIONS

Confessions are powerful indicators of guilt and can be perceived as the most damning form of evidence against an accused person by both professional (police, judge) and lay people (jury) in the justice system (see Henkel et al., 2008). Indeed, some scholars have suggested that if a confession is admitted as evidence into a trial, undergoing the remaining proceedings is a moot point (McCormick, 1972). Saul Kassin (1997) proffered that "in criminal law, confession evidence is a prosecutor's most potent weapon" (p. 221). Confessions derive their probative force from the fact that they are against the accused's self-interest and legal protections. These legal rights and protections, at least in Canada, are afforded to Canadians through the CCRF under Sections (7) Life, liberty, and security of person; (8) Security against unreasonable search or seizure; (9) Not being arbitrarily detained or imprisoned; (10) Being informed of reasons for arrest or detention, access to counsel, validity of detention determined via *habeus corpus* ("have the body"); (11) Being informed of proceedings in criminal and penal matters (e.g., informed of offence, tried within reasonable time); (12) Not being subjected to cruel and unusual treatment or punishment; (13) Self-incrimination; and (14) Assistance of an interpreter. A trilogy of SCC cases outline the legal protections available to suspects when subjected to a police interrogation. These cases include *R. v. Oickle* (voluntariness of a confession), *R. v. Singh* (right to silence and against self-incrimination), and *R. v. Sinclair* (right to counsel; see Dufraimont, 2011).

Given these many legal protections, it is difficult to understand why someone would falsely confess to a crime, especially murder. While French philosopher Albert Camus maintained that "a guilty conscience needs to confess," research related to confessions shows that many people falsely confess and they do so whether they have a guilty conscience or not. Considered as the foundational taxonomy of false confessions, Kassin and Wrightsman (1985) proposed three different types: Voluntary, Coerced-Internalized, and Coerced-Compliant. *Voluntary false confessions* may arise out of a person's need for notoriety, difficulty distinguishing fact from fantasy, desire for punishment to assuage a sense of guilt, or to protect someone else. For example, in 1932, almost 200 people falsely confessed to the kidnapping and murder of Charles Lindbergh's baby (see Kassin & Gudjonsson, 2005). *Coerced-internalized false confessions* may arise from evocative interrogation techniques with highly suggestible and/or vulnerable individuals (e.g., those with mental health problems, addictions, or brain dysfunction). One of the most sensational examples of *coerced-internalized false confessions* is the case of Paul Ingram, who falsely confessed to sexually assaulting his two daughters and spent 20 years in prison before being released (see Kassin, 2007). *Coerced-compliant false confessions*, which include many police-induced confessions, follow from coercive interrogation tactics that can entice a suspect to confess so as to escape further interrogation, gain a promised benefit, or avoid a threatened punishment. The Central Park Jogger case (discussed below) is an example of youth detainees falling victim to coercive interrogation tactics by police and confessing to a crime that none of them committed (see Kassin, 2002).

Kassin and Wrightsman's (1985) original taxonomy of false confessions, however, has not been without criticism. Others have since proposed some extended and refined versions of the false confession classification system (e.g., Davison & Forshaw, 1993; Gudjonsson, 1992, 2003; Kassin, 1997; Leo & Ofshe, 1997; McCann, 1998; Ofshe & Leo, 1997; see Kassin & Gudjonsson, 2004). For instance, McCann (1998) proposed adding a fourth category of false confessions: coerced-reactive false confessions. As defined by McCann (1998), *coerced-reactive false confessions* occur "when an individual (who may or may not be a criminal suspect) confesses in order to avoid or escape some coercive action that arises out of a relationship with one or more individuals other than police" (p. 449). An example is a victim of domestic violence claiming responsibility for a crime that was committed by their abuser in order to escape the abusive relationship, thus avoiding future victimization (see McCann, 1998, but cf. Kassin, 1998).

Another criticism of the original taxonomy model has been related to the terminology used to describe the confession typologies (e.g., "coerced" vs. "persuaded" vs. "pressured"; see Davison & Forshaw, 1993; Gudjonsson, 2003; Leo & Ofshe, 1997; Ofshe & Leo, 1997). For example, Leo and Ofshe (1997) and Ofshe and Leo (1997) offered a similar but extended version of Kassin and Wrightman's (1985) false confessions model that proposed five levels: voluntary, coerced-compliant, stress-compliant, noncoerced persuaded, and coerced-persuaded. Leo and Ofshe (1997) and Ofshe and Leo (1997) agree with Kassin and Wrightman (1985) that a *voluntary false confession* can arise from the accused being manipulated in some fashion – either by legal police tactics or their own perceptions – but add that this type of confession might be rooted in other motivations such as a desire to help the real perpetrator. Ofshe and Leo also agree with Kassin and Wrightman that a *coerced-compliant false confession* is the result of classical coercive police tactics. According to Ofshe and Leo (1997), a *stress-compliant false confession* is the result of the accused feeling the effects of excessive physical or mental stressors during the interrogation, but they make a point to note that this is distinct from a *coerced-compliant false confession* where threats and/or promises are made by the interrogator. Finally, as the terminology suggests, the difference between a *noncoerced-persuaded false confession* and a *coerced-persuaded false confession* is simply whether any strong-arming practices on the part of the police are applied (Leo & Ofshe, 1997; Ofshe & Leo, 1997; see also Leo, 2009). Gudjonsson (2003) further added to the classification debate for false confessions. Specifically, Gudjonsson maintains that there are three types of false confessions, as proposed by Kassin and Wrightman (1985) – albeit, he uses the language "pressured" versus "coerced" when referring to internalized and compliant false confessions (e.g., pressured-internalized false confession; pressured-compliant false confession) – but added that consideration of the potential sources of influence (i.e., pressure) to give a confession can come from *internal* (e.g., pressure from within the individual, such as the need to confess for notoriety or the mistaken belief that they committed the crime when in fact they did not; applies only to voluntary false confession), *custodial* (e.g., pressure from the police during the interrogation, such as applying coercive persuasive tactics; applies to pressured-internalized and pressured-compliant false confessions), or *noncustodial* sources (e.g., pressure from sources outside of the police, such as family, friends, jail cellmate, undercover police officer; applies to pressured-internalized and pressured-compliant false confessions; see Gudjonsson, 2003). Despite there being some debate among scholars about the best classification system to use for false confession, there is certainly agreement that false confessions do occur and can be the initial catalyst that leads to wrongful convictions.

To be clear, none of the above false confession case examples (real or fictionalized for illustrative purposes) employed the Mr. Big technique. The atmosphere of criminality surrounding Mr. Big, however, is designed to entice individuals to admit the truth about their supposed crimes – similar to that of a coercive police interrogation. That same atmosphere, however, can entice a lie, especially if a suspect is seeking admiration, affirmation, friendship, or financial gain.

False confessions long predate Mr. Big operations, of course. Brothers Jesse and Stephen Boorn each confessed to the murder of their brother-in-law, Russell Colvin, and narrowly escaped hanging. Colvin disappeared from Manchester, Vermont, in 1812 only to reappear seven years later, alive and well (Bluhm Legal Clinic Center on Wrongful Convictions, n.d.). Renowned Harvard University psychologist Hugo Münsterberg (1909) warned that "untrue confessions" can be the result of being "under the spell of overpowering influences" (p. 147). Münsterberg was troubled by the hanging of a youth who had confessed to a crime that Münsterberg and others were convinced he had not committed. Arguments in defence of the youth were challenged repeatedly with the assertion that it would be "inconceivable that any man who was innocent of it should claim the infamy of guilt" (Münsterberg, 1909, p. 142). The prevalence of false confessions in wrongful conviction cases was not understood, however, until the 1980s and the advent of DNA evidence. Today, we know that false confessions are common, accounting for approximately 15–30 per cent of DNA-exoneration cases (Garrett, 2008; Scheck et al., 2000; see Innocence Project, 2022).

CLINICAL FORENSIC PSYCHOLOGY AND MR. BIG OPERATIONS

Saul Kassin maintains that "[t]here's no one kind of person who can give a false confession. It can happen to anybody" (Starr, 2019).

While that may be true, some people are simply more vulnerable than others to becoming ensnared in Mr. Big stings and then falsely confessing to crimes for which they are not responsible. A comprehensive review by Kassin et al. (2010) identified certain factors that increase one's risk to falsely confess in certain situations. These include youth and immaturity, intellectual disability, mental illness, and personality traits (e.g., suggestibility, compliance). Situational risk factors for false confessions include prolonged interrogation time, presentations of false evidence, and tactics like "maximization" (intended to convey the interrogator's conviction that the suspect is guilty and can exaggerate the seriousness of the offence) and "minimization" (offers the suspect moral justification and face-saving excuses for criminal conduct) – all features of Mr. Big operations. Kassin et al. (2010) maintain that interrogation techniques that combine psychological pressures ("we know you did it") and escape hatches ("but we understand why and can help") can easily entice an innocent person to confess. Other risk factors for false confessions include stress, fatigue, and history of trauma. Even innocence can be a risk factor for false confessions. As Kassin (2008) explains, innocent people tend to believe that truth and justice will prevail and that their innocence will be apparent to juries and others.

Moore (2019) characterized Mr. Big operations as being psychologically manipulative. Manipulative effects would be exacerbated with vulnerable suspects (immature, compliant, rendered desperate by greed or need). Kassin et al. (2010) found youth and mental impairment to be significant vulnerabilities for police-induced (coerced) false confessions. Of the first 200 DNA exonerations in the United States, 35 per cent of the false confessors were 18 years or younger and/or had a developmental disability. One sample of wrongful convictions found that 44 per cent of the exonerated juveniles and 69 per cent of exonerated persons with mental disabilities were wrongly convicted because of false confessions (see Gross et al., 2005). In Canada, Kyle Unger was only 19 when he became the target of a Mr. Big operation. Though he repeatedly declared his innocence and contradicted himself on the details of the crime, Unger's false confession sealed his fate. He served 14 years in prison for the 1990 murder of 16-year-old Brigitte Grenier, before being exonerated based on DNA evidence (see Innocence Canada, 2022).

In an opinion editorial on the Central Park Jogger case, Kassin (2002) explained how attributes associated with young age (e.g., heightened suggestibility and obedience to authority, immature decision-making abilities) can be perilous when confronted with prolonged and manipulative interrogation tactics. This 1989 case involved five Black and Latino youth from Harlem – Kevin Richardson (14), Raymond Santana (14), Antron McCray (15), Yusef Salaam (15), and Korey Wise (15) – being convicted of raping and assaulting a White woman in Central Park, NY. Four of the five youth confessed to the crime and all served between 6 and 12 years before their sentences were vacated when DNA evidence linked a convicted serial rapist and murderer (Matias Reyes) to the crime (for more information on the Central Park Five, see the Netflix documentary *When They See Us*; Skoll et al., 2019).

Individuals with intellectual and cognitive disabilities are overrepresented in false confession cases (see Gudjonsson, 2003). Like youth, these individuals can be imperiled by greater suggestibility and susceptibility to influence, desire to please and reliance on authority figures, tendency to feign competence, and willingness to accept blame for negative outcomes (Perske, 2004, as cited in Kassin et al., 2010). Personality traits like conscientiousness and agreeableness are associated with greater compliance and increased risk for false confessions (Bègue et al., 2015). Certain types of psychopathology have also been linked to false confessions. Disorders characterized by disruptions in neurodevelopment (e.g., attention deficit hyperactivity disorder [ADHD] – see description of ADHD below); disturbances in mood, anxiety, perception, cognition (e.g., schizophrenia spectrum), and conduct (e.g., impulse control); trauma- and stressor-related disorders (e.g., PTSD); personality and substance use disorders all have been linked to false confessions (see Kassin et al., 2010). See the *Diagnostic and Statistical Manual of Mental Disorders* (*DSM-5*; American Psychiatric Association, 2013) for more information on these disorders.

The distinguishing features of ADHD – inattention, hyperactivity, and impulsivity – make it a particularly risky disorder with regard to false confessions, and its prevalence among incarcerated populations (see Gudjonsson & Sigurdsson, 1994) suggests the potential magnitude of the problem. Research shows that people with ADHD are inclined to cope with persistent questioning by uttering "don't know" replies, which can make them appear to be evasive and raise police suspicions (Gudjonsson et al., 2007). At the same time, they may be more compliant. The rate of self-reported false confessions in one incarcerated sample was significantly higher among those who were currently symptomatic for ADHD than others (41% and 18%, respectively; Gudjonsson et al., 2008). Individuals with prominent traits of antisocial personality disorder (ASPD) tend to lie for short-term instrumental gain with little consideration to longer-term consequences. Perhaps unsurprisingly, they are inclined to make false denials but also to make false confessions – depending on their need at the time (see Kassin et al., 2010).

Twenty-year-old Cody Bates (*R. v. Bates*, 2009) had diagnoses of both ADHD and ASPD when he became the target of a Mr. Big operation. He also had a severe substance use disorder; indeed, he operated a cocaine ring in Calgary. Bates's mental health deteriorated following the Mr. Big operation as he became more paranoid and distrustful of others, unable to distinguish police from non-police (Bates, 2018; *R. v. Bates*, 2009). Today, the former "cocaine king" is helping others who struggle with addictions (Nelson, 2018; see Bates, 2018). Andy Rose, who confessed to shooting two German travellers in Chetwynd, BC, in 1983, only to have DNA evidence prove otherwise in 2001, was an alcoholic. At one point in the operation, Mr. Big operatives insisted that Rose have a drink and reconsider his story. Rose was adamant that he was telling the truth and that a beer would not change his story; nonetheless, the pressure persisted. After hours of drinking, Rose complied with the two officers' request and stated: "We'll go with I did it, okay?" (Keenan & Brockman, 2010, p. 10).

Kyle Ledesma also suffered with addiction, both personal and family. His mother was a crack-cocaine user, which led to her incarceration, and his father suffered with addiction related to his residential school experience (*R. v. Ledesma*, 2020). Throughout his time as the target of a Mr. Big operation, Ledesma was addicted to alcohol and cannabis and used both substances daily. Undercover officers often provided him with money to purchase alcohol and transportation to liquor stores to procure it. Reportedly, Ledesma was highly intoxicated during many of the undercover scenarios. On one occasion, undercover officers plied Ledesma with so much alcohol prior to his meeting with Mr. Big that he vomited twice before arriving at the location. Upon arriving for his interrogation, he was given even more alcohol by Mr. Big (*R. v. Ledesma*, 2020, p. 13).

Many of these risk factors for false confessions would apply in the Nelson Hart case. Hart's chronological age seems to have exceeded his social, emotional, and intellectual maturity. His development may have been impacted by his chronic and severe epilepsy. His mother described him as being "like a child in a man's body" and his wife, Jennifer, commonly referred to him as "my son" (Köhler, 2013). Hart struggled to live independently; he was poorly educated, rarely employed, and often reliant on social assistance. Although he may not have had a problem with substances, he did have a problem with gambling. Jennifer described him as "demanding, morose, uncommunicative, and obsessed with video lottery terminal gambling at the local bar" (Stobbe, 2021, p. 67). A person with Hart's profile would have relished the attention and friendship of someone like Steph Sauve (a name that suggests smoothness and sophistication) and would have found it hard to resist invitations to collaborate. Like Cody Bates, Hart grew paranoid in the aftermath of the Mr. Big sting and was resistant to offers of assistance from lawyers, thinking that, like the Mr. Big operatives, they were part of a conspiracy to betray him.

A recent book by Mark Stobbe (2021) titled *The Mr. Big Sting: The Cases, The Killers, The Controversial Confessions* characterizes the Hart case as a "murky" one. At the end of the day, there are no clear villains or victims other than Karen and Krista. Nonetheless, the case changed Canadian legal history and will impact future cases – or not. Interestingly, since *R. v. Hart* (2014), only one Mr. Big confession has been excluded due to abuse of process (*R. v. Laflamme*, 2015; see Lutes, 2020).

SUMMARY AND CONCLUSIONS

> *A confession provides powerful evidence of guilt, but only if it is true.*
>
> – (R. v. Hart, *2014)*

The *R. v. Mack* (2014) case clearly outlines the many ramifications of a guilty confession:

> Of all types of evidence tendered by the Crown in criminal prosecutions, confessions are the most persuasive. The power of a confession, in effect, is akin to reversing the burden of proof. The

> presumption of innocence gives way to an assumption of guilt. An accused who has confessed will never be treated the same as an accused who either denies commission of the offence or exercised the right to remain silent, and will be met with suspicion and judged more harshly throughout the trial process. Not the least of which is because, if the accused hopes to counter the confession, he must enter the witness box, but does so with his credibility already greatly compromised. If a recantation of the confession is what the accused offers, it is natural for such evidence to be disbelieved, and that the accused be found to be deceptive and/or lying under a sworn oath to avoid a murder conviction. (*R. v. Mack*, 2014)

Police argue that Mr. Big operations solve cases that lack forensic evidence or have gone cold. If not for a Mr. Big operation on Michael Bridges, teenager Erin Chorney might still be considered a missing person (Keenan & Brockman, 2010, p. 15). Sometimes Mr. Big yields surprising results, such as in *R. v. Yakimchuk* (2017), when the target confessed to a murder from years earlier that was not the focus of the undercover operation. Mr. Big operations also can establish a suspect's innocence, as in the case of Gregory Parsons. In 1994, Parsons was convicted for the 1991 murder of his mother, Dolly Carroll, who had been stabbed 52 times. Four years later (1998), Parsons was exonerated based on DNA evidence, and four years after that (2003), Brian Doyle (a "friend" of Parsons) was convicted based on the results of a Mr. Big sting (see *R. v. Doyle*, 2003). Police cite impressive conviction rates (e.g., 75%) as a result of Mr. Big operations and maintain that such operations are better than the alternative of doing nothing.

Police contend that they are seeking the truth when they implement Mr. Big stings. But Mr. Big operations come at a cost, and those costs can be substantial. The financial costs of Mr. Big operations can range from thousands to millions (Keenan & Brockman, 2010). The *R. v. Ledesma* (2020) case is considered inexpensive at roughly $37,000. The three-year Mr. Big operation to find those responsible for the murder of four RCMP officers in Mayerthorpe, AB, in 2005 was $2 million, and eliciting a confession from Vancouver crime figure Salvatore Ciancio for the murder of seven individuals cost $4 million. Nelson Hart's Mr. Big operation cost over $400,000. Most recently, the

Nova Scotia case of *R. v. Buckley* (2018) exceeded $300,000 (*R. v. Buckley*, 2018; Murphy & Anderson, 2016). Expenses included running job fairs, smashing cars, and paying for trips to see the Montreal Canadiens play. Buckley confessed to killing his mother, but his confession was deemed inadmissible.

Paramount among the costs of Mr. Big operations are suspects' loss of legal rights, including loss of liberty and security of person (CCRF, S.7). In a democracy, the loss of one person's rights is a threat to all persons' rights. Mr. Big operations are shrouded in secrecy, not subject to judicial authorization, and not easily monitored or scrutinized. "Secrecy in any government is an invitation to an abuse of power" (C. E. S. Franks, as cited in Keenan & Brockman, 2010, p. 21). The lack of oversight means a high potential for abuse of process, including entrapment, coercion, railroading, and taking advantage of a suspect's vulnerabilities (e.g., mental health and addiction problems, financial need, or social isolation). According to Dalhousie University law professor Adelina Iftene (2016, p. 168), by employing Mr. Big operations, "the state is virtually taking control of one's life, takes advantage of his greed or addictions, and uses them to obtain indirectly what it is forbidden by law to obtain directly."

In addition to financial and legal costs, Mr. Big operations can impose severe psychological costs. Targets of the operations can suffer the Lucifer effect (i.e., when good people do bad things due to the influence of iniquitous social contexts on behaviour; Zimbardo, 2007) and the Hawthorne effect (i.e., when individuals modify their behaviour in response to being observed; Landsberger, 1958). Targets also can suffer deleterious mental health effects – such as increased paranoia, distrust, avoidance of others, or fear of betrayal – after discovering that their new "friends" were not real, their new circumstances were an elaborate ruse, and they themselves were pawns in an undercover operation. Nelson Hart, Cody Bates, Kyle Unger, and others must have questioned their own sanity. When someone is presented with a false narrative designed to make them question their own reality (perceptions, memories, beliefs), it is disorientating and distressful. Colloquially it is called "gaslighting" and is considered to be a malicious power tactic (see Abramson, 2014, p. 2). It is no less malicious if implemented by the state.

CRITICAL THINKING QUESTIONS

1. Do you think the benefits of Mr. Big sting operations (obtaining a confession, securing convictions, solving cold cases) outweigh the costs (financial, legal, psychological)?
2. In Canada, police investigators cannot explicitly lie to suspects about evidence that the police may or may not have on the suspect during an interview. Yet the foundation of the Mr. Big technique is built upon a fictitious scenario that is used to manipulate the suspect. Aren't the police just lying to the suspect by using this approach? And if so, why is lying to the suspect appropriate in the Mr. Big technique, but not during investigative interviews?
3. Despite the SCC ruling of *R. v. Hart* in 2014 (i.e., the Crown needs to demonstrate that the *probative* value of the Mr. Big evidence outweighs its *prejudicial* effects), the court did not outrightly prohibit its use in Canada. However, the Mr. Big technique has been prohibited in other jurisdictions worldwide (e.g., United States, United Kingdom, and Germany). Given the concerns related to false confessions and otherwise, should its use be abolished in Canada?

REFERENCES

Abramson, K. (2014). Turning up the lights on gaslighting. *Philosophical Perspectives, 28*(1), 1–30. https://doi.org/10.1111/phpe.12046

American Psychiatric Association. (2013). *Diagnostic and statistical manual of mental disorders* (5th ed.).

Bates, C. (2018). *The devil's pupil.* Word Alive Press.

Bègue, L., Beauvois, J. L., Courbet, D., Oberlé, D., Lepage, J., & Duke, A. A. (2015). Personality predicts obedience in a Milgram paradigm. *Journal of Personality, 83*(3), 299–306. https://doi.org/10.1111/jopy.12104

Bluhm Legal Clinic Center on Wrongful Convictions. (n.d.). *First wrongful conviction Jesse Boorn and Stephen Boorn.* https://www.law.northwestern.edu/legalclinic/wrongfulconvictions/exonerations/vt/boorn-brothers.html

Bridges, A., & Dinh, V. (2019, December 9). Confessions and controversy: Murder case against husband of Sheree Fertuck latest test of "Mr. Big" tactic. *CBC News.* https://www.cbc.ca/news/canada/saskatchewan/mr-big-sting-saskatchewan-greg-fertuck-rcmp-police-canada-1.5388277

Canadian Charter of Rights and Freedoms. (1982). S 2, Part I of the Constitution Act, 1982, being Schedule B to the Canada Act 1982 (UK), 1982, c 11.

Connors, C. J., Patry, M. W., & Smith, S. M. (2019). The Mr. Big technique on trial by jury. *Psychology, Crime & Law, 25*(1), 1–22. https://doi.org/10.1080/1068316X.2018.1483507

Coughlan, S. (2015). Threading together abuse of process and exclusion of evidence: How it became possible to rebuke Mr. Big. *Supreme Court Law*

Review: Osgoode's Annual Constitutional Cases Conference, 71(1), 415–38. https://digitalcommons.osgoode.yorku.ca/sclr/vol71/iss1/16

Davison, S. E., & Forshaw, D. M. (1993). Retracted confessions: Through opiate withdrawal to a new conceptual framework. *Medicine, Science, and the Law, 33*(4), 285–90. https://doi.org/10.1177/002580249303300403

Dawson, W. E. (2011). *The use of "Mr. Big" in undercover operations* (Paper 5.2 in Criminal Law: Special Issues). Continuing Legal Education Society of British Columbia. https://online.cle.bc.ca/CoursesOnDemand/ContentByCourse/Papers?courseId=4202

Dufraimont, L. (2011). The interrogation trilogy and the protections for interrogated suspects in Canadian law. *Supreme Court Law Review: Osgoode's Annual Constitutional Cases Conference, 54*(1), 309–34. https://digitalcommons.osgoode.yorku.ca/sclr/vol54/iss1/11

Duszara, P., Bailey, S., Gatien, J., Rosenstein, H., & Travis, D. (Executive Producers). (2018–20). *The Detectives* [TV series]. WAM Media GRP.

East, M. D. (2017). *A free licence: The lack of external checks on police undercover operations* [Unpublished honours dissertation]. University of Otago – Te Whare Wananga o Otago. https://www.otago.ac.nz/law/research/journals/otago719258.pdf

FPT Heads of Prosecutions Committee. (2018). *Innocence at stake: The need for continued vigilance to prevent wrongful convictions in Canada*. https://www.ppsc-sppc.gc.ca/eng/pub/is-ip/is-ip-eng.pdf

Garrett, B. L. (2008). Judging innocence. *Columbia Law Review, 108*(55), 55–142. https://scholarship.law.duke.edu/faculty_scholarship/3863/

Government of Canada. (2019, April 25). False confessions. In *Innocence at stake: The need for continued vigilance to prevent wrongful convictions in Canada*. https://www.ppsc-sppc.gc.ca/eng/pub/is-ip/ch4.html

Gross, S. R., Jacoby, K., Matheson, D. J., Montgomery, N., & Patel, S. (2005). Exonerations in the United States from 1989 through 2003. *Journal of Criminal Law and Criminology, 95*(2), 523–60. https://repository.law.umich.edu/articles/1590/

Gudjonsson, G. H. (1992). *The psychology of interrogations, confessions, and testimony*. Wiley.

Gudjonsson, G. H. (2003). *The psychology of interrogations and confessions: A handbook*. Wiley.

Gudjonsson, G. H., & Sigurdsson, J. F. (1994). How frequently do false confessions occur? An empirical study among prison inmates. *Psychology, Crime & Law, 1*(1), 21–6. https://doi.org/10.1080/10683169408411933

Gudjonsson, G. H., Sigurdsson, J. F., Bragason, O. O., Newton, A. K., & Einarsson, E. (2008). Interrogative suggestibility, compliance and false confessions among prisoners and their relationship with attention deficit hyperactivity disorder (ADHD) symptoms. *Psychological Medicine, 38*(7), 1037–44. https://doi.org/10.1017/S0033291708002882

Gudjonsson, G. H., Young, S., & Bramham, J. (2007). Interrogative suggestibility in adults diagnosed with attention-deficit hyperactivity disorder (ADHD): A potential vulnerability during police questioning. *Personality and Individual Differences, 43*(4), 737–45. https://doi.org/10.1016/j.paid.2007.01.014

Henkel, L. A., Coffman, K. A., & Dailey, E. M. (2008). A survey of people's attitudes and beliefs about false confessions. *Behavioral Sciences and the Law, 26*(5), 555–84. https://doi.org/10.1002/bsl.826

Iftene, A. (2016) The "Hart" of the (Mr.) Big problem. *Criminal Law Quarterly, 63*, 151. https://ssrn.com/abstract=2896890

Innocence Canada. (2022). Kyle Unger. http://www.innocencecanada.com/exonerations/kyle-unger/

Innocence Project. (2022). DNA exonerations in the United States. https://innocenceproject.org/dna-exonerations-in-the-united-states/

Kassin, S. M. (1997). The psychology of confession evidence. *American Psychologist, 52*(3), 221–33. https://doi.org/10.1037/0003-066X.52.3.221

Kassin, S. M. (1998). More on the psychology of false confessions. *American Psychologist, 53*(3), 320–1. https://doi.org/10.1037/h0092166

Kassin, S. M. (2002, November 1). False confessions and the jogger case. *The New York Times*. https://www.nytimes.com/2002/11/01/opinion/false-confessions-and-the-jogger-case.html

Kassin, S. M. (2007). Internalized false confessions. In M. P. Toglia, J. D. Read, D. F. Ross, & R. C. L. Lindsay (Eds.), *The handbook of eyewitness psychology, Vol. 1: Memory for events* (pp. 175–92). Lawrence Erlbaum.

Kassin, S. M. (2008). False confessions: Causes, consequences, and implications for reform. *Current Directions in Psychological Science, 17*(4), 249–53. https://doi.org/10.1111/j.1467-8721.2008.00584.x

Kassin, S. M., Drizin, S. A., Grisso, T., Gudjonsson, G. H., Leo, R. A., & Redlich, A. D. (2010). Police-induced confessions: Risk factors and recommendations. *Law and Human Behavior, 34*(1), 3–38. https://doi.org/10.1007/s10979-009-9188-6

Kassin, S. M., & Gudjonsson, G. H. (2004). The psychology of confessions: A review of the literature and issues. *Psychological Science in the Public Interest, 5*(2), 33–67. https://doi.org/10.1111/j.1529-1006.2004.00016.x

Kassin, S. M., & Gudjonsson, G. H. (2005). True crimes, false confessions. *Scientific American Mind, 16*(2), 24–31. https://doi.org/10.1038/scientificamericanmind0605-24

Kassin, S. M., & Wrightsman, L. S. (1985). Confession evidence. In S. Kassin & L. Wrightsman (Eds.), *The psychology of evidence and trial procedure* (pp. 67–94). SAGE Publications.

Keenan, K. T., & Brockman, J. (2010). *Mr. Big: Exposing undercover investigations in Canada*. Fernwood.

Köhler, N. (2013, October 31). The case of Nelson Hart: 2 girls, 3 years and a mystery 'Mr. Big.' *Maclean's*. https://www.macleans.ca/politics/the-case-of-nelson-hart-2-girls-3-years-and-a-mystery-mr-big/
Landsberger, H. A. (1958). *Hawthorne revisited*. Cornell University.
Leo, R. A. (2009). False confessions: Causes, consequences, and implications. *Journal of the American Academy of Psychiatry and the Law Online, 37*(3), 332–43. https://pubmed.ncbi.nlm.nih.gov/19767498/
Leo, R. A., & Ofshe, R. J. (1997). The social psychology of police interrogation: The theory and classification of true and false confessions. *Studies in Law, Politics and Society, 16*, 189–251. https://ssrn.com/abstract=1141368
Lutes, C. (2020). Hart failure: Assessing the Mr. Big confessions framework five years later. *Manitoba Law Journal, 43*(4), 209–44. https://journals.library.ualberta.ca/themanitobalawjournal/index.php/mlj/article/view/1218
Luther, K., & Snook, B. (2016). Putting the Mr. Big technique back on trial: A re-examination of probative value and abuse of process through a scientific lens. *Journal of Forensic Practice, 18*(2), 131–42. https://doi.org/10.1108/JFP-01-2015-0004
McCann, J. T. (1998). A conceptual framework for identifying various types of confessions. *Behavioral Sciences and the Law, 16*(4), 441–53. https://doi.org/10.1002/(SICI)1099-0798(199823)16:43.0.CO;2-W
McCormick, C. T. (1972). *Handbook of the law of evidence* (2nd ed.). West.
Moore, T. E. (2019). *Mr. Big undercover operations: Who is deceiving whom?* [Master's thesis]. Glendon College, York University. https://arcabc.ca/islandora/object/mru%3A447/datastream/PDF/download/citation.pdf
Moore, T. E., Copeland, P., & Schuller, R. A. (2009). Deceit, betrayal and the search for truth: Legal and psychological perspectives on the Mr. Big strategy. *Criminal Law Quarterly, 55*(3), 348–404. https://www.glendon.yorku.ca/timmoore/wp-content/uploads/sites/222/deceit-betrayal-Mr-Big.pdf
Münsterberg, H. (1909). *On the witness stand: Essays on psychology and crime*. Doubleday.
Murphy, B., & Anderson, J. (2016). Confessions to Mr Big: A new rule of evidence? *International Journal of Evidence & Proof, 20*(1), 29–48. https://doi.org/10.1177/1365712715613485
Nelson, C. (2018, December 10). Nelson: Former Calgary cocaine king now on a mission to save lives. *Calgary Herald*. https://calgaryherald.com/news/local-news/former-calgary-cocaine-king-saves-lives-rather-than-taking-them
Ofshe, R. J., & Leo, R. A. (1997). The decision to confess falsely: Rational choice and irrational action. *Denver University Law Review, 74*(4), 979–1122. https://digitalcommons.du.edu/cgi/viewcontent.cgi?article=1986&context=dlr

Puddister, K., & Riddell, T. (2012). The RCMP's "Mr. Big" sting operation: A case study in police independence, accountability and oversight. *Canadian Public Administration, 55*(3), 385–409. https://doi.org/10.1111/j.1754-7121.2012.00229.x

R. v. Bates (C.W.), 2009, 468 A.R. 158 (QB).

R. v. Beaulac, 1999, 1 SCR 768.

R. v. Buckley, 2018, NSSC 1 CRBW No. 461375.

R. v. Doyle, 2003, NLSCrD 20.

R. v. Hart, 2002, SSC 52.

R. v. Hart, 2014, SCC 52.

R. v. Laflamme, 2015, QCCA 1517.

R. v. Ledesma, 2020, ABQB 117.

R. v. Mack, 2014, SCC 3.

R. v. Rose, 1983, SSC.

R. v. Todd, 1901, CCC 514.

R. v. Yakimchuk, 2017, ABCA 101.

RCMP. (2015, May 1). Undercover operations. *Royal Canadian Mounted Police*. https://bc-cb.rcmp-grc.gc.ca/ViewPage.action?siteNodeId=23&languageId=1&contentId=6941

Scheck, B., Neufeld, P., & Dwyer, J. (2000). *Actual innocence*. Doubleday.

Skoll, J., King, J., Rosenthal, J., De Niro, R., Welsh, B., Winfrey, O., & DuVernay, A. (Executive Producers). (2019). *When they see us* [Video]. Netflix. http://www.netflix.com

Smith, S. M., Stinson, V., & Patry, M. W. (2009). Using the "Mr. Big" technique to elicit confessions: Successful innovation or dangerous development in the Canadian legal system? *Psychology, Public Policy, and Law, 15*(3), 168–93. https://doi.org/10.1037/a0016962

Smith, S. M., Stinson, V., & Patry, M. W. (2010). High-risk interrogation: Using the "Mr. Big Technique" to elicit confessions. *Law and Human Behavior, 34*(1), 39–40. https://doi.org/10.1007/s10979-009-9203-y

Starr, D. (2019, June 14). The confession – A psychologist has shown how police questioning can get innocent people to condemn themselves. *Science, 364*(6445), 1022–6. https://doi.org/10.1126/science.364.6445.1022

Stobbe, M. (2021). *The "Mr. Big" sting: The cases, the killers, the controversial confessions*. ECW Press.

Sukkau, E., & Brockman, J. (2015). "Boys, you should all be in Hollywood": Perspectives on the Mr. Big investigative technique. *UBC Law Review Society, 48*(1), 47–77. https://www.thefreelibrary.com/%22Boys%2C+you+should+all+be+in+Hollywood%22%3A+perspectives+on+the+Mr.+Big...-a0403916551

United States v. Burns, 2001, 1 SCR 283, SCC 7.

Zimbardo, P. (2007). *The Lucifer effect: Understanding how good people turn evil*. Random House.

CHAPTER TWO[1]

"What Life?" Eyewitness Testimony

The Case of Anthony Hanemaayer

With Elle Lévesque, Juliana Khoury, and Christopher J. Lively

In the early morning hours (about 5:00 a.m.) of 29 September 1987, a man climbed through the bedroom window of a 15-year-old girl in Scarborough, ON. He jumped on her back, covered her mouth, and threatened her with a knife. The mother, awakened by the noise, thought the girl had fallen out of bed and went into the hall and turned on the light. She screamed at the man sitting on top of her daughter. The mother, who was not wearing her glasses, saw the perpetrator for only moments in the dark bedroom before he fled the scene in a white vehicle. The mother would later testify that she and the assailant stared at one another for 45 seconds, during which time she studied the man's face very closely, before he leapt up and "raised his arms up in the air and roared at me like a lion." The daughter later testified that less than 30 seconds elapsed from the time her mother entered the bedroom to when the assailant fled (Moles & Sangha, n.d.; *R. v. Hanemaayer*, 2008).

The mother described the man to police as follows: 6′0″; 170 lb; 19 years old; with sandy brown, wavy hair; slim build; wearing a black leather jacket and blue jeans. She also helped with a composite drawing and viewed roughly 100 photographs at the police station. At the station, she recalled two particular characteristics: his very small ears and piercing blue eyes. Believing that the perpetrator was likely stalking her daughter and their house, the mother launched her own investigation – searching local construction sites for possible suspects (*R. v. Hanemaayer*, 2008).

Five days after the assault, 19-year-old Anthony Hanemaayer quit his job at a construction company. The construction company later received a call from the mother who asked if anyone they employed fit her description of the assailant. She was told by a woman working in the office of the personnel department that the description sounded like Hanemaayer. Indeed, with blonde/brown hair and blue eyes, Hanemaayer did fit the description. Hanemaayer, however, did not own a white car and typically opted to ride to work in a company car with coworkers rather than driving his own black Firebird (Innocence Canada, n.d.-b). The mother forwarded the information to police. Two months after the break-in, the mother selected Hanemaayer from a photo lineup of 12 individuals. She later admitted, upon cross-examination, that Hanemaayer's photograph was the least clear of all the pictures in the array. On 18 December 1987, Hanemaayer was arrested and charged in his home in Newmarket, ON. He denied any knowledge of the crime (*R. v. Hanemaayer*, 2008).

By the time his trial began, Hanemaayer had been incarcerated for six months. During this time, the Crown offered Hanemaayer two deals, both of which he refused, while maintaining his innocence. On the first day of the trial, the mother positively identified Hanemaayer as the assailant (Innocence Canada, n.d.-b). Hanemaayer later claimed in an interview that, at that point, he felt like everyone in the courtroom looked at him as if he were guilty (CBC Radio, 2017). He had no one to support his alibi that he was home at the time of the offence because his wife had left him and wasn't speaking to him "as a result of his charge." Given the mother's confidence in her testimony and the prospect of a 6–10-year sentence if found guilty, Hanemaayer's lawyer advised that he change his plea. Just two days into the trial, Hanemaayer accepted the Crown's offer of a plea bargain and confessed to a crime he did not commit. He would later explain that he "lost his nerve." Apparently, he found the homeowner to be a very convincing witness and could tell that his lawyer was not making any headway in convincing the judge otherwise (Moles & Sangha, n.d.).

Twenty years later, Hanemaayer explained his dilemma at the time: "Back then, I was nineteen, I was scared, I would have been scared to go in federal prison because of the charge. So, in other words, basically I had to take the deal. I didn't want to do the ten years. I was already inside. I figured I'd just do another eight months and get out, just get it over and done with…. As the trial proceeded, the trial was going real bad, I could see in everybody's eyes, the Crown, the judge, I could see the way it was … guilty … they had me guilty before I could even prove my innocence" (CBC News, 2008).

Hanemaayer was sentenced to two years less a day and would serve his time in an Ontario provincial prison. After eight months, he was released on parole. He attempted to move on with his life. He married again and fathered two children, but that marriage too ended in divorce. In 2008 came an interesting turn of events. Two lawyers for the Association in Defence of the Wrongly Convicted (AIDWYC; now Innocence Canada) were reviewing the case of another wrongly accused man (Robert Baltovich) when they discovered that Paul Bernardo had confessed to the crime for which Hanemaayer had been convicted (Innocence Canada, n.d.-b). In 2005, Bernardo's lawyer had emailed a police officer of the Sex Crimes Unit listing 18 sexual assaults and other offences he believed to be unsolved, one of which was the crime for which Hanemaayer had been convicted. Police interviewed Bernardo in April 2006 and, following an investigation, confirmed that Bernardo, not Hanemaayer, had committed the crime (*R. v. Hanemaayer*, 2008). Blonde-haired and blue-eyed Bernardo would have fit the witness's description of the assailant (see chapter 7 for more information on the Bernardo case).

Shockingly, Hanemaayer was not apprised of these developments. Neither police nor the Crown prosecutor informed him about Bernardo's confession. In fact, Hanemaayer had no knowledge of Bernardo's confession until he was contacted by AIDWYC lawyers. In 2008, AIDWYC/Innocence Canada took on Hanemaayer's case. Police opened a new investigation and re-interviewed the victim's mother and Hanemaayer. The mother reasserted her confidence that it was Hanemaayer and not Bernardo. She was adamant that it could not have been Bernardo because the *modus operandi* was different. Hanemaayer maintained his innocence. By 25 June 2008, the Ontario Court of Appeal acquitted Hanemaayer of the crime that he never committed. Since his exoneration, it appears that Anthony Hanemaayer has sought solace from this horrific life experience through creative writing (Innocence Canada, n.d.-b). Below is an excerpt of his work entitled "What life?":

How can a "sorry" reverse the damage done?
Within my being, the demons and ghosts haunt my every breath, my every action
A life of irreversible suffering, nightmares, shattered dreams
Faith, a distant hope, an illusion
What will become of me?
How can I look to the future when I have been robbed of all that I was?
All that I could have become?
Alone.
My life stolen.
Where is the justice? How can a wrong be made right?
Faith and hope no more, separated from society
Withdrawn from the world, so I ask
"What life?"

– Anthony Hanemaayer (Innocence Canada, n.d.-b)

PREVALENCE AND CAUSES OF WRONGFUL CONVICTION

Unfortunately, the case of Anthony Hanemaayer is not unique. There are other people similar to Hanemaayer who have been unfairly served by the justice system, but have gone on to be vindicated through some form of exculpatory evidence – but at what cost? Being accused of a crime you did not commit often brings stigma, and lay people may often form negative perceptions about the exoneree, especially those from racialized groups (see, e.g., Hamovitch et al., 2022; Zannella et al., 2020). Moreover, people like Hanemaayer and a select group of other exonerees are merely just the ones we know about. On any given day, approximately 38,000 Canadian adults are incarcerated in provincial, territorial, and federal institutions. About 14,000 are in federal custody, meaning that they are serving sentences of 2+ years under the supervision of the Correctional Service Canada (see Malakieh, 2020). Among these numbers are an estimated 140–280 people (1%–2%) who are serving sentences they do not deserve and are wrongfully convicted. A wrongful conviction means that an innocent person has been found guilty of a crime. While 140–280 people may not sound like many, Blackstone's Ratio asserts that it is "better that ten guilty persons escape, than that one innocent suffer" (Oxford Reference, 2022; see also chapters 3 and 5). Indeed, the problem is of such a magnitude that, in December 2019, Prime Minister Justin Trudeau instructed the minister of justice and attorney general of Canada to "[e]stablish an independent Criminal Case Review Commission to make it easier and faster for potentially wrongfully convicted people to have their applications reviewed" (Trudeau, 2019). Innocence Canada, a nonprofit legal organization based in Toronto, ON, assists people in making such applications. Since its founding in 1993, Innocence Canada has helped to exonerate 24 innocent people, with 90 cases currently under review (Innocence Canada, n.d.-a)

Many factors can contribute to a wrongful conviction, and many cases involve a combination of factors. Causes of wrongful convictions include eyewitness identification error (e.g., Leighton Hay), false confessions (e.g., Romeo Phillion), Mr. Big stings (e.g., Kyle Unger; see also chapter 1), false guilty pleas and plea bargaining (e.g., Maria Shepherd), investigative tunnel vision (e.g., Thomas Sophonow), systemic discrimination (e.g., Donald Marshall Jr.), errors in forensic science (e.g., hair microscopy in the James Driskell case), jailhouse informants (e.g., Guy Paul Morin), youth vulnerability (e.g., David Milgaard), professional misconduct (e.g., Stephen Truscott; Frank Ostrowski – one of the four George Dangerfield cases), and the role of expert witnesses (e.g., William Mullins-Johnson – one of five Dr. Charles Smith cases). See Innocence Canada (n.d.-c) for information related to the example cases listed above; see Hickman et al. (1989) for information related to the Donald Marshall Jr. case, specifically.

Of all the aforementioned factors, eyewitness identification error is one of the leading causes of wrongful convictions. Consider the fact that of the 873 cases in the National Registry of Exonerations (a joint project of the University of Michigan Law School and the Center on Wrongful Convictions at the Northwestern University School of Law), eyewitness identification errors occurred in 76 per cent (n = 667) of cases (see Gross & Shaffer, 2012). Smith and Cutler's (2013) analysis of 1,198 cases of wrongful convictions found that eyewitness error occurred in 50 per cent of the cases. According to the US Innocence Project

(2020), eyewitness identification error was a contributing factor in 70 per cent of 356 DNA-exonerated convictions. While DNA analysis has been a godsend to many wrongfully convicted, it is not an option in most cases as most do not include biological evidence that can be DNA tested. In those cases, investigators must rely on other forms of evidence. In turn, many wrongfully convicted persons must rely on less definitive options (e.g., eyewitness testimony) to prove their innocence. When the prosecution depends on eyewitness identification, "the risk of a miscarriage of justice is notorious" (*Gage v. HM Advocate*, 2011).

CLINICAL FORENSIC PSYCHOLOGY AND EYEWITNESS TESTIMONY

> *No matter what eyewitness testimony is in the court of law, it is the lowest form of evidence in the court of science.*
>
> *– Neil deGrasse Tyson (as cited in McAfee & d'Entremont, 2017)*

Researchers have been studying eyewitness testimony for over 100 years (see Münsterberg, 1909). Eyewitnesses can err in two ways: by failing to identify the guilty or falsely identifying the innocent. The American Psychological Association estimates that one in three eyewitnesses make an erroneous identification (Wise et al., 2014). Eyewitness errors can occur for many reasons and at different points in an investigation; if early, it "can set in motion a chain of errors causing an innocent person to be charged and leading the trier of fact towards a guilty verdict" (Government of Canada, 2019). Eyewitness testimony relies on memory and, as Münsterberg (1909) cautioned so many years ago, "Justice would less often miscarry if all who are to weigh evidence were more conscious of the treachery of human memory" (p. 44). Much of what we know about memory dates back to experiments conducted by Hermann Ebbinghaus in the 1880s. With his "forgetting curve," Ebbinghaus (1885) visually depicted the degradation of memory for meaningless information (e.g., nonsense syllables), with roughly 50 per cent of information irretrievable after one hour. Ebbinghaus's research was recently replicated by Murre and Dros (2015), who confirmed the following: memories fade gradually unless effort is made at retention, the greatest decrement occurs shortly after learning, meaningful information is easier to remember, recency and primacy effects occur, and psychological factors (e.g., stress, sleep) impact retention.

Atkinson and Shiffrin (1968) proposed a three-stage model of memory processing: encode, store, and retrieve. *Encoding* involves the input of information that begins with perception and attention. For instance, we notice something in our environment (e.g., a "creepy" person) and we process that information either automatically (without conscious awareness) or with conscious effort. Information is organized according to details like time, space, frequency, and meaning of words. At this stage, environmental factors (e.g., lighting of the crime scene, duration of event, proximity to perpetrator, presence of a weapon) and physical aspects of the witness (e.g., vision, hearing, attention, intoxication) can affect the accuracy of the memory. Once the information is encoded, it moves to *storage* via sensory memory (sights, sounds, tastes, smells, tactual sensation) then to short-term memory (temporary, limited capacity) followed by long-term memory (continuous intake, infinite capacity). Once stored, memories can be *retrieved* through *recall* (without cues) or *recognition* (identifying information once reencountered). For example, the police may ask you to describe the "creepy" person you saw (i.e., retrieved through recall memory) or to indicate if that person is included in a photo array or lineup (i.e., retrieved through recognition memory).

The Atkinson-Shiffrin model is based on the belief that we process memories in the same way that a computer processes information. Memory, however, is more akin to a living document than a hard drive. That is, memory is subject to continual editing and updating, and is vulnerable to distortion – such as reconstructions in how events transpired. Memories can be influenced by many factors throughout the encoding and storage process including, but not limited to, schema or mental models of the world (i.e., the way we organize information based on our knowledge, beliefs, attitudes, and expectations); source amnesia (i.e., predilection to forget origin of information); hindsight (20/20) bias (i.e., events seem more obvious and predictable once they have happened); confabulation (i.e., creation of false memories without intention to deceive); and state of the individual during the encoding, storage, and retrieval processes (i.e., being under the influence of substances, fatigue, experiencing anxiety or stress; see Neath & Surprenant, 2003; see also Openstax, 2022).

Figure 2.1. Thomas Sophonow was tried three times and imprisoned for four years for the 1981 murder of donut-shop clerk Barbara Stoppel. He was acquitted in 1985 (another wrongful conviction related to faulty eyewitness testimony).
Picture courtesy of *Winnipeg Free Press*.

Misconceptions about memory have fed into myths about eyewitness testimony, including the following, all of which are not true (see Tupper et al., 2015), and miscarriages of justice (see Sophonow, 1984).

1. **All eyewitness testimony is unreliable.** While the salience of highly publicized wrongful conviction cases can make it seem like no eyewitness testimony should be trusted, truth be known, most eyewitnesses are reporting on crimes about people they know. Consider that about 90 per cent of sexual assault victim-survivors know their assailant (see Brooks-Hay, 2020). Indeed, eyewitness testimony figures prominently and positively in many cases. One study found that most of the 189 cold cases held by the District of Columbia's Metropolitan Police Department (US) were reopened

because of new eyewitnesses coming forward (63%) versus DNA testing (3%; Davis et al., 2014).

2. **Not all eyewitnesses are vulnerable to bias.** Bias can easily be introduced by seemingly harmless decisions made by police. The case of *R. v. Sophonow* (1984; see figure 2.1) illustrates how eyewitness testimony can be subtly influenced leading to eyewitness error and wrongful conviction (see Yarmey, 2003). Sophonow was convicted of the brutal murder of Barbara Stoppel in a donut shop in Winnipeg, MB. As would later be revealed, Sophonow had an ironclad alibi and could not have committed the crime. Nonetheless, a number of eyewitnesses described a man who looked like Sophonow being in the donut shop, and incorrectly picked Sophonow out of photo and in-person lineups. The composite drawing of the suspect (a tall man with dark hair, wearing a cowboy hat) resembled the picture of Sophonow that was used in the lineup. One eyewitness, who had seen the composite drawing of the suspect, later picked Sophonow out of the lineup of photographs. Other eyewitnesses were shown a photo lineup where Sophonow appeared to be a foot taller than the rest of the suspects. Eyewitnesses who felt unsure received cues from the police as to whom was the correct choice. Three out of the four eyewitnesses were unable to identify the suspect in the photo lineup, but nevertheless proceeded to testify at the trial that Sophonow was the man they witnessed leaving the crime scene. Unfortunately, judges and juries are often unaware of how police construct and conduct lineups and the perils of improper procedures. See below for an important discussion related to the best practices and recommendations for lineup procedures.
3. **Confidence is a good indicator of reliability.** Research by Gary Wells and others has demonstrated that eyewitness confidence can be manipulated (e.g., selection being confirmed by police officers), but also inflated through repeated tellings. Wells et al. (1998, 2020) have recommended that police ask eyewitnesses to rate their confidence in their identification decision immediately after they make it (prior to any feedback) and that rating should be used in court. Perhaps in no case is the fallibility of eyewitness confidence better illustrated than in the Ronald Cotton case. In 1984, Cotton was convicted of the rape of Jennifer Thompson. She

was very confident of Cotton's guilt and made a compelling witness for the prosecution. But she was wrong, and Cotton served 11 years before being exonerated by DNA (Thompson-Cannino et al., 2009).

4. **Consistency is a good indicator of reliability**. While consistency is appealing, discrepancies in an eyewitness's account can arise due to frailties of memory or police asking different questions (Fisher et al., 2009). Consistency across cowitnesses can be especially appealing but likewise should be treated with caution and confirmed as being truly independent. Research shows that cowitnesses can (inadvertently) come up with a common version of events by either blending original and postevent information or complying with the version of the most confident witness (Skagerberg & Wright, 2008).
5. **Expert witnesses are unnecessary**. In *R. v. Mohan* (1994), the Supreme Court of Canada established formal criteria for determining when expert testimony should be admitted into court. The expert is to assist the court by providing evidence based on their specialized knowledge and experience, which is deemed to be beyond the purview of jury members or judge. The importance of expert evidence is highlighted by the findings of Benton et al. (2006) that only 41 per cent of jury-eligible Americans believed that police lineup instructions can impact the accuracy of an eyewitness identification, and only 50 per cent knew that eyewitness confidence is highly susceptible to outside influences (see also Wise et al., 2014; see also the discussion about Saul Kassin and false confessions in chapter 1). In 1975, researcher Dr. Elizabeth Loftus became the first North American psychologist to provide expert testimony on eyewitness memory and misidentification. Since then, she has testified in over 250 cases, including, most recently and controversially, Ghislaine Maxwell, but also Ted Bundy, Rodney King, Harvey Weinstein, the Menendez brothers, the Oklahoma City Bombing, and Thomas Sophonow. The enquiry into the *R. v. Sophonow* (1984) case led to a number of recommendations, including that judges should willingly admit expert testimony (i.e., psychologists) on the nature of eyewitness memory (see Yarmey, 2003). Unfortunately, no expert witness testified at the 1987 trial of Anthony Hanemaayer, who was tried and convicted solely on the basis of eyewitness testimony.

RECALL AND RECOGNITION PROCEDURES OF PERPETRATORS

Elizabeth Loftus is one of the world-leading authorities on research related to memory and, in particular, eyewitness memory. She has spent a lifetime demonstrating that there are many factors that can influence an eyewitness's memory (e.g., Loftus, 2003, 2019; Loftus & Palmer, 1974; Loftus & Zanni, 1975). For example, recall memory can be impacted by inaccurate information presented after an event, in what is known as the misinformation or postevent effect (see Loftus, 2005). This means that something as simple as the choice of words used by police during witness questioning can impact memory. For instance, asking how fast the cars were going when they *contacted/bumped/collided / smashed* will elicit increasingly higher estimates of speed (Loftus & Palmer, 1974). Similarly, asking "Did you see *the* broken light?" versus "Did you see *a* broken light?" can colour an eyewitness's memory of the event and elicit different responses (Loftus & Zanni, 1975). Thus, when asking an eyewitness to recall information about a crime or culprit, it is extremely important that interviewing officers closely monitor their word choice and question structure to avoid pitfalls that may introduce misinformation into the respondent's memory. Using productive questions (i.e., open-ended questions that start with "Tell," "Explain," or "Describe"; e.g., "Describe the person you saw at the party") as compared to unproductive questions (i.e., closed-ended or suggestive questions; e.g., "The culprit got away in a white car, didn't he?") has been shown to not only protect against questioners introducing misinformation to witnesses' testimony, but also render much longer and more detailed responses that can aid in an investigation or examination of facts; this fact has been demonstrated by research examining questioning practices at various stages of the justice system (e.g., police interviews, lawyer direct- and cross-examinations, and judicial questioning; see Lively et al., 2020, 2022; Milne & Bull, 2003; Snook et al., 2012).

Recognition memory, by contrast, involves a process of comparison and can be impacted by different factors including race, weapons, and stress. For instance, eyewitnesses are significantly more apt to remember, and correctly identify, the face of an individual of the same race (cross-race effect). The effect has been demonstrated in numerous studies, including a Canadian-based study by Jackiw et al. (2008), who confirmed the effect in both Caucasian and First Nations samples. The presence of a weapon can also impact memory by focusing the eyewitness's attention to the exclusion of other information (weapon focus effect; Steblay, 1992; see Fawcett et al., 2013). Also, it is commonly assumed that memories for violent, stressful, or emotional events (e.g., "flashbulb memories") are so well-encoded as to be impervious to error during retrieval; however, these too have been found to be vulnerable to distortion (see Lacy & Stark, 2013).

Recognition memory can also be affected by the way a lineup or photospread is constructed and conducted – factors that have become known as system variables within eyewitness identification research. System variables refer to anything that can influence an eyewitness's ability to remember information accurately and is under the complete control of the justice system (e.g., type of lineup constructed, feedback from lineup administrator). Comparatively, estimator variables refer to dispositional and situational factors as they relate to the witnessed event itself and, importantly, can neither be changed nor controlled by the justice system (e.g., room lighting, viewing obstructions, state of witness; see Wells, 1978). A white paper on lineups written by Gary Wells and colleagues (1998) considered how best to utilize system variables under the control of the justice system (e.g., lineup procedures) and offered a number of recommendations for best practices at the time. More recently, Wells and colleagues (2020) provided an updated commentary related to lineup policy and procedures that has incorporated newly gained knowledge from eyewitness research conducted over the past two decades. The current best practice recommendations, as pertaining to lineups and eyewitness identification procedures more broadly, include the following (see Wells et al., 2020):

1. **Pre-lineup interview**. As soon as is practically possible and prior to presenting a suspect lineup, a police officer should interview the eyewitness about what happened (i.e., collect descriptive details of crime and culprit), and note if there were any conditions of the crime event itself that might impact the reliability of information (e.g., amount of light present, obstructed view of crime/culprit); this entire pre-lineup interview should also be video-recorded.

2. **Evidence-based suspicion.** Reasonable evidence needs to exist before an individual can be alleged to be involved with the crime at hand and be further used as a suspect in a lineup procedure. Moreover, any evidence in support of this should be included in writing before the lineup procedure takes place.
3. **Double-blind procedures.** Lineups should be conducted through a "double-blind" process such that both the lineup administrator and eyewitness identifier are neither privy to who the suspect is, nor have knowledge whether the suspect is present or absent in the lineup. This blinded procedure helps to protect the lineup administrator from inadvertently influencing the eyewitness's selection, while also protecting the eyewitness identifier from being pressured to make a selection.
4. **Lineup fillers.** Lineups should be constructed so that there is only one suspect and five fillers (i.e., people known to not be the culprit). Additionally, the physical and context features of the lineup fillers should be similar enough to the suspect so that the suspect does not unfairly stand out (recall the case of *R. v. Sophonow*, 1984, above).
5. **Pre-lineup instructions.** Eyewitness should be provided with specific instructions before the lineup is shown. Specifically, they should be informed that the lineup administrator is not aware of who the suspect is; that the suspect might not be included in the lineup; that they have the option to say "I don't know" as opposed to giving a "yes" or "no" answer; and that the investigation will continue regardless of the lineup procedure outcome.
6. **Immediate confidence statement.** A statement of how confident the eyewitness is with their identification decision should be taken immediately, regardless of whether their decision is "yes," "no," or "I don't know."
7. **Video-recording.** The entire lineup process and procedure – from the pre-lineup interview through to the eyewitness's confidence statement – should be audio- and video-recorded. Recordings of this nature serve to protect all parties involved by accurately capturing the conditions under which the information was collected. Moreover, given that the passage of time can result in memory vulnerabilities (i.e., forgetting), an audio-video recording of the lineup procedures, actions of the lineup administrator, and

decisions made by the eyewitness can protect again misinformation being adopted post event.

8. **Avoid repeated misidentification.** Repeated lineup procedures should not be conducted using the same suspect and eyewitness. Regardless of the eyewitness's decision (i.e., correctly/incorrectly identified/rejected) about the suspect from the original lineup, the suspect should not be shown to the same witness again in a new lineup with new filler suspects.
9. **Showups.** In contrast to a lineup procedure that shows to the eyewitness an array of people who may or may not be the suspect, a showup procedure only shows the suspect to the eyewitness. When possible, a lineup procedure is preferred (vs. a showup). However, in cases where a showup procedure is necessary, all of the recommendations mentioned above for lineups should be applied.

The above recommendations should be followed regardless of whether the lineup is shown simultaneously (i.e., presenting all photos or live persons at the same time and requiring the eyewitness to make a relative judgment) or sequentially (i.e., presenting each photo or live person one at a time and requiring the eyewitness to make an absolute judgment; see Lindsay & Wells, 1985; see also Lindsay, 1999). In cases where a child witness is invited to offer eyewitness identification, research has found that children have trouble with sequential lineup procedures, often leading to incorrect identifications (Lindsay et al., 1997). To help with this, developmental forensic psychologists created the elimination lineup that involves a two-judgment process (see Pozzulo & Lindsay, 1999; see also Pica & Pozzulo, 2017). In the elimination lineup, a child witness is asked to make a relative judgment followed by an absolute judgment. More specifically, the child witness is presented all photos or live persons and is asked to pick who *looks* like the perpetrator of the crime (i.e., relative judgment). Following this decision, the child is then asked to look at this particular photo/person and compare it against their memory of the perpetrator to determine if it *is* the perpetrator (i.e., absolute judgment). For a review of the effectiveness of various lineup procedures, see meta-analyses carried out by Steblay and colleagues (2001, 2003).

SUMMARY AND CONCLUSIONS

It will stay with me forever, for as long as I live. I can never leave that past.
– Anthony Hanemaayer (CBC News, 2008)

Like all wrongfully convicted persons, Anthony Hanemaayer continues to bear the burden of having his name linked to a heinous crime. In Hanemaayer's case, his name is also linked to a heinous criminal, Paul Bernardo. It is important to bear in mind that a wrongful conviction of an innocent person means a guilty (and dangerous) person remains at large. It is possible that, if police had not been so focused on Anthony Hanemaayer, the Scarborough Rapist (Paul Bernardo) could have been apprehended sooner and before he emerged as Ken of the Ken and Barbie Killers (see chapter 7).

Wrongful convictions are costly, not only for individuals like Thomas Sophonow, Ronald Cotton, and Anthony Hanemaayer, but also for our system of justice. As a society, we have agreed that a false negative (guilty person going free) is preferable to a false positive (innocent person being convicted). The presumption of innocence is protected by the Canadian Charter of Rights and Freedoms (CCRF) Section 11(d) (see Government of Canada, 2021). Wrongful convictions imperil the freedom of all of us. One of the most famous opening lines in literature is found in Franz Kafka's (1925) *The Trial*: "Somebody must have made a false accusation against Joseph K., for he was arrested one morning without having done anything wrong" (p. 1). Imagine what it must feel like to be wrongfully accused, let alone wrongfully convicted, of a crime. Imagine what it must feel like to discover that the rightful perpetrator confessed, and you were not told!

While it is easy to understand how eyewitnesses can make honest mistakes, it is much more difficult to comprehend how other witnesses (e.g., police, prosecutors, medical experts) make such inexcusable errors. For instance, Gross et al. (2020) reviewed 2,400 exonerations recorded in America between 1989 and 2019, 93 of whom had escaped a death sentence. Results showed that over half (54%) of the cases involved official misconduct: police in 34 per cent, prosecutors in 30 per cent, and a combination of both in other cases. Only 4 per cent of prosecutors were disciplined; three were disbarred. Police officers were disciplined in 19 per cent of the cases and, of those, 80 per cent were convicted of crimes, such as Chicago police

Sergeant Ronald Watts, who led a group of officers who planted drug or gun evidence, leading to 66 false convictions (Jackman, 2020).

Canada is not immune to professional misconduct leading to wrongful convictions. Forensic child pathologist Dr. Charles Smith was responsible for five murder convictions (now quashed) in Ontario: William Mullins-Johnson, Dinesh Kumar, Louise Reynolds, Lianne Gagnon, and Tammy Marquardt – all of whom were convicted for the deaths of their own or related children (Mahoney & Bonoguore, 2010)! Manitoba crown prosecutor George Dangerfield was responsible for four murder convictions (now quashed) in Manitoba: Frank Ostrowski, Thomas Sophonow, Kyle Unger, and James Driskell (Innocence Canada, n.d.-d). Professional misconduct is especially galling, given that not everyone is at equal risk for wrongful conviction nor equally likely to have their case reviewed. Some people are particularly vulnerable – Indigenous people, racialized Canadians, women, youth, persons with disabilities – and they need professionals to do their jobs well.

The reasons why some groups are more vulnerable to being wrongfully convicted are the same reasons that these groups are overrepresented throughout the criminal justice system. For example, Indigenous persons "are more likely to be arrested, charged, detained in custody without bail, convicted, and imprisoned" (FPT Heads of Prosecution Committee, 2018, p. 231). According to the 2016 Canadian Census, about 5 per cent of the Canadian population was Indigenous, yet 24 per cent of federally sentenced offenders were Indigenous. In 2020, over 30 per cent of individuals in federal custody and 42 per cent of the female inmate population were Indigenous (Office of the Correctional Investigator, 2020). The reasons for higher incarceration rates among Indigenous people are many and include both distal (e.g., colonialism, disruption of cultural practices, poverty, discrimination) and proximal factors (adverse childhood experiences, chronic life stress; see Mushquash et al., 2021). These factors also include "language and translation difficulties, inadequate and insensitive defence representation, pressures to plead guilty and racist stereotypes that associate Aboriginal people with crime" (Roach, 2015, p. 203).

Women, youth, and persons with disabilities also are at risk for succumbing to pressures to plead guilty. Police may appeal to "a mother's sense of responsibility for the welfare of her children to elicit confessions to criminal acts," and avoidance of a custodial sentence that would separate the mother from her children (see Parkes & Cunliffe, 2015, p. 234). Parkes and Cunliffe (2015) suggest that certain types of wrongful convictions disproportionately affect women, and Indigenous women in particular. For example, a woman who kills an abusive partner and pleads guilty to manslaughter, rather than going to trial for murder and pleading self-defence, may be excluded from a future criminal conviction review process because they denied an available defence. Young people are more susceptible to pressure from authority figures to waive their rights or to accept a guilty plea (see *R. v. L.T.H.*, 2008, paras. 1 and 24). False guilty pleas may lead to shorter sentences but can reduce chances of exoneration for wrongfully convicted individuals (see Government of Canada, 2019).

According to Edwin Grimsley (2012), a case analyst with the Innocence Project in New York, 70 per cent of those exonerated by DNA evidence were racialized persons, a disproportionate overrepresentation given that approximately 60 per cent of the American population are non-Latino White. In Canada, of the 24 exonerated Canadians, six (25%) are racialized persons: O'Neil Blackett (Black), Leighton Hay (Black), Dinesh Kumar (Indian), Tammy Marquardt (Indigenous), William Mullins-Johnson (Indigenous), and Maria Shepherd (Asian). Four of the 24 (17%) are women, which is noteworthy, given that less than 5 per cent of incarcerated persons are women (see Innocence Canada, n.d.-c).

While some people are at greater risk to be wrongfully convicted, we all are at risk if our criminal justice system fails and is compromised. All participants in the system (police, courts, corrections) must embrace Blackstone's Ratio "that it is better that ten guilty persons escape, than that one innocent suffer" (Oxford Reference, 2022; see also chapters 3 and 5), and professionals within the system must be held to a higher standard. Indeed, there is something quite despicable about professional misconduct given that professionals bear the responsibility of being self-regulated. Professionals are supposed to be trustworthy. It is noteworthy that, of Dante's nine circles of hell, the deepest is for treachery – those who betray trust or special relationships are to be frozen in a lake of ice (Alighieri, 1472/1982). Such persons are deemed to be even more contemptible than those who commit violence against others (i.e., the seventh circle of hell).

CRITICAL THINKING QUESTIONS

1. In the Ronald Cotton case, we now know from exonerating DNA evidence that the victim, Jennifer Thompson, misidentified Ronald Cotton as Bobby Poole – her actual perpetrator (see Thompson-Cannino et al., 2009). The points discussed above related to the challenges that eyewitnesses face when recalling a criminal event are also applicable to those who are (incorrectly) accused of crimes and asked for an alibi. Indeed, as was the case for Ronald Cotton, he misremembered his whereabouts for the time in question (i.e., he stated that he was with friends when he was actually at his mother's house – both exculpating actions in their own regard), a statement that was ultimately damning for him from the point of view of investigators and ultimately the court jury. What sort of "checks and balances" do you think could be incorporated into police investigative practices that would better evaluate such (misremembered) alibi claims from the accused, and assist eyewitnesses/victims to a crime to remember accurate and complete details?
2. Do you think "brain-" or "memory-training" could help improve an individual's ability to report accurate eyewitness testimony? Why or why not? Could training of any kind be helpful in this domain?
3. Are there any protective measures that the people (i.e., police officers, judges, juries) evaluating these claims (i.e., eyewitness testimony, alibis) can utilize to render better judgments of this information?
4. Do you think you would be a "good" eyewitness? Why or why not? What things have you learned in this chapter that challenge and/or confirm any assumptions you may have had about eyewitness testimony?

NOTE

1. This chapter benefitted from a number of undergraduate students at St. Francis Xavier University in Antigonish, NS, who worked on an Innocence Canada project in 2021. These students included Juliana Khoury, Jenna MacIntosh, Mercedes Hustler, Kierra Maika, Jasonique Moss, Allison Hancock, Dafina Kozhani, Gracie Grieve, and Rachel Jollimore.

REFERENCES

Alighieri, D. (1982). *Inferno* (A. Mandelbaum, Trans.). Bantam Classics. (Original work published 1472)

Atkinson, R. C., & Shiffrin, R. M. (1968). Human memory: A proposed system and its control processes. *Psychology of Learning and Motivation, 2*, 89–195. https://doi.org/10.1016/S0079-7421(08)60422-3

Benton, T. R., Ross, D. F., Bradshaw, E., Thomas, W. N., & Bradshaw, G. S. (2006). Eyewitness memory is still not common sense: Comparing jurors, judges and law enforcement to eyewitness experts. *Applied Cognitive Psychology, 20*(1), 115–29. https://doi.org/10.1002/acp.1171

Brooks-Hay, O. (2020). Doing the "right thing"? Understanding why rape victim-survivors report to the police. *Feminist Criminology, 15*(2), 174–95. https://doi.org/10.1177/1557085119859079

CBC News. (2008, June 20). Ontario man wants assault conviction overturned after Bernardo confession. *CBC News*. https://www.cbc.ca/news/canada/ontario-man-wants-assault-conviction-overturned-after-bernardo-confession-1.719749

CBC Radio. (2017, December 29). Out in the open: Living in the shadow of a notorious killer. *CBC Radio*. https://www.cbc.ca/radio/outintheopen/past-lives-1.4439905/living-in-the-shadow-of-a-notorious-killer-1.4440068

Davis, R. C., Jensen, C., & Kitchens, K. E. (2014). *Cold-case investigations: An analysis of current practices and factors associated with successful outcomes*. Center on Quality Policing. https://www.ojp.gov/pdffiles1/nij/grants/237558.pdf

Ebbinghaus, H. (1885). Forgetting curve. In H. Ebbinghaus, *Memory: A contribution to experimental psychology*. MCW: University of Berlin.

Fawcett, J. M., Fawcett, E., Peace, K. A., & Christie, J. (2013). Of guns and geese: A meta-analytic review of the "weapon focus" literature. *Psychology, Crime and Law, 19*(1), 35–66. https://doi.org/10.1080/1068316X.2011.599325

Fisher, R. P., Brewer, N., & Mitchell, G. (2009). The relation between consistency and accuracy of eyewitness testimony: Legal versus cognitive explanations. In R. Bull, T. Valentine, & T. Williamson (Eds.), *Handbook of psychology of investigative interviewing: Current developments and future directions* (pp. 121–36). Wiley Blackwell. https://doi.org/10.1002/9780470747599.ch8

FPT Heads of Prosecution Committee. (2018). *Innocence at stake: The need for continued vigilance to prevent wrongful convictions in Canada – Report of the Federal/Provincial/Territorial Heads of Prosecutions Subcommittee on the Prevention of Wrongful Convictions*. https://www.ppsc-sppc.gc.ca/eng/pub/is-ip/is-ip-eng.pdf

Gage v. HM Advocate. (2011). HCJAC 40. https://www.scotcourts.gov.uk/search-judgments/judgment?id=fa5c86a6-8980-69d2-b500-ff0000d74aa7

Government of Canada. (2019, April 25). Chapter 8 – False guilty pleas. In *Innocence at stake: The need for continued vigilance to prevent wrongful convictions in Canada – Report of the Federal/Provincial/Territorial Heads of Prosecutions Subcommittee on the Prevention of Wrongful Convictions*. https://www.ppsc-sppc.gc.ca/eng/pub/is-ip/ch8.html

Government of Canada. (2021, September 1). Section 11(d) – Presumption of innocence. In *Canadian charter of rights and freedoms*. https://www.justice.gc.ca/eng/csj-sjc/rfc-dlc/ccrf-ccdl/check/art11d.html

Grimsley, E. (2012, September 26). *What wrongful convictions teach us about racial inequality*. Innocence Project. https://innocenceproject.org/what-wrongful-convictions-teach-us-about-racial-inequality/

Gross, S. R., Possley, M. J., Roll, K. J., & Stephens, K. H. (2020). *Government misconduct and convicting the innocent: The role of prosecutors, police, and other law enforcement*. National Registry of Exonerations. https://www.law.umich.edu/special/exoneration/Documents/Government_Misconduct_and_Convicting_the_Innocent.pdf

Gross, S. R., & Shaffer, M. (2012). *Exonerations in the United States, 1989–2012: Report by the National Registry of Exonerations*. http://www.law.umich.edu/special/exoneration/Documents/exonerations_us_1989_2012_full_report.pdf

Hamovitch, L., Zannella, L., Rempel, E., Graf, H., & Clow, K. (2022). "You are not the tenant I am looking for": An analysis of landlords' responses to rental inquiries from wrongfully convicted individuals. *Wrongful Conviction Law Review, 3*(1), 34–59. https://doi.org/10.29173/wclawr71

Hickman, T. A., Poitras, L. A., & Evans, G. T. (1989). *Royal commission on the Donald Marshall, Jr., prosecution: Digest of findings and recommendations*. https://novascotia.ca/just/marshall_inquiry/_docs/Royal%20Commission%20on%20the%20Donald%20Marshall%20Jr%20Prosecution_findings.pdf

Innocence Canada. (n.d.-a). *About us*. https://innocencecanada.com/about-us/

Innocence Canada. (n.d.-b). *Anthony Hanemaayer*. https://www.innocencecanada.com/exonerations/anthony-hanemaayer/

Innocence Canada. (n.d.-c). *Exonerations*. https://www.innocencecanada.com/exonerations/

Innocence Canada. (n.d.-d). *Stories of innocence*. https://www.innocencecanada.com/stories-of-innocence/

Innocence Project. (2020, December 17). *Eyewitness identification reform*. https://innocenceproject.org/eyewitness-identification-reform/

Jackiw, L. B., Arbuthnott, K. D., Pfeifer, J. E., Marcon, J. L., & Meissner, C. A. (2008). Examining the cross-race effect in lineup identification using Caucasian and First Nations samples. *Canadian Journal of Behavioural Science/Revue canadienne des sciences du comportement, 40*(1), 52–7. https://doi.org/10.1037/0008-400x.40.1.52

Jackman, T. (2020, September 16). More than half of all wrongful criminal convictions are caused by government misconduct, study finds. *Washington Post*. https://www.washingtonpost.com/crime-law/2020/09/16/more-than-half-all-wrongful-criminal-convictions-caused-by-government-misconduct-study-finds/

Kafka, F. (1925). *The trial*. Verlag Die Schmiede, Berlin.

Lacy, J., & Stark, C. (2013). The neuroscience of memory: Implications for the courtroom. *Nature Review Neuroscience, 14*(9), 649–58. https://doi.org/10.1038/nrn3563

Lindsay, R. C. L. (1999). Applying applied research: Selling the sequential line-up. *Applied Cognitive Psychology, 13*(3), 219–25. https://doi.org/10.1002/(SICI)1099-0720(199906)13:3 3.0.CO;2-H

Lindsay, R. C. L., Pozzulo, J., Craig, W., Lee, K., & Corber, S. (1997). Simultaneous lineups, sequential lineups, and showups: Eyewitness identification decisions of adults and children. *Law and Human Behavior, 21*(4), 391–404. https://doi.org/10.1023/A:1024807202926

Lindsay, R. C. L., & Wells, G. L. (1985). Improving eyewitness identifications from lineups: Simultaneous versus sequential lineup presentation. *Journal of Applied Psychology, 70*(3), 556–64. https://doi.org/10.1037/0021-9010.70.3.556

Lively, C. J., Fallon, L., Snook, B., & Fahmy, W. (2020). Seeking or controlling the truth? An examination of courtroom questioning practices by Canadian lawyers. *Psychology, Crime & Law, 26*(4), 343–66. https://doi.org/10.1080/1068316X.2019.1669595

Lively, C. J., Fallon, L., Snook, B., & Fahmy, W. (2022). Objection, your honour: Examining the questioning practices of Canadian judges. *Psychology, Crime & Law*. Advanced online publication. https://doi.org/10.1080/1068316X.2022.2030737

Loftus, E. F. (2003). Memory in Canadian courts of law. *Canadian Psychology, 44*(3), 207–12. https://doi.org/10.1037/h0086940

Loftus, E. F. (2005). Planting misinformation in the human mind: A 30-year investigation of the malleability of memory. *Learning and Memory, 12*(4), 361–6. https://doi.org/10.1101/lm.94705

Loftus, E. F. (2019). Eyewitness testimony. *Applied Cognitive Psychology, 33*(4), 498–503. https://doi.org/10.1002/acp.3542

Loftus, E. F., & Palmer, J. C. (1974). Reconstruction of automobile destruction: An example of the interaction between language and memory. *Journal of Verbal Learning and Verbal Behavior, 13*(5), 585–9. https://doi.org/10.1016/S0022-5371(74)80011-3

Loftus, E. F., & Zanni, G. (1975). Eyewitness testimony: The influence of the wording of a question. *Bulletin of the Psychonomic Society, 5*(1), 86–8. https://doi.org/10.3758/BF03336715

Mahoney, J., & Bonoguore, T. (2010, August 10). 14 cases tainted by Charles Smith's evidence. *Globe and Mail*. https://www.theglobeandmail.com/news/national/14-cases-tainted-by-charles-smiths-evidence/article562711/

Malakieh, J. (2020). Adult and youth correctional statistics in Canada, 2018/2019. *Statistics Canada*. https://www150.statcan.gc.ca/n1/pub/85-002-x/2020001/article/00016-eng.htm

McAfee, D. G., & d'Entremont, Y. (2017). *No sacred cows: Investigating myths, cults, and the supernatural.* Pitchstone.

Milne, R., & Bull, R. (2003). *Investigative interviewing: Psychology and practice.* Wiley.

Moles, R., & Sangha, B. (n.d.). *Networked knowledge – Law report R. v. Hanemaayer*, 2008 ONCA 580. http://netk.net.au/Canada/Hanemaayer.asp

Münsterberg, H. (1909). *On the witness stand: Essays on psychology and crime.* Doubleday.

Murre, J. M. J., & Dros, J. (2015). Replication and analysis of Ebbinghaus' forgetting curve. *PLoS ONE, 10*(7). https://doi.org/10.1371/journal.pone.0120644

Mushquash, C., Lund, J., Toombs, E., & Grol, C. (2021). Colonialism and cultural disruption: Intergenerational pathways to incarceration for Indigenous Peoples. In C. Cesaroni (Ed.), *Canadian prisons: Understanding the Canadian correctional system* (pp. 169–92). Oxford University Press.

Neath, I., & Surprenant, A. M. (2003). *Human memory* (2nd ed.). Thomson Wadsworth.

Office of the Correctional Investigator. (2020, January 21). *Indigenous people in federal custody surpasses 30%: Correctional Investigator issues statement and challenge.* https://www.oci-bec.gc.ca/cnt/comm/press/press20200121-eng.aspx

Openstax. (2022). *Memory.* https://openstax.org/books/psychology-2e/pages/8-introduction

Oxford Reference. (2022). Blackstone ratio. https://www.oxfordreference.com/view/10.1093/oi/authority.20110803095510389

Parkes, D., & Cunliffe, E. (2015). Women and wrongful convictions: Concepts and challenges. *International Journal of Law in Context, 11*(3), 219–44. https://doi.org/10.1017/S1744552315000129

Pica, E., & Pozzulo, J. (2017). The elimination-plus lineup: Testing a modified lineup procedure with confidence. *Journal of Investigative Psychology and Offender Profiling, 14*(3), 294–306. https://doi.org/10.1002/jip.1477

Pozzulo, J. D., & Lindsay, R. C. L. (1999). Elimination lineups: An improved identification procedure for child eyewitnesses. *Journal of Applied Psychology, 84*(2), 167–76. https://doi.org/10.1037/0021-9010.84.2.167

Roach, K. (2015). The wrongful conviction of Indigenous people in Australia and Canada. *Flinders Law Journal, 17*(2), 203–62. http://www.austlii.edu.au/au/journals/FlinLawJl/2015/7.html

R. v. Hanemaayer, 2008, ONCA 580.

R. v. L.T.H., 2008, SCC 49.

R. v. Mohan, 1994, 2 SCR 9.

R. v. Sophonow, 1984, 2 SCR 524.

Skagerberg, E. M., & Wright, D. B. (2008). The prevalence of co-witnesses and co-witness discussions in real eyewitnesses. *Psychology, Crime & Law, 14*(6), 513–21. https://doi.org/10.1080/10683160801948980

Smith, A. M., & Cutler, B. L. (2013). Introduction: Identification procedures and conviction of the innocent. In B. L. Cutler (Ed.), *Reform of eyewitness identification procedures* (pp. 3–21). American Psychological Association. https://doi.org/10.1037/14094-001

Snook, B., Luther, K., Quinlan, H., & Milne, R. (2012). Let 'em talk! A field study of police questioning practices of suspects and accused persons. *Criminal Justice and Behavior, 39*(10), 1328–39. https://doi.org/10.1177/0093854812449216

Steblay, N. M. (1992). A meta-analytic review of the weapon focus effect. *Law and Human Behavior, 16*(4), 413–24. https://doi.org/10.1007/BF02352267

Steblay, N., Dysart, J., Fulero, S., & Lindsay, R. C. L. (2001). Eyewitness accuracy rates in sequential and simultaneous lineup presentations: A meta-analytic comparison. *Law and Human Behavior, 25*(5), 459–74. https://doi.org/10.1023/A:1012888715007

Steblay, N., Dysart, J., Fulero, S., & Lindsay, R. C. L. (2003). Eyewitness accuracy rates in police showup and lineup presentations: A meta-analytic comparison. *Law and Human Behavior, 27*(5), 523–40. https://doi.org/10.1023/A:1025438223608

Thompson-Cannino, J., Cotton, R., & Torneo, E. (2009). *Picking Cotton: Our memoir of injustice and redemption*. Macmillan.

Trudeau, J. (2019, December 13). *Minister of Justice and Attorney General of Canada mandate letter.* https://pm.gc.ca/en/mandate-letters/2019/12/13/archived-minister-justice-and-attorney-general-canada-mandate-letter

Tupper, N., Sauerland, M., Hope, L., Merckelbach, H., & Efendic, E. (Eds.). (2015). Seeing and believing: Common courtroom myths in eyewitness memory. *The Inquisitive Mind.* https://www.in-mind.org/article/seeing-and-believing-common-courtroom-myths-in-eyewitness-memory?page=5

Wells, G. L. (1978). Applied eyewitness-testimony research: System variables and estimator variables. *Journal of Personality and Social Psychology, 36*(12), 1546–57. https://doi.org/10.1037/0022-3514.36.12.1546

Wells, G. L., Kovera, M. B., Douglass, A. B., Brewer, N., Meissner, C. A., & Wixted, J. T. (2020). Policy and procedure recommendations for the collection and preservation of eyewitness identification evidence. *Law and Human Behavior, 44*(1), 3–36. https://doi.org/10.1037/lhb0000359

Wells, G. L., Small, M., Penrod, S., Malpass, R. S., Fulero, S. M., & Brimacombe, C. A. E. (1998). Eyewitness identification procedures: Recommendations for lineups and photospreads. *Law and Human Behavior, 22*(6), 603–47. https://doi.org/10.1023/A:1025750605807

Wise, R. A., Sartori, G., Magnussen, S., & Safer, M. A. (2014). An examination of the causes and solutions to eyewitness error. *Frontiers in Psychiatry*, 5. https://doi.org/10.3389/fpsyt.2014.00102

Yarmey, A. (2003). Eyewitness identification: Guidelines and recommendations for identification procedures in the United States and in Canada. *Canadian Psychology, 44*(3), 181–9. https://doi.org/10.1037/h0086938

Zannella, L., Clow, K., Rempel, E., Hamovitch, L., & Hall, V. (2020). The effects of race and criminal history on landlords' (un)willingness to rent to exonerees. *Law and Human Behavior, 44*(4), 300–10. https://doi.org/10.1037/lhb0000419

CHAPTER THREE

Trial by Media: Pretrial Publicity

The Case of Dennis Oland

With Ethan Draper, Elle Lévesque, and Christopher J. Lively

> *The media is the most powerful entity on earth. They have the power to make the innocent guilty and to make the guilty innocent, and that's power.*
>
> *– Malcolm X (1965)*

In July 2011, 69-year-old New Brunswick businessman Richard Oland was found dead in his Saint John office. Lying in a pool of blood from 45 blows to the head, neck, and upper body (MacKinnon, 2016), his death was deemed a homicide. Prosecutor Paul Veniot later described the violence as gratuitous: "way beyond what was required to cause Richard Oland's death" (Blatchford, 2015).

Although suspicion fell early on Dennis Oland, it was not until November 2013 that the 51-year-old was charged with the second-degree murder of his father. What implicated Dennis Oland was that he seemed to have been the last person to see his father alive. He had visited his father at his downtown Saint John office that evening, claiming to have left at 6:30 p.m. His father's cell phone (which has never been found) received its last message at 6:44 p.m. pinging off a cell tower near a wharf in Rothesay, NB, where Dennis later testified that he had gone in search of his children. Dennis and Richard's relationship was a contentious one. As Richard's only son, Dennis claimed that he faced a great deal of pressure and high expectations from his father, describing him as a man who could not be friends with his son (MacKinnon, 2013). Nonetheless, Richard had come to his son's aid during his 2009 divorce, providing Dennis with a $500,000 financial arrangement so that he could retain the ancestral home. Recently, Dennis had fallen into arrears (bounced two interest payments of $1,666.67 to his father including one the day before his father's murder), and his prospects for regaining a financial foothold did not look promising. Forensic accountants would testify that in the months leading up to his father's murder, Dennis's financial situation was becoming dire. Apparently, the CIBC Wood Gundy employee was living beyond his means by up to $14,000 per month (MacKinnon, 2015b). While deeply indebted to his father, it seems Dennis resented the idea that his 69-year-old father may have been planning to marry his mistress of eight years.

Another piece of incriminating evidence against Dennis involved the suit jacket he was wearing on the day of the murder. Oland claimed he had been wearing a navy blazer, but video footage showed that he was wearing a brown sport coat. The sport coat in question was dry cleaned before police confiscated it as evidence, at which time an investigator rolled it up into a 30-centimetre by 30-centimetre paper bag with his bare hands. The sport coat was not forensically examined for four months (MacKinnon, 2015c), and was later found to have traces of blood on it that were confirmed to be that of his late father.

While there were factors that implicated Dennis Oland, certain key pieces of information were missing. The time of death could not be confirmed, and no murder weapon was ever found. The crime scene had not been adequately secured and was contaminated before forensic testing. A back door that might have served as an escape route for the killer was not tested for evidence (MacKinnon, 2017). A footprint that did not match either of the Olands' seized footwear was never identified (Sadler, 2020). Although a few bloodstains matching Richard's DNA were found on Dennis's brown sport coat, no significant blood was found in his car or on his shoes. Given the violence of the assault, this lack of significant blood was perplexing.

JURY SELECTION IN THE OLAND CASE

Selecting a jury for the Oland trial was bound to be a challenge. New Brunswick is a small province (population of less than 800,000), and even its largest city, Saint John, is small (approximately 70,000). For most trials in New Brunswick, only about 300 people would be summoned for the jury panel. For the Oland trial, a record 5,000 prospective jurors (almost 17 times the normal jury pool) were summoned to a local hockey arena. The pool was larger than those for the trials of serial killer Allan Legere ("Monster of the Miramichi"; *N* = 500), Paul Bernardo (*N* = 1,500), Luka Magnotta (*N* = 1,600), or Robert "Willie" Pickton (*N* = 3,500) (Mackinnon, 2015a). It was hoped that such a large pool would yield 12 impartial jurors, but this was not guaranteed in a province where the name "Oland" is ubiquitous. The case was very highly publicized in the Saint John region, leading to some concerns over the court's ability to conduct a fair trial. Nonetheless, 16 jurors were empanelled: 12 jurors plus 4 alternates. On 16 September 2015, the longest trial in the province's history (65 days) began and, in December 2015, Dennis Oland was found guilty of the second-degree murder of his father, Richard Oland. When New Brunswick's "trial of the century" ended, Dennis Oland had been found guilty and sentenced to life imprisonment with parole eligibility after 10 years. The jury had deliberated for 30 hours (Sadler, 2020).

Ten months later, the New Brunswick Appeal Court overturned Oland's conviction "on the grounds of misdirection in the [trial] judge's instructions with respect to postoffence conduct evidence, specifically [Oland's] false statement to the police regarding the jacket he was wearing at the material times" (MacKinnon, 2017). Pretrial publicity and community sentiment surrounding the case were presumed to have played an undue role in Dennis Oland being found guilty despite the case being built on circumstantial (vs. forensic) evidence. Dennis Oland believed that everyone "had their own opinions of his guilt before the first trial began" (Sadler, 2020). Oland and others placed blame on the local Saint John police and their "tunnel vision" detective work, saying, "A small-town police force decided that I killed my father" (Sadler, 2020). Oland argued that many believed he "must have done it" due to his wealthy upbringing and life as a "rich kid from Rothesay" (Sadler, 2020).

For his second trial in October 2018, Oland requested to be tried by judge-alone, arguing that prejudicial pretrial publicity impeded his right to a fair trial. His lawyers cited "thousands" of media reports, social media postings, two bestselling books, The Fifth Estate documentary, *The Richard Oland Case: Murder in the Family,* plus CBC's online publication of Dennis Oland's full videotaped statement to police on 7 July 2011 (i.e., the day Richard Oland's body was discovered) as evidence of the magnitude and bias of pretrial publicity. The defence reported the results of a public opinion poll that found that 27 per cent of respondents ($N = 401$) in the Saint John area believed Oland was guilty, 18 per cent believed he was not guilty, and 55 per cent said they did not know or preferred not to say. Of those who indicated they would "very much" like to serve on Oland's jury, nearly 46 per cent believed he was guilty. The defence team explored the option of a change of venue, but a telephone poll of over 1,200 jury-eligible residents in Saint John, Moncton, and Fredericton found no significant difference between jurisdictions. Again, about 45 per cent of respondents who said they "very much" wanted to serve believed Oland was guilty. Oland's request for a judge-alone trial was denied; however, during the jury selection process, the judge was forced to declare a mistrial after learning that a Saint John police officer conducted "improper" background checks on prospective jurors – alleged witness tampering that could have proved advantageous to the Crown (MacKinnon, 2018).

Justice Terrence Morrison decided to hear the case alone, without a jury. The retrial lasted 44 days and included 61 witness testimonies and 309 pieces of evidence (Campbell, 2019). In July 2019, with insufficient evidence to satisfy the standard of beyond a reasonable doubt, Dennis Oland was found not guilty of the second-degree murder of his father (Campbell, 2019). In commenting on the acquittal, Greg Marquis (2019), University of New Brunswick professor and Oland trial author, said the judge found "too many gaps, too many unknowns and too much reasonable doubt. It is not a black-and-white thing, but in the end reasonable doubt trumps everything" (Campbell, 2019). In his closing statements, sentencing judge Terrence Morrison concluded: "There is much to implicate Dennis Oland in this crime.... But more than suspicion is needed in order to convict someone of murder – probability is not enough" (Levenson-King, 2019). To date, Richard Oland's murder remains a mystery.

EFFECTS OF PRETRIAL PUBLICITY ON IMPARTIALITY

Impartiality of a tribunal (court) refers to the absence of bias – bias arising from a personal interest in the case, bias directed at the accused's cultural or racial group, but also bias arising from pretrial publicity or notoriety of the accused (*R. v. Sherratt*, 1991). Interestingly, bias pertaining to the nature of the offence (e.g., negative perceptions of persons charged with sexual assault) is not as big a concern as other forms of bias (*R. v. Find*, 2001). Impartiality does not require that the juror's mind be a blank slate, nor that they disregard all opinions, beliefs, knowledge, and other accumulations of life experience, nor everything they have heard or learned about the case from media sources. Impartiality means that the juror is expected to be "indifferent between the Queen and the accused" (*R. v. Find*, 2001).

Pretrial publicity refers to media coverage of a case prior to trial (see Studebaker & Penrod, 1997). High-profile cases can attract a lot of media attention, especially if they involve (a) sexual or sordid elements; (b) a particularly heinous crime; and/or (c) defendants who are famous, infamous, or otherwise well-known in their local area (Morris, 2003). Media reporting that emphasizes the dastardliness of the defendant's actions, deleterious effects on victims, compelling evidence against the defendant, and/or opinions about the defendant's guilt expressed by police, prosecution, political figures, or celebrities can be quite prejudicial (Penrod, 2021). As an example, former US president Donald Trump once took out a full-page newspaper advertisement that called for the death penalty for the five teenagers accused in the 1989 Central Park Jogger case – all of whom were later DNA-exonerated (see chapter 1). Negative pretrial publicity, especially when extensive, can threaten the defendant's right to a fair trial. If the public is flooded with prejudicial information, it can be difficult for the courts to find truly impartial jurors who have not been affected by the publicity. This can result in verdicts being decided, not on the basis of trial evidence, but by media attention – "trial by media" (see Chancellor, 2019; Suresh & George, 2021).

Media play an important role in the adjudication of justice. Media are the fourth pillar (estate) of democracy (after executive, legislative, and judicial branches), and a responsible press is considered to be the "handmaiden of effective judicial administration, especially in the criminal field.... The press does not simply publish information about trials but guards against the miscarriage of justice by subjecting the police, prosecutors, and judicial processes to extensive public scrutiny and criticism" (*Vickery v. Nova Scotia Supreme Court [Prothonotary]*, 1991). In pretrial publicity cases, the concern is not publication of facts but the misrepresentation of evidence, dissemination of discreditable incidents from an accused's past, or undue speculation as to the accused's guilt or innocence.

RESEARCH ON PRETRIAL PUBLICITY

Pretrial publicity can cut many ways depending on the type (defendant or victim) and the slant (positive or negative). Factors such as gender (of both the jurors and defendant), defendant ethnicity, criminal history, type of crime being tried, and even acceptance of rape myths can impact perceptions and overall decisions made at trial (see, e.g., Belyea & Blais, 2021; Clow et al., 2013; Hammond et al., 2011; Hans & Doob, 1976; Maeder et al., 2012). Ruva (2018) provides a valuable overview of research findings on pretrial publicity derived from (a) surveys of actual or potential jurors, (b) jury simulation research/experiments, and (c) meta-analyses. Highlights from Ruva's (2018) research are provided below, but readers are encouraged to consult the original source and references. Not surprisingly, most research has focused on *negative-defendant* pretrial publicity because it is most prevalent and most apt to jeopardize a defendant's right to a fair trial, especially in high-profile cases. Research shows that jurors who are exposed (vs. not exposed) to negative-defendant pretrial publicity are more likely to find the defendant guilty and to view the defendant as less credible. *Positive-defendant* pretrial publicity is most apt to appear in trials involving sexual assault or murder, or where the defendant is a celebrity or police officer. Jurors exposed (vs. not exposed) to positive-defendant pretrial publicity are more inclined to vote not guilty and to view the defendant as more credible. *Negative-victim* pretrial publicity involves using pejorative language to describe victims and/or portraying their actions as contributing to their victimization. Negative-victim pretrial publicity is prevalent for certain types of crime (e.g., sexual assault, interpersonal violence), and has been found to impact jurors' decision-making. For example, when mock-jurors were presented with anti-victim (vs. pro-victim) stories, they were more likely to believe that the defendant was not guilty and that the victim was lying (see Ruva, 2018).

According to Ruva (2018), in some high-profile cases, multiple types of pretrial publicity (e.g., negative-defendant and negative-victim) can be present. What little research there is suggests that juror exposure to *mixed pretrial publicity* might result in a reduction of bias. It is thought that cases of mixed pretrial publicity will increase with greater accessibility to media sources, including social media. While negative-defendant pretrial publicity is especially problematic given its ability to taint the jury pool and jeopardize the defendant's right to a fair trial, all types or slants of pretrial publicity can influence jury decision-making. For example, both positive-defendant and negative-victim pretrial publicity can challenge the prosecution's burden of proving guilt. Better understanding the influence of pretrial publicity on juror bias is important.

Research shows that the biasing effects of pretrial publicity arise from its influence on the following: (a) how jurors interpret trial evidence, (b) how they form impressions of defendants and defence, (c) how they respond emotionally, and (d) their ability to discriminate the source of information (pretrial publicity vs. trial evidence). For example, pretrial publicity exposure influences what evidence jurors attend to, how much weight they assign to each piece of the evidence, and whether they interpret the evidence as supporting the defence or prosecution. A biasing effect can also occur based on when information is presented to jurors. For instance, research related to the serial position effect has demonstrated that the order of information presented can result in primacy (information presented first) and recency effects (information presented last); the discovery of this phenomenon is credited to Hermann Ebbinghaus (1913). Also, if jurors are able to construct a complete and coherent narrative of what happened based on early pretrial publicity information, then they will ignore or devalue later pretrial publicity or trial information (evidence) that does not fit with their narrative. Compounding the effect, jurors exposed to pretrial publicity are predisposed to prefer a particular side. For example, jurors exposed to negative-defendant pretrial publicity (vs. positive-defendant or no pretrial publicity) are inclined to rate the prosecution more favourably (higher in likeability and ability) and the defence less favourably. Pennington and Hastie's (1986, 1991) story model of jury decision-making explains how jurors exposed to negative-defendant pretrial publicity arrive at court with a version of events wherein the defendant is not credible and likely guilty. Subsequent trial evidence is then encoded in a manner that agrees with this anti-defendant narrative (see Ruva, 2018).

Pretrial publicity that activates emotions can have a more potent effect on jurors' decisions than factual pretrial publicity. For example, negative-defendant pretrial publicity can elicit negative emotions, such as anger, disgust, anxiety, or sadness, but not all negative emotions are equally impactful. Anger appears to be the most powerful emotion for influencing juror perceptions, beliefs, reasoning, choices, and punitiveness. Increased juror anger increases the likelihood that they will vote guilty. Ruva (2018) suggests that when people are angry (vs. sad or anxious) they are less cautious in their decision-making, more influenced by stereotypes, more confident in their preconceived judgments, and less inclined to consider additional information.

Another mechanism through which pretrial publicity can bias jurors' decisions is via source memory. Jurors exposed to pretrial publicity can misattribute information provided only in the pretrial publicity with information provided during the trial. Ruva et al. (2021) warn that increased delay between pretrial publicity exposure and trial testimony, and increased delay between evidence presented early in trial and jury deliberations, can exacerbate the effect. A longer delay between encoding and retrieval of information increases source misattributions. These findings fit with Steblay et al.'s (1999) meta-analysis, which found that pretrial publicity effects increased as the delay between pretrial publicity exposure and verdict decision increased. Pretrial publicity information misattributed to the trial could influence decisions of guilt.

Bruschke (1999, 2016) challenges the evidence for "strong" pretrial publicity effects, arguing that people tend to have poor memories and, if anything, would be inclined to forget pretrial publicity information. Bruschke suggests that the intense spotlight on trial evidence would override pretrial publicity (i.e., elaboration likelihood model of persuasion; see Petty & Cacioppo, 1986a, 1986b) and that the long delays between arraignment and trial in real life should mitigate the effects of pretrial publicity. Bruschke et al. (1999, 2016) have found evidence for "weak" pretrial publicity effects but conclude that pretrial publicity findings remain equivocal: "You can't say it always matters, and you can't say it never matters" (CSUF News, 2020).

Findings from a study on one of Canada's most high-profile cases seem to support Bruschke's scepticism about "strong" pretrial publicity effects. Freedman and Burke (1996) assessed pretrial publicity effects in the case of Paul Bernardo, one of the most sensational and highly publicized cases in Canadian history (see chapter 7). Participants in the study were visitors to the Ontario Science Centre who were asked how much they had heard about the case, then provided a possible scenario of what the trial would contain. Results showed that participants with greater exposure to pretrial publicity were more likely to think Bernardo was guilty. After reading the trial transcript, however, the effect of pretrial publicity virtually disappeared. Knowledge that Bernardo had been charged with other counts of rape seemed to account for the small residual effect.

Clearly, more research on pretrial publicity effects is warranted. For now, however, the preponderance of evidence (see Ruva, 2018) gives cause for concern about its influence on trial integrity and defendants' rights.

REMEDIES FOR REDUCING OR AMELIORATING PRETRIAL PUBLICITY BIAS

In high-profile cases where a widespread bias may exist in the community and it is expected that some jurors may be incapable of setting aside this bias (such as the case of Dennis Oland), despite the trial judge's instructions to jurors to set aside their biases, at least four options are available for increasing the likelihood of securing an impartial jury.

1. **Change of venue**: As the name implies, the trial is moved to a location where the pretrial publicity has been less voluminous and/or negative. This option is seldom granted – notable exceptions being Paul Bernardo's trial, which was moved from St. Catharine's to Toronto, and the trial of Kelly Ellard (the

15-year-old convicted for the swarming death of Reena Virk in 1997), which was moved from Victoria to Vancouver. Relocating a trial will not always produce a jury entirely unaware of the issues surrounding the case (Morris, 2003), and there exists little research on its efficacy. Advances in technology (internet and social media coverage of cases) have removed geographical boundaries, and for those cases that capture national attention, finding a venue where a defendant can receive a fair trial might prove extremely challenging.

2. **Adjournment** (delay of trial): Contrary to courts' beliefs that a delay will diminish or eliminate the biasing effects of pervasive and prejudicial pretrial publicity, social science research suggests it is unlikely to be an effective remedy. Memory traces may persist due to the retention enhancement effects of distributed or spaced learning; emotional pretrial publicity is resistant to delay; media typically reinstates the pretrial publicity at the time of pretrial hearings; and 90 per cent of people are online and accessing news from online media sources, blogs, and social media stories and videos (e.g., YouTube, Netflix, podcasts). See Ruva (2018) and Morris (2003).
3. **Challenges for cause**: During the jury selection process, the judge may allow lawyers to challenge jurors "for cause" if there is reason to believe that the jury pool may contain people who are not "indifferent" between the Crown and the accused – in other words, people who are not able to set aside their biases (see chapter 4).
4. **Jury deliberations**: Although commonly assumed that jury deliberation enables jurors to correct errors, reject irrelevant information, and control biases, research findings suggest otherwise (Ruva, 2018). Indeed, research shows that deliberation can actually intensify pretrial publicity bias via group polarization effects, in which the responses of groups are more extreme than those of individuals (Moscovici & Zavalloni, 1969). For example, Kramer et al. (1990) found that pretrial publicity's biasing effect was stronger in juries than in jurors. Similarly, Kerr et al. (1999) found that jurors exposed to pretrial publicity were more likely to vote guilty after deliberation than prior to it. Ruva and Guenther (2015) found that jurors not exposed to pretrial publicity were less likely to vote guilty after deliberation versus prior to it, in what has been called

a leniency shift (Kerr, 1994). The leniency shift does not seem to apply in cases with negative-defendant pretrial publicity, where jurors are just as likely to vote guilty after deliberations as prior to them. Most recently, Ruva et al. (2021) have reported on a study with mock jurors deliberating on the case of *New Mexico v. Gilbert* (1998). Among other things, this study shows that courts should not rely on jury deliberation to correct the bias associated with pretrial publicity – "doing so may result in an increase or spread of bias" – and that all parties should be concerned about pretrial publicity as it can just as easily challenge prosecutors' ability to attain a guilty verdict.

PRETRIAL PUBLICITY AND THE DENNIS OLAND CASE

Richard Oland's brutal murder and Dennis Oland's arrest were bound to generate a media storm. This case had all the ingredients for a pretrial publicity case: a high-profile defendant, well known in his local area; a heinous crime of patricide (see below); and even somewhat sordid elements like Dennis Oland's perturbance over his father's "mistress." The Oland family are considered "one of a handful of dynasties who had for the past century controlled the economy in the province [NB] like the Rockefellers and the Vanderbilts had once controlled New York City" (Levinson-King, 2019). At the time of his death, Richard Oland was the sole director of three investment and real estate companies with assets estimated to be worth about $36 million. By comparison, his son, Dennis, was deeply in debt.

Determining how pretrial publicity affected the outcomes of the Dennis Oland trials requires that we consider the types and slants of pretrial publicity in the case. For example, Dennis Oland could be seen as a *negative-defendant* (privileged, entitled, "a rich kid from Rothesay") or a *positive-defendant* (well groomed, seemingly mild-mannered, family man, no criminal history). Richard Oland could be seen as a *negative-victim* (hard-nosed businessman, argumentative, adulterer). The day after his murder, Richard's wife, Constance, would describe her deceased husband to police as a "strong and controlling" man who could be verbally and emotionally abusive with their two daughters, Lisa and Jackie, but especially with his only son, Dennis

(Kimber, 2015). On the other hand, Richard Oland could be seen as a *positive-victim* (good community citizen, philanthropist).

The Oland case might fit the profile of a mixed pretrial publicity case: *negative-defendant* and *negative-victim*. *Negative-defendant* pretrial publicity places the burden on the defence team to ensure their client is not denied his right to a fair trial by an impartial jury; both *positive-defendant* and *negative-victim* pretrial publicity place the burden of proving guilt on the prosecution. The mixed outcomes of the two trials might reflect the mixed pretrial publicity. Moreover, the considerable delay (two years) in bringing Dennis Oland to trial might have exacerbated the pretrial publicity impact.

SUMMARY AND CONCLUSIONS

> *The minds of the jurors are the test tubes of the judicial system. They must be kept clean of extraneous matter if justice is to be done.*
>
> *– Greenspan (1984; as cited in Freedman & Burke, 1996)*

The Dennis Oland case is significant for a number of reasons: (a) the Oland family are a Canadian dynasty – along with the Irvings and the McCains, the Olands are "old money" families; (b) crimes of patricide are not common, especially not in such family dynasties; (c) this was the longest and most expensive trial in New Brunswick history; (d) it boasted the largest jury panel in Canadian history; (e) police conduct and misconduct plagued the investigation, including the jury selection process in the second trial; and (f) it is a case with a conclusion but no closure – a murderer has eluded conviction.

It is difficult to assess the impact of pretrial publicity on the Dennis Oland case. Community sentiment ran high and Dennis Oland may have been correct in thinking that everyone had prejudged the outcome. Both Dennis and Richard Oland seemed to cultivate mixed views in the court of public opinion. Interestingly, the alleged crime of patricide was seldom mentioned in the many media accounts of the case. Patricide is a recurring theme in Greek and Roman mythology, with fathers like Saturn and Zeus often fearing that their sons would kill them. In Chinese lore, people who commit patricide (or matricide) will be struck by lightning as punishment. Parental homicide (or parricide) is rare. Oram et al. (2013) found only 251 cases reported between 1997 and 2008 in England and Wales. Bourget et al. (2007) found that parricide accounted for 7 per cent of homicides in the province of Quebec between 1990 and 2005: 64 parents (27 mothers and 37 fathers). Bourget et al.'s sample included 56 perpetrators: 52 sons and 4 daughters and nine cases of double parricide. About 15 per cent of perpetrators (8/56) attempted suicide following the parricide. A psychiatric motive (stemming from depression or psychotic illness) was determined in most cases (65.5%). One study of 10 men charged with patricide found that the fathers had been significantly more punitive than the mothers, and the mothers had been more overprotective and tolerant than the fathers (Singhal & Dutta, 1990). In cases where family abuse occurred, the parricide is often committed using exaggerated and excessive violence (Bourget et al., 2007). Men who committed parricide against their fathers were often motivated by long-term conflict (Liettu et al., 2009), and the homicide was almost always committed in the house of the victim. Mental disorders commonly found among parricide perpetrators include substance misuse, depression, borderline personality disorder, and schizophrenia. Devaux et al. (1974) reported attempted suicide in 17 per cent of all perpetrators.

POSTSCRIPT TO THE DENNIS OLAND CASE

Less than a year after being found not guilty of murder, Dennis Oland was placed under a restraining order for alleged intimate partner violence against his wife, Lisa Andrik-Oland. The allegations, as reported in the *National Post* (see MacDonald, 2021), were contained in an application for an emergency intervention order filed on 10 June 2020, at a shelter for abused women in Saint John, NB. In her handwritten notes, Lisa Andrik-Oland describes Dennis Oland as an angry, violent man who was losing control and suffering from posttraumatic stress disorder. "I am not sure what he will do, but he has PTSD and has had many episodes where he is not controlling his actions and becomes aggressive," she wrote. "It is getting worse because he is less and less in control. He is not getting a reaction from me and he can't handle it.... I am not safe in my own house." She recounts a specific incident during a visit to Toronto in June 2018 in which "Dennis used a belt to tie my hands behind my back; there was a physical altercation," and "[p]eople in the next room called police." Because the incident occurred five months before Oland's retrial was set to begin, Andrik-Oland claims she told police that "everything was OK." Andrik-Oland also describes a "beach incident" in September 2019, when Oland allegedly bound her hands and feet with rope and pulled her down a dirt path. She alleges that he threw her over his shoulder and dropped her head first toward some rocks. According to Andrik-Oland's account, there was "[a] lot of blood," and "Dennis started this with a mental breakdown." She continued, "He dropped me, head first, down on to the rocks ... my head split – cut – I got a cut and there was blood everywhere.... As you can imagine, my husband was accused of quite the crime, where there was a lot of blood. So, when he saw this he completely freaked out," adding that "Dennis continued to sit at edge of property to monitor my movements for a few (hours)." Andrik-Oland goes on to say that "[h]e monitors my movements to my mother's home" and accuses her husband of sending "hate email and text" messages.

This is a confusing account, clearly composed by a woman (Lisa Andrik-Oland) in distress. This is the first report of Dennis Oland having posttraumatic stress disorder (PTSD), but the specific trauma is not known – unexpected death of his father, being accused of the murder, two criminal trials, time served in a maximum-security prison (i.e., Atlantic Institution in Renous, NB), or a combination of all of the above. While the genesis of his trauma is not specified, his wife's comments seem to suggest that he was triggered by all the blood at the "beach incident" because it reminded him of all the blood at the scene of his father's murder. Given that he claims not to have been at the scene of Richard Oland's death, perhaps Dennis was traumatized by the evidence presented in court during his trials. For more information on the potential traumatic impact of trial evidence, see chapter 5.

CRITICAL THINKING QUESTIONS

1. What do you think: Did Dennis Oland murder his father? What factors suggest his culpability in the murder? What factors are exculpatory?
2. Do you think that pretrial publicity influences jury/judge verdicts?
3. Does the allegation of interpersonal violence against his wife affect your perception of Dennis Oland?

REFERENCES

Belyea, L., & Blais, J. (2021). Effect of pretrial publicity via social media, mock juror sex, and rape myth acceptance on juror decisions in a mock sexual assault trial. *Psychology, Crime & Law*, advanced online publication. https://doi.org/10.1080/1068316X.2021.2018440

Blatchford, C. (2015, September 18). Could Dennis Oland have gone from killer to happy shopper in 68 minutes? *National Post*. https://nationalpost.com/opinion/christie-blatchford-could-dennis-oland-go-from-killer-to-happy-shopper-in-68-minutes

Bourget, D., Gagné, P., & Labelle, M. E. (2007). Parricide: A comparative study of matricide versus patricide. *Journal of the American Academy of Psychiatry and the Law Online, 35*(3), 306–12. https://pubmed.ncbi.nlm.nih.gov/17872550/

Bruschke, J., Gonis III, A., Hill, S. A., Fiber-Ostrow, P., & Loges, W. (2016). The influence of heterogeneous exposure and pre-deliberation queries on pretrial publicity effects. *Communication Monographs, 83*(4), 521–34. https://doi.org/10.1080/03637751.2016.1182639

Bruschke, J., & Loges, W. E. (1999). Relationship between pretrial publicity and trial outcomes. *Journal of Communication, 49*(4), 104–20. https://doi.org/10.1111/j.1460-2466.1999.tb02819.x

Campbell, F. (2019, July 19). Author on Dennis Oland's not guilty verdict: "Reasonable doubt trumps everything." *SaltWire*. https://www.saltwire.com/nova-scotia/news/author-on-dennis-olands-not-guilty-verdict-reasonable-doubt-trumps-everything-334712/

Chancellor, L. (2019). Public contempt and compassion: Media biases and their effect on juror impartiality and wrongful convictions. *Manitoba Law Journal, 42*(3), 427–44. https://journals.library.ualberta.ca/themanitobalawjournal/index.php/mlj/article/view/1121

Clow, K. A., Lant, J. M., & Cutler, B. L. (2013). Perceptions of defendant culpability in pretrial publicity: The effects of defendant ethnicity and participant gender. *Race and Social Problems, 5*, 250–61. https://doi.org/10.1007/s12552-013-9102-1

CSUF News. (2020). The jury's still out on the effects of pretrial publicity: Human communication scholar finds limited impact on cases. https://news.fullerton.edu/2020/02/pretrial-publicity-effect-is-limited/

Devaux, C., Petit, G., Perol, Y., & Porot, M. (1974). Enquête sur le parricide en France [Investigation concerning parricide in France]. *Annales Medico Psychologiques, 1*(2), 161–8. https://pubmed.ncbi.nlm.nih.gov/4848990/

Ebbinghaus, H. (1913). *On memory: A contribution to experimental psychology*. Teachers College.

Freedman, J. L., & Burke, T. M. (1996). The effect of pretrial publicity: The Bernardo case. *Canadian Journal of Criminology, 38*(3), 253–70. https://doi.org/10.3138/cjcrim.38.3.253

Hammond, E. M., Berry, M. A., & Rodriguez, D. N. (2011). The influence of rape myth acceptance, sexual attitudes, and belief in a just world on attributions of responsibility in a date rape scenario. *Legal and Criminological Psychology, 16*(2), 242–52. https://doi.org/10.1348/135532510X499887

Hans, V. P., & Doob, A. N. (1976). Section 12 of the Canada Evidence Act and the deliberation of simulated juries. *Criminal Law Quarterly, 18*, 235–53. https://scholarship.law.cornell.edu/cgi/viewcontent.cgi?article=1480&context=facpub

Kerr, N. L. (1994). The effects of pretrial publicity on jurors. *Judicature, 78*(3), 120–7. https://heinonline.org/HOL/LandingPage?handle=hein.journals/judica78&div=32&id=&page=

Kerr, N. L., Niedermeier, K. E., & Kaplan, M. F. (1999). Bias in jurors vs. bias in juries: New evidence from the SDS perspective. *Organizational Behavior and Human Decision Processes, 80*(1), 70–86. https://doi.org/10.1006/obhd.1999.2855

Kimber, S. (2015, April 1). *Spilled secrets: The Richard Oland murder mystery*. Stephen Kimber. https://stephenkimber.com/spilled-secrets-the-richard-oland-murder-mystery/

Kramer, G. P., Kerr, N. L., & Carroll, J. S. (1990). Pretrial publicity, judicial remedies, and jury bias. *Law and Human Behavior, 14*(5), 409–38. https://doi.org/10.1007/BF01044220

Levinson-King, R. (2019, July 19). Richard Oland: A millionaire, a murder and a mystery killer. *BBC News*. https://www.bbc.com/news/world-us-canada-49024677

Liettu, A., Säävälä, H., Hakko, H., Räsänen, P., & Joukamaa, M. (2009). Mental disorders of male parricidal offenders. *Social Psychiatry and Psychiatric Epidemiology, 44*(2), 96–103. https://doi.org/10.1007/s00127-008-0419-9

MacDonald, M. (2021, May 4). "A lot of blood": Dennis Oland's wife accused him of intimate partner violence. *National Post*. https://nationalpost.com/news/canada/a-lot-of-blood-dennis-olands-wife-accused-him-of-intimate-partner-violence-2

MacKinnon, B. (2013, September 6). Documents shed new light on Oland murder investigation. *CBC News*. https://www.cbc.ca/news/canada/new-brunswick/documentsshed-new-light-on-oland-murder-investigation-1.1699119

MacKinnon, B. (2015a, September 8). Jury selection in Dennis Oland's murder trial begins in Saint John. *CBC News*. https://www.cbc.ca/news/canada/new-brunswick/dennis-oland-jury-selection-day-one-1.3215856

MacKinnon, B. (2015b, November 6). Dennis Oland was less than honest with wife about cash crunch, jury hears. *CBC News*. https://www.cbc.ca/news/canada/newbrunswick/oland-trial-finances-wife-accountant-1.3307173

MacKinnon, B. (2015c, December 22). Saint John police's handling of Richard Oland murder investigation to be reviewed. *CBC News*. https://www.cbc.ca/news/canada/new-brunswick/oland-investigation-police-commission-1.3376852

MacKinnon, B. (2016, February 11). Dennis Oland pressured to confess to father's murder by police. *CBC News*. https://www.cbc.ca/news/canada/new-brunswick/dennisoland-police-murder-confession-1.3436687

MacKinnon, B. (2017, January 3). Dennis Oland's new murder trial date could be set today. *CBC News*. https://www.cbc.ca/news/canada/new-brunswick/dennis-olandnew-trial-date-murder-1.3918940

MacKinnon, B. (2018, November 28). Police waited over a year to interview paramedics, Oland murder trial hears. *CBC News*. https://www.cbc.ca/news/canada/new-brunswick/dennis-oland-murder-retrial-noises-paramedics-funeral-1.4922809

Maeder, E., Dempsey, J., & Pozzulo, J. (2012). Behind the veil of juror decision making: Testing the effects of Muslim veils and defendant race in the courtroom. *Criminal Justice and Behavior, 39*(5), 666–78. https://doi.org/10.1177/0093854812436478

Marquis, G. (2019). *Truth & honour: The Oland family murder case that shocked Canada* (2nd ed.). Nimbus.

Morris, J. (2003). The anonymous accused: Protecting defendants' rights in high-profile criminal cases. *Boston College Law Review, 44*(3). https://lawdigitalcommons.bc.edu/bclr/vol44/iss3/6

Moscovici, S., & Zavalloni, M. (1969). The group as a polarizer of attitudes. *Journal of Personality and Social Psychology, 12*(2), 125–35. https://doi.org/10.1037/h0027568

New Mexico v. Gilbert, 1998, case #D-202-CR-199700660, Albuquerque District.

Oram, S., Flynn, S. M., Shaw, J., Appleby, L., & Howard, L. M. (2013). Mental illness and domestic homicide: A population-based descriptive study. *Psychiatric Services, 64*(10), 1006–11. https://doi.org/10.1176/appi.ps.201200484

Pennington, N., & Hastie, R. (1986). Evidence evaluation in complex decision making. *Journal of Personality and Social Psychology, 51*(2), 242–58. https://doi.org/10.1037/0022-3514.51.2.242

Pennington, N., & Hastie, R. (1991). A cognitive theory of juror decision making: The story model. *Cardozo Law Review, 13*, 5001–39. https://heinonline.org/HOL/LandingPage?handle=hein.journals/cdozo13&div=30&id=&page=

Penrod, S. D. (2021). Pretrial publicity. *Oxford Bibliographies*. https://www.oxfordbibliographies.com/view/document/obo-9780199828340/obo-9780199828340-0290.xml

Petty, R. E., & Cacioppo, J. T. (1986a). *Communication and persuasion: Central and peripheral routes to attitude change*. Springer-Verlag.
Petty, R. E., & Cacioppo, J. T. (1986b). The elaboration likelihood model of persuasion. *Advances in Experimental Social Psychology, 19*, 123–205. https://doi.org/10.1016/S0065-2601(08)60214-2
R. v. Find, 2001, SCC 32.
R. v. Sherratt, 1991, SCR 509.
Ruva, C. L. (2018). From the headlines to the jury room: An examination of the impact of pretrial publicity on jurors and juries. In M. K. Miller & B. H. Bornstein (Eds.), *Advances in psychology and law* (pp. 1–39). Springer International. https://doi.org/10.1007/978-3-319-75859-6_1
Ruva, C. L., Diaz Ortega, S. E., & O'Grady, K. A. (2021). What drives a jury's deliberation? The influence of pretrial publicity and jury composition on deliberation slant and content. *Psychology, Public Policy, and Law, 28*(1), 32–52. https://doi.org/10.1037/law0000310
Ruva, C. L., & Guenther, C. C. (2015). From the shadows into the light: How pretrial publicity and deliberation affect mock jurors' decisions, impressions, and memory. *Law and Human Behavior, 39*(3), 294–310. https://doi.org/10.1037/lhb0000117
Sadler, C. (2020, March 21). The Oland murder. *CBC News*. https://www.cbc.ca/tv/features/the-oland-murder
Singhal, S., & Dutta, A. (1990). Who commits patricide? *Acta Psychiatrica Scandinavica, 82*(1), 40–3. https://doi.org/10.1111/j.1600-0447.1990.tb01352.x
Steblay, N. M., Besirevic, J., Fulero, S. M., & Jimenez-Lorente, B. (1999). The effects of pretrial publicity on juror verdicts: A meta-analytic review. *Law and Human Behavior, 23*(2), 219–35. https://doi.org/10.1023/A:1022325019080
Studebaker, C. A., & Penrod, S. D. (1997). Pretrial publicity: The media, the law, and common sense. *Psychology, Public Policy, and Law, 3*(2–3), 428–60. https://doi.org/10.1037/1076-8971.3.2-3.428
Suresh, N., & George, L. C. (2021). Trial by media: An overview. *International Journal of Law Management and Humanities, 4*(2), 267–72. https://doi.org/10.24919/2308-4863/40-2-43
Vickery v. Nova Scotia Supreme Court (Prothonotary), 1991, SCR 671.
X, M., & Haley, A. (1965). *The autobiography of Malcolm X*. Grove Press.

CHAPTER FOUR

Fault Lines in the "Rock of Ages": Trial by Jury

The Cases of Donald Marshall Jr., Cindy Gladue, and Colten Boushie

With Ethan Draper

> *Trial by jury is a fundamental institution, a veritable "rock of ages," in our system of criminal justice in Canada.*
> *– Michael A. Johnstone brief (Law Reform Commission of Canada, 1989)*

On 2 November 1971, Donald Marshall Jr., a 17-year-old Mi'kmaq youth from Membertou First Nation (see figure 4.1), was sentenced to life imprisonment for the stabbing death of Sandy Seale, a 17-year-old Black youth. After 11 years and one month in federal custody, Donald Marshall Jr. was released on 28 July 1982. At the time, the Appeals Division of the Nova Scotia Supreme Court ruled that "no reasonable jury could, on that evidence, find Donald Marshall, Jr. guilty of the murder," while maintaining that "any miscarriage of justice is, however, more apparent than real" (Province of Nova Scotia, n.d.). Despite the court's assertion that no miscarriage of justice had occurred, Marshall's wrongful conviction led to an enquiry into the Nova Scotia justice system. One of the revelations from the enquiry was that, at the time of Marshall's conviction in 1971, no Indigenous person had ever sat on a jury in Nova Scotia (Nova Scotia v. Nova Scotia, 1989, p. 176). Due to Canada's jury secrecy rule (CCC Section 649; see chapter 5), the commission could not question any of the

Figure 4.1. In 2000, Donald Marshall Jr. (seen here with Governor General, Adrienne Clarkson) was presented with The Wolf Award by Grandfather William Commanda. The Wolf Award (represented by a large grey wolf statue) acknowledges excellence in working toward enhancing respect and understanding between cultures and races. The award is meant to serve as a reminder to never give up the dream of unity. For more information see http://www.wolfproject.com/individuals.htm.
Picture courtesy of Dr. L. Jane McMillan.

R. v. Marshall (1971) jurors. In an interview with a reporter, however, one of the jurors explained the reasoning behind the verdict: "With one redskin and one Negro involved, it was like two dogs in the field – you knew one of them was going to kill another. I would expect more from a white person. We are more civilized" (Roach, 2020). It is worth noting that, until 1964, no municipal police officers in the Maritime provinces were people of colour.

In theory, juries are designed to be impartial (without bias) and representative of the community whence they derive; in practice, they often fall short of this ideal. As microcosms, juries reflect the same biases and prejudices about people's colour and culture as seen in the larger society. In addition to the Marshall case, Canada has a litany of controversial and wrongful convictions by all-White juries.

In 1991, the Manitoba Aboriginal Justice Inquiry found that lawyers for two White defendants used six peremptory challenges to exclude visibly Indigenous people in a racially charged case arising from the murder of Helen Betty Osborne. The 19-year-old Cree woman from Norway House, MB, had been abducted, repeatedly raped, brutally beaten, stabbed with a screwdriver over 50 times, and murdered. Four young White men were implicated in her death; only one was ever convicted. The enquiry into Osborne's murder revealed that 18 of 105 prospective jurors in the case were Aboriginal. In Saskatchewan, all-White juries convicted two young White men of manslaughter (vs. murder) in the death of Pamela George, a 28-year-old Indigenous woman from Saulteaux First Nation, in 1996; acquitted a White man in the death of William Kakakaway of the White Bear First Nation in 2001; and acquitted two of three White men charged for the sexual assault of a 12-year-old Indigenous girl in Tisdale in 2003. In 2011, Connie Oakes, a Cree woman from Nekaneet First Nation, SK, was wrongfully convicted of murder by an Alberta jury with no visible Indigenous representation. Oakes's conviction was overturned in 2016 (Roach, 2020).

An all-White jury acquitted the man who murdered Cindy Gladue. Gladue was a 36-year-old Cree and Métis mother of three who died an agonizing death in a blood-soaked bathtub at the Yellowhead Inn in Edmonton, AB, in June 2011. An autopsy determined Gladue suffered a "catastrophic, unusual and fatal" injury to her vaginal area. While it was evident that the injury had been caused by blunt force, what was disputed in court was whether it resulted from consensual "rough sex" or sexual assault. The forensic pathologist suggested that the injury could have been caused by a fist or hand placed in the vagina, causing it to "stretch beyond its limits." Defendant Bradley Barton, a White 42-year-old long-distance truck driver from Mississauga, ON, claimed that he had arranged to pay Gladue for "rough sex" and admitted that he caused the injury but denied knowing that Gladue was hurt. He said he was shocked to find her dead the following morning. The Crown argued that Barton performed a sexual act on Gladue that caused the severe vaginal wound while she was unconscious, and then put her in the room's bathtub and left her to bleed to death. Medical experts confirmed that Gladue had four times the legal limit of alcohol in her system, which would have precluded her ability to consent. A forensic analysis of Barton's computer revealed that, nine days before Gladue's death, he had entered a search for "vaginas getting ripped or torn by large objects" (Canadian Press, 2021a).

In March 2015, an Edmonton jury found Bradley Barton not guilty of the first-degree murder of Cindy Gladue. The verdict sparked an outcry among the Indigenous community with rallies and calls for justice for Indigenous women. Indigenous rights lawyers were outraged that Gladue had been repeatedly referred to as a "Native girl" and a prostitute. Adding insult to injury, Gladue's preserved vaginal tissue had been presented in court. "It was utterly dehumanizing, and it ignored Indigenous laws on caring for the dead," said Lise Gotell, a gender studies professor at the University of Alberta and vice-chair of the Women's Legal Education and Action Fund (LEAF), one of 16 groups that intervened in the Barton case before the Supreme Court (Women's Legal Education & Action Fund, 2020).

In 2017, the Alberta Court of Appeal set aside Barton's acquittal and, in 2019, the Supreme Court ordered a new trial. During the retrial, two jurors had to be removed for bias. One juror expressed the view that working in the sex trade was "bad" and that Gladue would have lived had she not exchanged sex for money. A second juror was removed for endeavouring to unduly sway the opinion of other jurors. The judge issued repeated admonishments to the jurors not to rely on stereotypes and prejudices about sex workers and Indigenous persons in considering the case. Jurors were reminded of the traumatic effects of colonialism on Indigenous culture. In February 2021, 10 years after the death of Cindy Gladue, Bradley Barton was convicted of manslaughter in her death and sentenced to 12.5 years (Canadian Press, 2021b).

TRIAL BY JURY

While it cannot be concluded that a miscarriage of justice transpired in any of these cases, public confidence in the verdicts suffered from the lack of visible Indigenous representation on the jury. In the courtroom, the jury serves as proxy for the public, acting on behalf of society (*R. v. Kokopenace*, 2015). Trials by jury serve to engage public interest in the administration of justice, act as a vehicle of public education, and lend the weight of community standards to trial verdicts. As outlined in Clause 39 of the Magna Carta, "No free man is to be arrested, or imprisoned, or disseised, or outlawed, or exiled, or in any other way ruined, nor will we go against him or send against him, except by the lawful judgment of his peers or by the law of the land" (Summerson, n.d.). In 1215, this meant that nobility would be judged by their fellow nobles rather than the king; today, this means an accused will be judged by a jury of fellow citizens or "jury of one's peers."

The right to be judged by a jury of one's peers for indictable offences was codified in the Criminal Code of 1892 and now is protected by the Canadian Charter of Rights and Freedoms (Government of Canada, 2021b). Anyone tried for an indictable offence can elect to have a *preliminary enquiry* to determine if sufficient evidence exists to proceed to trial. If evidence is deemed sufficient, a trial will be scheduled and a jury will be empanelled. *Indictable* offences are those that are most serious (e.g., murder or treason) and/or carry a maximum penalty of more than five years imprisonment. Anyone charged with an indictable offence has the right to trial by jury. By comparison, *summary* offences are the least serious (e.g., causing a disturbance) with a maximum fine of $5,000 and a maximum jail term of less than two years. Summary offence cases are heard by judges. *Hybrid* offences, as the name implies, fall between indictable and summary. Hybrid offences (e.g., sexual assault) can proceed "summarily" (heard by judge) or "by indictment" (trial by jury), depending on the Crown's choice.

The goal in empanelling a jury is to select 12 persons who will satisfy the dual imperatives of *impartiality and representativeness* as outlined in *R. v. Sherratt* (1991). Impartiality means that jurors must be "indifferent between the Queen and the accused" (*R. v. Find*, 2001), which is to say that jurors must have no particular leanings (interest, sympathy, prejudice) toward one side or the other. Jurors must be without bias. Representativeness means that the composition of the jury should reflect a "cross-section of society, honestly and fairly chosen." This does not mean that an accused is entitled to a particular number of individuals of their race on either the panel or the jury (*R. v. Kokopenace*, 2015).

CLINICAL FORENSIC PSYCHOLOGY AND JURIES

Impartiality Matters

A fox should not be on a jury at a goose's trial
– Thomas Fuller, 1608–1661 (Mieder et al., 1991, p. 116)

People who harbour prejudicial attitudes toward someone's skin colour, ethnic heritage, culture, or occupation could be like foxes at a goose's trial if selected for jury duty. The Canadian Charter of Rights and Freedoms (CCRF) Section 11(d) guarantees that accused people have the right to be presumed innocent until proven guilty "in a fair and public hearing by an independent and impartial tribunal" (Government of Canada, 2021a). An impartial tribunal means a court without bias, such as bias arising from a personal interest in the case (*R. v. Hubbert*, 1975, 1977), prejudice arising from pretrial publicity or notoriety of the accused (*R. v. Sherratt*, 1991; see chapter 3), or prejudice against the accused's social or racial group (*R. v. Williams*, 1998).

In cases with a high likelihood of juror prejudice (i.e., partiality), the judge may allow for jurors to be questioned about potential bias. In the landmark *R. v. Williams* (1998) case, an Indigenous man named Victor Williams applied to question potential jurors about racial bias under the Criminal Code of Canada (Government of Canada, 2022). In support of his application, Williams filed evidence of widespread racism against Indigenous people in Canadian society: "Williams said he understood that it was very unlikely that any Indigenous person would be on his jury, but he hoped that 'the 12 people that try me are not Indian haters'" (Roach, 2020). The trial judge allowed potential jurors to be asked two questions: "(1) Would your ability to judge the evidence in the case without bias, prejudice or partiality be affected by the fact that the person charged is an 'Indian'? (2) Would your ability to judge the evidence in the case without bias, prejudice, or partiality be affected by the fact that the person charged is an Indian and the complainant is White?" (Roach, 2020). Of the 43 panel members who were questioned, 12 (28%) were dismissed for risk of bias.

Such questions were not asked of jurors in the Colten Boushie case. Indeed, there was no screening for potential racial bias, despite

Figure 4.2. On 9 August 2016, 22-year-old Colten Boushie from Red Pheasant First Nation was shot dead in rural Saskatchewan by a 56-year-old White farmer, whom he had approached for help with a flat tire. Picture courtesy of Zola, a Montreal-based street artist and activist.

widespread evidence of prejudice in the community. Moreover, the all-White jury was given no specific instructions about the danger of bias predicated on stereotypes with respect to Indigenous victims and witnesses. Colten Boushie (see figure 4.2) was a 22-year-old Cree man from the Red Pheasant First Nation in rural Saskatchewan. On 9 August 2016, Boushie and four other Indigenous youth drove onto the property of Gerald Stanley because their vehicle had a flat tire. Stanley was a 56-year-old White farmer. A confrontation arose between Stanley and the Indigenous youth that resulted in Stanley shooting and killing Boushie. On 11 August 2016, Stanley was charged with second-degree murder. In the ensuing weeks, public opinion in the surrounding communities grew sharply divided along racial lines about the right to defend one's property. Saskatchewan premier Brad Wall appealed to citizens to "rise above intolerance," beseeching them to stop their "racist and hate-filled comments on social media" (Roach, 2020).

When Stanley was released on bail, a commentator quipped that this was a privilege "that too many Indigenous people have themselves been denied for far lesser crimes." In April 2017, a preliminary enquiry determined there was sufficient evidence to proceed to trial and, in January 2018, a jury panel of 750 citizens was summoned to the empanelling process in Battleford, SK (Edwards, 2018). Seven women and five men (plus two alternates) were selected to serve. On the first day of the trial, two jurors were excused and replaced by the alternates. None of the 14 jurors was visibly Indigenous, and suspicions grew about the questionable use of peremptory challenges (see below). On 9 February 2018, following a two-week trial, the jury acquitted Gerald Stanley of culpability in the death of Colten Boushie.

Stanley's acquittal provoked debate about peremptory challenges, jury representativeness, and CCC Section 649 – the secrecy rule that prevents jurors from disclosing information about jury deliberations (see chapter 5). Prior to 2019, Canadian lawyers could reject jurors in two ways: challenges for cause and peremptory. The Crown and defence were granted a certain number of peremptory challenges (20 each in murder trials; 12 each for most other crimes). Peremptorily, each could reject potential jurors ostensibly only on the basis of name, address, occupation, physical appearance, and/or demeanour. With social media, of course, a lot more information is readily available. Given that no explanation was required, lawyers could reject jurors of the same (or different) race, gender, or background as the defendant with impunity. This led to a number of controversial rulings, including in the Colten Boushie case, where many Indigenous groups argued that peremptory challenges were used to block Indigenous persons and ensure an all-White jury. Despite intense and prejudicial pretrial publicity, there had been no challenges for cause to assess potential racial bias among prospective jurors. Within two months of Stanley's acquittal, the federal government imposed a ban on peremptory challenges (Bill C-75), which the Supreme Court upheld in 2020.

The Marshall, Gladue, and Boushie cases revealed serious crevices/fissures in the "rock of ages" and, after each trial, calls for jury reform grew louder. Each case illustrates shortcomings in the jury selection process – lack of diversity and perception of fairness, plus an appalling lack of cultural sensitivity. It is evident today that Donald Marshall Jr. was not arrested, prosecuted, or judged by his peers. In the Gladue case, the *impartiality* of the jury was threatened by two jurors having to be removed for bias and all jurors needing repeated judicial admonishments not to rely on stereotypes and prejudices about sex workers and Indigenous persons. In the Boushie case, the *representativeness* of the jury was threatened by the allegation that peremptory challenges were used to preclude participation of Indigenous candidates and challenges for cause were not used to tease out potential racial bias.

REPRESENTATIVENESS MATTERS

In 2018, results of a two-year investigation by Toronto Star reporters showed that 71 per cent of all jurors in 52 juries in Toronto and Brampton were White, despite the fact that most residents in both municipalities were visible minorities. In the Greater Toronto Area, only 7 per cent of jurors were Black although 46 per cent of defendants were Black (see Martis, 2021).

Representativeness begins with the summoning of citizens to comprise a panel or array of potential jurors (see figure 4.3). These are lay persons, over the age of 18, who are drawn at random from the community (e.g., from health registration lists). The size of the panel will vary depending on the trial. In high-profile cases, like the Dennis Oland and Paul Bernardo trials, the array can be quite large (5,000 and 980, respectively; see chapter 3). Eventually, however, the panel gets whittled down to 12 persons via a process that can include both exemptions and challenges for cause. (Note: in some cases, the judge may consider it advisable to increase the number of jurors to 13 or 14 persons; however, only 12 can deliberate in the rendering of a verdict.) Exemptions can include excusals for financial hardship, age or infirmity, medical reasons, conflict of interest, type of employment (e.g., seasonal), and so forth.

One of the difficulties in constructing a truly representative jury is that about one fifth of prospective jurors fail to appear when summoned. In the Boushie-Stanley (2018) case, 750 people were called to serve on the jury but only 178 people appeared in court in Battleford,

Figure 4.3. "The Jury," oil on canvas painting by John Morgan (1861).

SK (Edwards, 2018). There are many reasons why people don't show up for jury duty, including that they don't understand it is mandatory; they have responsibilities to work and family (child and elder care); poor compensation (per diem of $20 to $100 in most provinces and territories); accessibility and language challenges; transportation costs; sense of alienation from the criminal justice system; and, for some, the mistaken belief that a criminal history precludes participation. While a Criminal Code conviction generally is a barrier to serving as a juror, in some provinces exceptions are made for certain summary offences. For example, in Ontario, rendering a false statement under oath, committing an indecent act, impersonating a police officer, or pretending to practise witchcraft do not preclude your potential to serve. Convictions for more serious indictable offences, however, are disqualifying unless you have been pardoned, which costs money. Other barriers include how prospective jurors are recruited, whether by electoral list, health registration, or drivers' licence, and how summons are issued – by mail versus electronically.

All these barriers disproportionately affect Indigenous persons and other minority groups. Even if they can make it to the courthouse, they can be among the first to be dismissed. In reviewing the transcript and media reports of jury selection in the Boushie case, Roach (2020) estimated that only about 20 of the 178 jurors (11%) who were available to serve were Indigenous, well below the 30 per cent Indigenous adult population in the district. According to Roach (2020), even if the underrepresentation of Indigenous people had been challenged, the challenge likely would have failed under current law, as determined by the Supreme Court of Canada majority decision in *R. v. Kokopenace* (2015).

Because jury duty is mandatory, there are legal consequences to not showing up to serve. In most provinces and territories, however, consequences (e.g., fines of $1,000 and up to three months in prison) are seldom imposed. One exception is Newfoundland and Labrador (NL) where fines are imposed and citizens can face six months in prison for not appearing. The province's absenteeism rate is less than 1 per cent the lowest in the country. Out of 2,908 summons issued recently in NL, only 24 prospective jurors failed to show (Hildebrandt, 2013a, 2013b).

DIVERSITY MATTERS

Social psychologist George Herbert Mead (1929) characterized society as "unity in diversity" (p. 396). Another social psychologist, Samuel Sommers (Tufts University), studies group diversity and is unequivocal in asserting that the racial composition of a jury matters. Commenting on the recent verdict in the Derek Chauvin trial (March-April 2021), the Minneapolis police officer convicted of murder in the death of African American George Floyd, Sommers proffered that the diversity of the jury may have contributed to a more just trial outcome. The jury consisted of five men and seven women, six of whom were White, four were Black, and two were multiracial. According to Sommers (as cited in Mekouar, 2021), "Bias seems more likely when we have homogeneous, or non-diverse, juries. With diverse juries seems to come more wide-ranging and representative discussion of facts in the case."

In a review article, Sommers (2008) summarized the theoretical and empirical evidence for the benefits of diversity in juries. For example, diverse jury trials are seen as significantly fairer than the same trials with homogeneous, all-White juries. Sommers cites evidence from organizational and management studies that shows that group diversity improves group creativity, information sharing, flexibility, and thoughtfulness. Some studies show that when groups are able to weather the initial conflict that diversity can engender, heterogeneous groups often exhibit superior performance, problem-solving, and decision-making.

American legal scholars such as Bowers et al. (2001) have found that the greater the proportion of Whites to Blacks on a capital jury, the greater the likelihood that a Black defendant would be sentenced to death, especially when the victim was White. Similarly, majority-White (vs. majority-Latino) juries have been found to be harsher in their judgments of Latino defendants. An experiment with college students that manipulated the race of the defendant in a trial video presented to 12-person mock juries of differing racial compositions found that, across conditions, White jurors were more likely to vote guilty than were Black jurors, particularly when the defendant was Black.

One of the best predictors of a jury's final verdict is the distribution of votes taken predeliberation. According to Sommers (2008), a jury's racial composition can determine how predeliberation votes align, which in turn impacts the likelihood of the jury reaching a guilty verdict. Sommers (2006) found that a jury's racial composition impacts not only the content of its deliberations, but also its performance. Jury diversity seems to expand the range of perspectives, increases accuracy regarding the facts of the case, and leads to greater willingness to discuss controversial issues. Results reported by Sommers (2006) showed that, predeliberation, White mock jurors on diverse juries were less likely to believe that the Black defendant was guilty than were Whites on all-White juries. Given that these differences emerged predeliberation, they cannot be attributed to the exchange of information between jurors. Recent research by Peter-Hagene (2019) found that, while jury diversity can increase cognitive depletion, it reduces racial disparity in verdicts and deliberation quality by improving the quality of deliberation for Black defendants.

Diversity among other court participants (e.g., judges) also matters. A *Globe and Mail* survey in 2012 found that of 100 federal appointments over a three-and-a-half year period, only two judges were racialized (Makin, 2012, as cited in Ruparelia, 2018). Subsequently, Way (2014) examined federal judicial appointments between April 2012 and May 2014 and found that, of 107 appointments, one judge was racialized and 90 were White (she was unable to determine the identity of the remaining 16). In 2010, a former BC judge, William Sundhu, estimated that only 50 to 60 judges in Canada were racialized (less than 3%). In BC, fewer than six provincial court judges of a total of 104 were racialized and no racialized judges were appointed between 2001 and 2008 (Sundhu, 2009). It is regrettable and, frankly, difficult to comprehend why the federal government does not keep statistics on the number of racialized appointments to the bench.

SUMMARY AND CONCLUSIONS

> *A jury is always a more orthodox body than any defendant brought before it; for blacks it is usually a whiter group, for poor people, a more prosperous group.*
>
> *– Howard Zinn, American historian, 1922–2010 (Zinn, 2018)*

In democratic countries, all citizens have the right to serve on juries, and all defendants have the right to be judged by a fair and impartial jury. The importance of impartial, representative, and diverse juries is not confined to issues of constitutionality or morality – these are essential to ensuring public confidence in jury verdicts, trial processes, and legitimacy of the criminal justice system in general. In the *R. v. Stanley* (2018) case, prospective jurors were not screened for racism or stereotypes about Indigenous people; the trial judge did not warn the jurors about anti-Indigenous sentiment; and the only reference to systemic issues affecting Indigenous peoples was when the trial judge twice enquired about an Eagle feather in the courtroom and conveyed the jury's concerns about it being waved (see Roach, 2020). This is difficult to understand given the intense and prejudicial pretrial publicity that led Premier Brad Wall to implore his fellow citizens to stop their "racist and hate-filled comments on social media" (Canadian Press, 2016). Suspicions were that peremptory challenges had been used to reject potential Indigenous jurors. Legal scholars contend that to challenge the representativeness of the jury would likely have failed under current law, which is based on archaic requirements of proof of intentional discrimination (*R. v. Kokopenace*, 2015). Polling conducted shortly after Stanley's acquittal showed that 59 per cent of respondents agreed that jury selection procedures should be reformed. Within months of Stanley's acquittal, the federal government banned peremptory challenges.

In 2018, prospective jurors in a Hamilton, ON, trial were asked whether the fact that the accused Peter Khill was White and the deceased victim Jon Styres was Indigenous would keep them from considering evidence without bias. In a case reminiscent of Colten Boushie and Gerald Stanley, Khill claimed he was "following his military training" (Khill had served as a part-time army reservist from 2007 to 2011) when he shot 29-year-old Styres twice at close range with a shotgun in the early morning hours of 4 February 2016. Allegedly, Styres was "in or near" Khill's truck. Khill testified that he fired in self-defence when he yelled, "Hey, hands up!" and Styres turned toward him with his hands moving up to "gun-height." Styres was unarmed. Khill was charged with and acquitted of second-degree murder. The verdict was appealed, and in October 2021, the Supreme Court overturned the acquittal. University of Toronto law professor Kent Roach commended the screening of jurors as a "good precaution" but bemoans the fact that it is so novel (Taekema, 2018). He is aware of only two other cases where jurors in Canada were asked about potential bias in cases involving Indigenous people.

Although trial by jury has survived since at least 1215, the cases outlined in this chapter reveal the fault lines in our "rock of ages" – the fissures created by threats to impartiality, representativeness, and diversity. Chapter 5 describes other challenges to trial by jury that need to be considered.

CRITICAL THINKING QUESTIONS

1. How would you answer if someone asked you these questions? (1) Would your ability to judge the evidence in the case without bias, prejudice, or partiality be affected by the fact that the person charged is Indigenous? (2) Would your ability to judge the evidence in the case without bias, prejudice, or partiality be affected by the fact that the person charged is Indigenous and the complainant is White?

2. Do you think that people can accurately self-report biases?
3. What do you think would work better: asking potential jurors to rate their perceptions on a Likert-like scale, using more open-ended and reflective questions, or perhaps have them respond to vignettes?

REFERENCES

Bowers, W. J., Steiner, B. D., & Sandys, M. (2001). Death sentencing in black and white: An empirical analysis of the role of jurors' race and jury racial composition. *Journal of Constitutional Law, 3*(1), 174–271. https://scholarship.law.upenn.edu/jcl/vol3/iss1/3/

Canadian Press. (2016, August 15). "Racist and hate-filled" comments after fatal shooting must stop: Brad Wall. *Global News*. https://globalnews.ca/news/2882523/brad-wall-says-racist-and-hate-filled-comments-after-fatal-shooting-must-stop/

Canadian Press. (2021a, February 20). Trucker Bradley Barton found guilty of manslaughter in death of woman in Edmonton hotel. *Global News*. https://globalnews.ca/news/7652061/edmonton-crime-bradley-barton-guilty-verdict/

Canadian Press. (2021b, June 26). "Legacy horrific" but Ontario trucker's retrial more sensitive to victim: Lawyers. *CTV News*. https://edmonton.ctvnews.ca/legacy-horrific-but-ontario-trucker-s-retrial-more-sensitive-to-victim-lawyers-1.5486861

Edwards, K. (2018, April 2). Saskatchewan officials skipped a step when they formed Gerald Stanley's jury. *Maclean's*. https://www.macleans.ca/news/canada/saskatchewan-officials-skipped-a-step-when-they-formed-gerald-stanleys-jury/

Government of Canada. (2021a, January 9). Section 11(d) – Presumption of innocence. *Charterpedia*. https://www.justice.gc.ca/eng/csj-sjc/rfc-dlc/ccrf-ccdl/check/art11d.html

Government of Canada. (2021b, January 9). Section 11(f) – Trial by jury. *Charterpedia*. https://www.justice.gc.ca/eng/csj-sjc/rfc-dlc/ccrf-ccdl/check/art11f.html

Government of Canada. (2022, February 18). Criminal Code. *Justice of Law*. https://laws-lois.justice.gc.ca/eng/acts/c-46/page-94.html

Hildebrandt, A. (2013a, May 27). Jury duty: Tracking no-shows and compensation across Canada. *CBC News*. https://www.cbc.ca/news/canada/jury-duty-tracking-no-shows-and-compensation-across-canada-1.1412886

Hildebrandt, A. (2013b, May 27). Who's to blame for juror no-shows: "Sad generation" or broken system? *CBC News*. https://www.cbc.ca/news/canada/who-s-to-blame-for-juror-no-shows-sad-generation-or-broken-system-1.1321595

Law Reform Commission of Canada. (1989). *Working paper 27: The jury in criminal trials*. Minister of Supply and Services Canada. http://www.lareau-law.ca/LRCWP27.pdf

Martis, E. (2021, October 16). Black in the jury box: Systemic barriers. *West End Phoenix*. https://www.westendphoenix.com/stories/black-in-the-jury-box-systemic-barriers

Mead, G. H. (1929). National mindedness and international mindedness. *International Journal of Ethics, 39*, 385–407. https://brocku.ca/MeadProject/Mead/pubs2/papers/Mead_1929c.html. https://doi.org/10.1086/intejethi.39.4.2377726

Mekouar, D. (2021, April 22). Why a jury's racial composition matters. *VOA News*. https://www.voanews.com/a/usa_all-about-america_why-jurys-racial-composition-matters/6204882.html

Mieder, W., Kingsbury, S. A., & Harder, K. B. (1991). *A dictionary of American proverbs*. Oxford University Press.

Nova Scotia (Attorney-General) v. Nova Scotia (Royal Commission into Marshall Prosecution), 1989, 2 SCR 788.

Peter-Hagene, L. (2019). Jurors' cognitive depletion and performance during jury deliberation as a function of jury diversity and defendant race. *Law and Human Behavior, 43*(3), 232–49. https://doi.org/10.1037/lhb0000332

Province of Nova Scotia. (n.d.). *Royal commission on the Donald Marshall Jr. prosecution*. Nova Scotia Archives. https://archives.novascotia.ca/marshall/

Roach, K. (2020). Juries, miscarriages of justice and the Bill C-75 reforms. *Canadian Bar Review, 315*. https://canlii.ca/t/sxj9

Ruparelia, R. (2018). Erring on the side of ignorance: Challenges for cause twenty years after Parks. *Canadian Bar Review, 267*. https://canlii.ca/t/28fz

R. v. Find, 2001, SCC 32.

R. v. Hubbert, 1975, 29 CCC 2d 279.

R. v. Hubbert, 1977, 15 NR 139 SCC.

R. v. Kokopenace, 2015, SCC 28.

R. v. Marshall, 1971.

R. v. Sherratt, 1991, SCR 509.

R. v. Stanley, 2018, SKQB 27.

R. v. Williams, 1998, 226 NR 162 SCC.

Sommers, S. R. (2006). On racial diversity and group decision making: Identifying multiple effects of racial composition on jury deliberations. *Journal of Personality and Social Psychology, 90*(4), 597–612. https://doi.org/10.1037/0022-3514.90.4.597

Sommers, S. R. (2008). Determinants and consequences of jury racial diversity: Empirical findings, implications, and directions for future research. *Social Issues and Policy Review, 2*(1), 65–102. https://doi.org/10.1111/j.1751-2409.2008.00011.x

Summerson, H. (n.d.). *Magna Carta project – 1215 Magna Carta – Clause 39*. The Magna Carta Project. https://magnacartaresearch.org/read/magna_carta_1215/Clause_39

Sundhu, B. W. (2009). *Terrorism trials and the judiciary: Does diversity matter?* [Unpublished master's thesis]. University of Oxford, Kellogg College.

Taekema, D. (2018, June 11). Prospective jurors in Peter Khill trial questioned about potential racial bias. *CBC News*. https://www.cbc.ca/news/canada/hamilton/peter-khill-jury-selection-1.4701156

Way, R. C. (2014). Deliberate disregard: Judicial appointments under the Harper government. Ottawa Faculty of Law Working Paper No. 2014-08. https://doi.org/10.2139/ssrn.2456792

Women's Legal Education & Action Fund. (2020, November 27). IAAW and LEAF continue to seek justice for Cindy Gladue. *Women's Legal Education and Action Fund*. https://www.leaf.ca/news/iaaw-and-leaf-continue-to-seek-justice-for-cindy-gladue/

Zinn, H. (2018). *You can't be neutral on a moving train: A personal history*. Beacon Press.

CHAPTER FIVE

Privilege or Punishment? Jury Service, Secrecy, and Stress

The Case of Tori Stafford

With Ryanne Chisholm

> With the exception of voting, for most citizens the honor and privilege of jury duty is their most significant opportunity to participate in the democratic process.
>
> – *SCOTUS* (Powers v. Ohio, *1991, p. 407)*

Jury duty may be an honour, a privilege, and an opportunity but, as Mark Farrant would remind us, it is the last compulsory form of service in Canada since the abolition of military conscription. Farrant was a juror in the 2014 trial of 31-year-old Farshad "Shawn" Badakhshan. Badakhshan was found guilty of second-degree murder in the stabbing death of his 23-year-old girlfriend, Carina Petrache, in 2010. Petrache was a student at Toronto Metropolitan University, and, after stabbing her, Badakhshan set fire to the rooming house where they both lived. He was convicted in April 2014 but one month later and prior to sentencing, he committed suicide in a Toronto jail.

Farrant had served as jury foreman for the four-month trial and, for him, the trial didn't end in April 2014 (see Clairmont, 2017). In the aftermath of the trial, Farrant was haunted by certain images, such as one autopsy close-up of Petrache's face and neck wounds. Apparently, the photo was displayed on a large courtroom screen for a long time. Farrant also was haunted by the victim's bloody handprints on a wall, which reminded him of his children's handprints on walls at home. After killing Petrache, Badahkshan tried to set himself on fire and was severely disfigured. Apparently, his facial expressions were masked by gruesome scarring, and this image haunted Farrant. As Farrant's stress and anxiety mounted, he took to sleeping with a knife under his pillow, another taped underneath his couch, and arming himself when he left the house: "My daughter is watching me put multiple knives in my pocket" (Clairmont, 2017). Farrant called the courthouse for help, but none was available. Eventually, he found a therapist, received a diagnosis of posttraumatic stress disorder (PTSD), and joined a growing movement calling for mental health support for jurors (see Clairmont, 2017; Private Member Bill C-211, 2018).

Each year, thousands of Canadians are called to serve on a jury. Each year, some of these Canadians are seriously harmed in the performance of their civic duty. While jury duty may be an honour, a privilege, and an opportunity, it is mandatory and it can be traumatizing (see Previl, 2021).

CONSIDER THE FOLLOWING SCENARIO

You have received a letter summoning you for possible jury duty. You are instructed as to where and when to appear. Upon arrival, you realize that you are one of 447 people who comprise the jury panel (array) who will be screened for eligibility to serve. The judge asks if any panel member thinks they should be excused from sitting on this particular trial due to special interest in the case (e.g., having a child the same age as the victim) or conflict of interest (e.g., having a friend or relative involved in the case). The judge explains that whoever is chosen will be subject to a "considerable amount" of hardship and inconvenience. Panel member names are picked at random. When your name is picked, you are asked if you would be able to serve on the 12-person jury for at least three months, in case unexpected delays arise. You are told that most weeks the trial will sit Tuesdays to Fridays but, because of the time commitment and the nature of this particular case, compensation will be increased: $40 a day from the start, rising to $100 a day on the 25th day. You affirm that you will faithfully execute your juror duties, your primary duty being to listen to all the evidence and decide the facts of the case. You are reminded that all jury deliberations must be conducted in secrecy and that you must not talk about what transpires. If you do, you could be charged with a criminal offence under the Criminal Code of Canada (CCC) Section 649, which prohibits jurors from making any public comment about their deliberations or their reasons for a verdict. The penalty for running afoul of this law is a summary conviction, meaning the possibility of six months in prison, a fine of $5,000, or both.

As it turns out, you have been selected for the trial of a 31-year-old man charged with kidnapping, sexual assault causing bodily harm, and first-degree murder of an 8-year-old girl (see figure 5.1). The girl was last seen leaving school three years ago on 8 April 2009. That was the girl's first day to walk home alone, without having to be accompanied by her 14-year-old brother. She and her mother and brother had

Figure 5.1. 8 April 2009 was Tori Stafford's first day to walk home alone from school. She never made it. Three months later, her skeletonized remains were found and an 18-year-old woman and a 28-year-old man were in custody.
Picture courtesy of Rodney Stafford.

recently moved to a new house, and she had just redecorated her new room. She was looking forward to spending time with her father that evening. She didn't know that she was being watched by a couple – an 18-year-old woman and a 28-year-old man – who were sitting in a car in a parking lot across from the school. She didn't know that the man had instructed the woman to take "a young female because the younger they are the easier they are to manipulate" (Chilling Crimes, 2020).

Two minutes into her walk, the little girl was approached by the woman who may have seemed familiar as, it later was revealed, she had crossed paths with the girl's mother. The woman started talking about one of the girl's favourite topics – dogs – and lured the girl toward the car with the promise of seeing a puppy (see *R. v. Rafferty*, 2012). When they got close to the car, the woman pushed the little girl in the back, while the man yelled "Hurry up, hurry up!" The little girl was shoved to the floor and covered with the man's coat. They drove for two hours, the woman and the little girl talking all the while. The little girl shared how her favourite colour was purple and how she loved to dress up for Hallowe'en. They stopped three times: once, to purchase Percocet; second, for coffee and tea at Tim Hortons; and, finally, to buy a hammer and garbage bags. When the man entered Tim Hortons, the woman mouthed to the little girl, "I'm sorry."

As they approached the remote rural area where the little girl's body would be found 103 days later on 19 July 2009, the man began to masturbate. When they arrived at their destination, the woman left the car and walked away knowing what was going to happen (see Hembrey & Nixon, 2012). After the man raped the girl, he ordered the woman to take her to use the bathroom. The little girl grasped the opportunity to plead with the woman to stay with her and not let the man hurt her again. The woman apologized, reassured her she was a strong girl, and then returned her to the man. The little girl begged the woman to stay with her and the woman tried. She remained in the car and held the little girl's hand until it was intolerable – knowing what was going to happen – and she left (Blake & Stebner, 2012). The little girl screamed and screamed. When the woman couldn't tolerate the screaming any longer and the rape ended, she threw the little girl on the ground, kicked her, put a plastic bag over her head, and bludgeoned her to death with a hammer. The couple then put the

Figure 5.2. A heart-shaped tombstone with an angel on top marks the resting place of Victoria "Tori" Elizabeth Marie Stafford.
Picture courtesy of Rodney Stafford.

girl's body in garbage bags along with her butterfly earrings and Hannah Montana t-shirt and buried her under a pile of rocks. Her badly decomposed body, including some visible skeletonization, was discovered three months later, identifiable only through dental records (see figure 5.2).

During the trial, you visit the site where the girl's body was found; you hear from 62 witnesses, including the female coaccused, who describes the events in graphic detail. You are presented with 200 exhibits, including electronic and photographic evidence. Dr. Michael Pollanen, who conducted the postmortem examination, testifies to the mechanism and cause of death. Of the hundreds of photographs taken, he identifies 20 as essential, 3 of which are graphic in nature. Only one photo (#3) is deemed to have sufficient probative (vs. prejudicial) value and accepted into evidence. This photo depicts the little girl's body in its original position after removal of the garbage bags.

Dr. Pollanen explains that the photo illustrates the extent of decomposition, including complete destruction of the external genitalia, which precluded determination of whether she had been sexually assaulted. Photo #3 also shows the considerable damage to the left side of the skull, the Hannah Montana shirt on the upper portion of the body, and the naked lower body. It also shows that the body was found in a foetal position.

In weighing the evidentiary value of photo #3, the judge explains:

> The jury in this case will know from the outset that they are trying charges relating to the abduction, rape and murder of a young child. They will inevitably be hearing evidence that could be classified as horrific, and will be instructed that they are to disregard any emotional reaction to such evidence, and to decide the case without prejudice or sympathy. The extent to which their emotional reaction might be aggravated by seeing graphic photographic evidence during the course of the trial is, in my view, minimal. Indeed, in a trial such as this, they will probably expect to encounter such evidence along the way, and will be emotionally prepared for it. A mid-trial instruction just before this evidence is introduced will also assist in buffering their reaction. (*R. v. Rafferty*, 2012, ONSC 1098)

It is difficult to imagine how jurors in such a trial could easily disregard their emotional responses to the evidence and "decide the case without prejudice or sympathy." How could they not sympathize with this eight-year-old child who was viciously raped and murdered by two adults who preyed on her innocence and vulnerability? Even the female coaccused who dealt the fatal blow sympathized and empathized with the child:

> I kept having flashbacks. Sometimes it was like I wasn't even there. I realized I needed to do something so I turned back to the vehicle and ... when I saw what was going on, all I saw was myself when I was that age and all the anger and hate and rage that I'd had and blame that I still feel towards myself came boiling up out of me […]. I went back to the vehicle and I savagely murdered that little girl. (Blake & Stebner, 2012)

At least one juror found it difficult to adjudicate dispassionately. The juror later claimed that she simply could not "unsee" the months of brutal testimony, especially the graphic details about how the couple lured the little girl into their car. "My short-term memory was gone. I was angry. I was reliving the trial, but I was reliving it in the place where I was standing there at the crime scene, watching it happen over and over and over again. I couldn't get rid of the videos in my head playing" (Nasser, 2016). The juror, whose name is protected by a publication ban on jurors' names (CCC Section 649), subsequently was diagnosed with PTSD and compensated by the Province of Ontario for injuries sustained in the performance of her civic duty. Her compensation came shortly after Ontario announced a new Juror Support Program to provide free and easily accessible counselling services to anyone serving jury duty. Prior to this settlement, in 2014, the woman had applied to the Criminal Injuries Compensation Board. The board determined that she didn't meet its criteria for a "nervous shock claim." It did not accept that vicarious (vs. direct) exposure to a traumatic experience (e.g., viewing evidence) could cause emotional distress. The board concluded that it was "absurd to suggest that a jury member is a victim of a crime" (Nasser, 2016).

Jurors can be negatively impacted by revelations even after a trial ends, when they learn about the evidence that was not presented at trial. For example, jurors in this particular case did not know that, just one day before the little girl disappeared outside her elementary school, the male perpetrator had been searching Google with terms such as "underage rape," "real underage rape pictures," "nude preteen," and "best program to download child porn" (Hembrey, 2012a). Nor did jurors know that the man had recently consumed substantial amounts of child pornography, including videos depicting "how-to instructions for child sexual assault" and "snuff" films (Blatchford, 2012). During the *voir dire* (trial within a trial) session where the relative value of this evidence was adjudicated, the Crown described how a film found on the man's laptop, *Gardens of the Night*, centring around the abduction of an eight-year-old girl with blonde hair (like the victim) who is forced into prostitution, had been downloaded just 12 days prior to the abduction and murder (see Hembrey, 2012b). Two weeks after the abduction and murder, the man downloaded another film, *Karla* (see Bender, 2006), a fictionalized account of the sexual assaults and murders of two teenagers by Karla Homolka and Paul Bernardo in the 1990s. The judge ruled that the probative value of the films was outweighed by their potential to prejudice the jury (see Hembrey, 2012b).

At one time, Mark Farrant wondered if he was alone. "I can't be the only one who has suffered" (Clairmont, 2017). Farrant soon learned that there were many others like himself. Dave Kenyon (jury foreman in the second of four trials of Robert Badgerow) claims: "Mark and I both went through a lot of the same stuff. There's no way to prep for jury duty going in but there should be some kind of help coming out." The Badgerow case involved the first-degree murder of Diane Werendowicz, a 23-year-old nursing assistant who was sexually assaulted, strangled, and dumped in a ravine in Hamilton, ON, in 1981.

In fact, not only jurors suffer. Ontario Superior Court chief justice Patrick LeSage presided over Canada's most high-profile and arguably most emotionally charged trial – *R. v. Bernardo* (1995). "I didn't expect that the visual depiction of crime would be so traumatic," Chief Justice LeSage later recalled. "It was like being hit with a sledgehammer. It was a very traumatic experience to watch a crime being committed, particularly against wonderful, young children." The impact of the trial led the chief justice to recuse himself from posttrial proceedings to determine whether Bernardo should be declared a dangerous offender. "I concluded that I was not physically and mentally able to conduct the dangerous-offender hearing" (Makin, 2002).

CLINICAL FORENSIC PSYCHOLOGY AND JURY-RELATED STRESS

The symptoms that Mark Farrant, Dave Kenyon, and Chief Justice LeSage experienced posttrial are consistent with PTSD. In the fifth edition of the *Diagnostic and Statistical Manual of Mental Disorders* (*DSM-5*; American Psychiatric Association [APA], 2013), PTSD was moved from the category of anxiety disorders into a new category: Trauma- and Stressor-Related Disorders. The *DSM-5* retained the three traumatic exposure types from *DSM-IV/TR* and added a fourth: Criterion A1 – directly experiences the traumatic event; A2 – witnesses the traumatic event in person; A3 – learns that the traumatic event occurred to close family or friend; and A4 – repeated or extreme exposure to aversive details of a traumatic event (e.g., first responders collecting human remains; police officers repeatedly exposed to child abuse). Criterion A4 is intended to apply to work-related (vs. media) exposure and to workers who encounter the consequences of traumatic events as part of their professional responsibilities, such as military mortuary workers, forensic child abuse investigators, and presumably jurors.

PTSD includes four distinct symptom clusters: (a) *Intrusion*: reexperiencing traumatic events through spontaneous memories, recurrent dreams, flashbacks, or other intense or prolonged psychological distress; (b) *Avoidance*: efforts to avoid distressing memories, thoughts, feelings, or external reminders of the event; (c) *Negative alterations in cognitions and mood*: inability to remember key aspects of the event, persistent and distorted sense of blame of self or others, persistent negative emotional state (anger, guilt, shame, fear), detachment and estrangement from others, markedly diminished interest in activities; (d) *Arousal and reactivity*: exaggerated startle response, hypervigilance, irritability, angry outbursts, reckless or self-destructive behaviour, and sleep disturbances.

Little research has investigated the prevalence of PTSD symptoms associated with jury duty. The secrecy of jury deliberations (CCC Section 649) is intended to protect jurors from harassment, censure, or recrimination (see *R. v. Pan*; *R. v. Sawyer*, 2001), but it has seriously constrained research on juror experiences. Much of what we know comes from American studies. American psychiatrist Stanley Kaplan (1985) conducted one of the first qualitative studies into the health effects of jury duty. Following the 1982 Roselawn Murder – a highly publicized death-penalty trial of David Steffen, who murdered 19-year-old Karen Range in her home after posing as a door-to-door salesman – Kaplan interviewed 16 of the 17 jurors and alternates, two and four months posttrial. Kaplan (1985) found that 6 jurors met criteria for PTSD, depression, and/or specific phobia, while most others satisfied at least some diagnostic criteria for a mood or anxiety disorder (see also Kaplan & Winget, 1992).

Antonio (2008) analysed data from the Capital Jury Project (a large, ongoing study of juror decision-making and experiences) and found that 60 per cent of 1,198 former jurors reported being emotionally upset and 36 per cent reported insomnia and loss of appetite as a result of the trial. Among those who elaborated when asked if they found the experience to be emotionally upsetting, almost 30 per cent (n = 38/130) reported long-term side effects consistent with a traumatic stress reaction, such as intrusive thoughts/memories, flashbacks, and interpersonal difficulties. Seven of these individuals said that the trial had caused them to increase their drug and/or alcohol use. Among those who elaborated on psychological symptoms, almost half (n = 40/90) reported insomnia and nightmares, and almost two thirds (63%) complained of nightmares directly related to what they saw or heard during the trial.

Canadian researchers Lonergan et al. (2016) systematically reviewed the literature on the prevalence and severity of trauma-related symptoms resulting from jury duty. They also sought to identify factors associated with psychological distress among criminal (vs. civil) jurors. In the 18 studies (mainly American) that were reviewed, trauma-related symptoms (e.g., intrusive memories, nightmares, avoidance, hyperarousal, depression) were found in as many as 50 per cent of jurors. For a minority of jurors, symptoms persisted for months, although few would meet full diagnostic criteria for PTSD. Findings from the 14 quantitative studies that included survey interviews and validated measures of traumatic stress symptoms, depression, or other anxiety disorders revealed that most jurors (80%–88%) felt proud of their jury duty and 56–71 per cent would volunteer again if called. On the other hand, approximately 30–89 per cent of jurors reported that they found their experience to be "stressful," and between 14 per cent and 56 per cent believed that jury duty would cause emotional problems in most people.

Lonergan et al.'s (2016) review found that trial-related factors, including jury deliberations (e.g., tension between jurors, verdict decision-making, fear of making a mistake) and being sequestered, increased juror risk for posttrial stress and trauma-related symptoms. "You try to forget a lot of things," says "Anna" (aged 70), who served on a jury in a homicide case in Quebec 25 years ago. "It's the fear of getting it wrong. You try to be careful; you try to be fair. You listen closely to the evidence, to what the experts are saying. But in the end, it's just you and a lot of people you didn't know before, deciding whether to take someone's freedom away" (CBA National/ABC National, 2020).

Chopra (2002) investigated the taxing experience of jury duty in her doctoral dissertation work at Simon Fraser University. Chopra found that two thirds of 80 former jurors from the greater Vancouver area reported experiencing stress as a result of their jury experience, and nearly half said they believed that stress affected the decisions made by their fellow jurors. A substantial proportion (11.3%) reported symptoms consistent with a *DSM-IV* diagnosis of PTSD. One third said they had difficulty sleeping as a result of their trial memories, while almost 20 per cent said the experience left them feeling "more fearful" than before. Interestingly, 7 of the top 10 sources of juror stress related to reaching a verdict (including the threat of a hung jury) and the deliberation process. These findings suggest that a trial doesn't need to involve a grisly crime and ghastly evidence to be stressful. Findings support Anna's experience, whereby she attributes more stress to the daunting responsibility than to the evidence per se. "I was in distress all the time," Anna says. "I couldn't stop thinking about it. And when it's all over, they just thank you and say goodbye, and you're done. Nobody talked to us. Nobody asked us how we were doing" (CBA National/ABC National, 2020).

Other sources of juror stress identified by Lonergan et al. (2016) included fear of retaliation (which CCC Section 649 is meant to protect against), feelings of isolation, inability to discuss the trial with loved ones, limited compensation, the length of the trial and deliberations, the type of trial, the level of media attention, and the presentation of gruesome and graphic (emotionally disturbing) evidence and testimony. Not surprisingly, trials that involved violent crimes against a person (vs. property), especially if heinous, were significantly more apt to trigger PTSD symptoms. Long trials (i.e., at least 11 days) or interrupted trials and deliberations were associated with a greater number and severity of PTSD symptoms over time. Robertson et al. (2009) found that prolonged exposure to graphic evidence and profound empathy for the victim in certain trials can be especially traumatizing for jurors. Dispositional risk factors linked to stress and trauma included female gender and history of prior trauma. Women, especially those serving on a case that is relevant to prior personal trauma (e.g., sexual assault), are at particular risk for PTSD symptoms.

Lonergan et al.'s (2016) review provides compelling evidence that jury duty can be hazardous to one's health. The sum of the studies reviewed shows that, while most jurors may not meet the full diagnostic criteria for PTSD posttrial, a meaningful proportion experienced clinically significant PTSD-related symptoms, including intrusive memories, nightmares, insomnia, hypervigilance, avoidance behaviours, and interpersonal difficulties. Moreover, many jurors experienced clinical or subclinical levels of depression (i.e., persistent sadness, loss of interest, lack of energy, feelings of guilt/worthlessness), and substance misuse. Both of these disorders can be caused or complicated by exposure to a traumatic experience.

> "While it's true a small percentage of jurors have suffered extensive mental health trauma like myself due to graphic evidence, one of the top sources of stress of jurors is actually related to the verdict and deliberation process," she said. "So for many, once the trial ends, the agony begins. Feelings of guilt, shame, regret often set in, feelings you're told not to talk about with anyone." – Tina Daenzer, former juror in *R. v. Bernardo* (1995), was diagnosed with PTSD after serving as a juror on the case. (Previl, 2021)

COPING WITH JURY DUTY

> If lawmakers know what it is like for an ordinary person to be plucked from their life and plunked into the atrocities of a murder trial, perhaps they would see help is needed. Maybe they will understand the least we can do is care for jurors we have burdened with the critical and sometimes crippling duty. (Clairmont, 2017)

In response to a growing outcry by former jurors, in June 2017 the federal government launched its first study into mental health supports for jurors. The House of Commons Committee heard first-hand accounts from former jurors, as well as government representatives, lawyers, and psychologists with expertise on stress generally and stress associated with jury duty more specifically. In its 2018 report, *Improving Support for Jurors in Canada* (see Housefather, 2018), the committee offered recommendations for preventing or reducing the deleterious impact on jurors. These recommendations included (a) Pretrial information package with information on roles and responsibilities, compensation, legal concepts and mechanics, deliberation process, how to cope with the potential impact of jury duty, and how to access mental health assistance posttrial; (b) Posttrial debriefing with format, duration, and facilitator left to the discretion of judicial officials. This a rather controversial recommendation given that debriefings should be done by a mental health professional with specific training. Moreover, research shows that debriefing alone may be insufficient to mitigate risk for PTSD (see LeClerc, as cited in Housefather, 2018); and (c) Psychological support and services with no predetermined time limit for jurors to access. While stress- and trauma-related symptoms usually begin within the first three months postexposure, delayed expression for months or even years is not unusual (see *DSM-5;* APA, 2013).

Psychological treatments for PTSD include trauma-focused interventions that directly address memories, thoughts, and feelings related to the traumatic experience, and non-trauma-focused interventions (e.g., relaxation, stress inoculation training, and interpersonal therapy) that aim to reduce symptoms. According to the American Psychological Association (2017) and organizations focused on veterans' health, trauma-focused interventions constitute best practices in the treatment of PTSD in adults. These interventions include cognitive behavioural therapy (CBT), cognitive processing therapy (CPT), and prolonged exposure therapy (PE). Each of these interventions is founded on a large base of evidence showing their effectiveness. None outperforms the other largely because they share critical components. Each includes some combination of both cognitive techniques, such as restructuring (i.e., identifying and challenging maladaptive thoughts and beliefs about the event), and behavioural techniques, such as exposure (i.e., repeated exposure to traumatic memory). Exposure can be imaginal (e.g., writing the traumatic narrative, or reading the traumatic memory out loud) and/or *in vivo* (i.e., repeatedly approaching situations, places, and people they have been avoiding because of a fear response due to the traumatic event until distress decreases; see Watkins et al., 2018). Most recently, a number of studies have found support for Written Exposure Therapy (WET), a manualized exposure-based intervention for PTSD (Sloan et al., 2022). WET involves clients writing about a single traumatic event and the therapist focusing on the client's experiences while writing about the trauma, rather than the event itself. Sloan and colleagues (2022) developed WET in response to the demand for PTSD treatments that are effective but also easier to implement, more accessible and affordable, and with lower dropout rates than other trauma interventions. WET has been found to be effective with veterans and might be effective for some jurors. Anecdotal evidence from former jurors suggests that the trauma of jury duty in some ways resembles military service – isolation, difficulty talking about it, feeling detached and separate/different from others.

The House of Commons Committee (Housefather, 2018) also advised an amendment to CCC Section 649 – Secrecy Rule for Jury Deliberations – so that jurors would be permitted to discuss jury deliberations with designated mental health professionals posttrial. Section 649 imposes a lifelong prohibition on former jurors discussing what went on during the jury deliberation process with spouses, friends, or mental health professionals. Violations of Section 649 could result in a summary conviction. The "secrecy rule" is intended to protect the integrity of the trial process by protecting jurors from harassment or intimidation from others. Its unintended consequence is to leave former jurors feeling isolated, with no way to process their experience. Mark Farrant said when his jury duty was over, he felt partially relieved and as if he had just walked out of a vacuum. He expected there would be some sort of debrief from the court: orders on what he could discuss or a list of counsellors available to help him cope. But that didn't happen, and Farrant felt "forced to suffer in silence."

Another committee recommendation was for jurors to receive a daily allowance and compensation for related costs (e.g., care for dependent children or adults, travel, parking, and meals). As psychologist Dr. Patrick Baillie explained: "We talk about the jury as being this great democratic institution, but many people justifiably ask to be excused because they just can't afford to do it ... hardly a jury of one's peers." The committee recommended that jurors receive a daily allowance of at least $120 throughout the legal proceedings to be adjusted to reflect cost of living increases. Currently, per diem allowances run from $40 (ON) to $50 (AB) to $103 (QC). Quebec also reimburses jurors for mileage, parking, and meals and, on a judge's order, child care and counselling can be covered (see Krugel, 2018).

The committee also advised raising awareness among judges, coroners, and judicial officials who interact with jurors, such as sheriffs and bailiffs, of the potential impact of legal proceedings on the mental health of jurors in order to ensure an environment that is more responsive to their mental health needs. Of course, judges and lawyers are not immune to trial-related stressors and trauma. Jaffe et al. (2003) investigated vicarious trauma in a cross-section of American judges (N = 105) who attended different levels of court across the United States and a range of criminal, civil, and specialized courts. Vicarious trauma falls within the *DSM-5*'s fourth criterion for PTSD, which applies to work-related exposure. Jaffe et al.'s study found that almost two thirds of judges (63%) reported symptoms of work-related vicarious trauma, with women and more experienced judges (seven or more years) reporting more symptoms. Female judges reported more internalizing symptoms (e.g., anxiety), while judges with more experience reported more externalizing symptoms (e.g., anger, hostility).

Recently, doctoral candidate Carly Schrever (see Stanton, 2019) surveyed the psychological well-being of more than 150 Australian judges, magistrates, and other judicial officers and conducted in-depth interviews with 60. Overall, the judiciary appeared to be coping well with heavy workloads and harrowing crimes, although one third reported "moderate to severe" symptoms of vicarious traumatic stress and almost 20 per cent reported intrusion symptoms (reexperiencing) from dealing with traumatic material (evidence) and traumatized people.

A *Canadian Lawyer* article titled "Vicarious Trauma: The Cumulative Effects of Caring" sheds light on some of the horrors to which lawyers can be exposed (Shutt, 2015). For example, over 12 weeks between September and December 2014, five lawyers from the law firm Borden Ladner Gervais sat in a Montreal courtroom listening to the grisly details of the murder of Lin Jun, a 34-year-old international student at Concordia University. Lin Jun had been stabbed, dismembered, and cannibalized, and a video of his murder was posted online by 30-year-old Luka Magnotta from Scarborough, ON. The lawyers were representing Lin Jun's family. When they weren't listening to graphic testimony, they watched the horrors unfold in a video made by Magnotta. When not in the courtroom, the team of lawyers would be meeting to review evidence – including the video – and discussing the details of the case. As one of the lawyers, Amélie Gouin, put it: "It was hard to acknowledge this was real. We're used to seeing violence on TV, but we know it's fake. You need to reconcile that one human being did this to another" (Shutt, 2015).

SUMMARY AND CONCLUSIONS

> Our right to trial by jury depends on the willingness of all citizens to serve, but doing so should not be at the expense of a juror's own mental health.
>
> – *Tina Daenzer, former juror in* R. v. Bernardo *(Housefather, 2018)*

It is difficult to reconcile what Michael Rafferty and Terri-Lynne McClintic did to eight-year-old Tori Stafford in April 2009. The seduction (luring the child to the car with the promise of seeing a puppy), abduction, extreme sexual violence, and ultimately violent murder are the stuff of nightmares. It is not difficult to imagine Tori's fear, horror, and sense of helplessness; her glimpses of hope and ultimate betrayal when McClintic turned out to be as monstrous as Rafferty. What happened to Tori actually exceeds the magnitude of catastrophe as defined in the *DSM-5* (APA, 2013), which removed subjective responses (e.g., "intense fear, horror, or helplessness") and reference to "threat to physical integrity" that had been part of the criteria in earlier versions. Regardless of how it is defined, Tori's experience included the three elements common to all sources of trauma: it was unexpected, the person was unprepared, and there was nothing the person could do to stop it from happening. Events were beyond the individual's control. For those who participated in Rafferty's trial – judge, jurors, lawyers, and others – repeated exposure to the aversive details of the crime would elevate their risk for PTSD symptoms: intrusive thoughts (distressing memories, imaginal reenactments of the crime), efforts to avoid reminders, negative changes in mood and cognitions, and disruptions in physiological arousal (e.g., hypervigilance). Symptoms can be "especially severe and long lasting when the stressor is interpersonal and intentional (e.g., torture, sexual violence)" (APA, 2013, p. 275).

Recommendations from the House of Commons Committee (Housefather, 2018) were not ignored and encouraged activists to lobby for mental health services for jurors. Efforts to amend CCC Section 649 to allow jurors to discuss aspects of jury deliberations with a licensed health-care professional posttrial are being promoted by former jurors Tina Daenzer and Mark Farrant (chief executive officer of the Canadian Juries Commission), in collaboration with members of Parliament (e.g., Michael Cooper; see Cooper, 2019) and Senators Pierre-Hugues Boisvenu and Lucie Moncion. To that end, Senator Boisvenu tabled Bill S-206 in 2019 (see Previl, 2021). The bill's progress was delayed by COVID-19 but eventually it had its first reading on 14 December 2021 and currently is at second reading in the House of Commons. For updates on Bill S-206, see https://www.parl.ca/LegisInfo/en/bill/44-1/s-206.

Other potential benefits to amending Section 649 include allowing research into jury decision-making. Because jurors cannot be interviewed posttrial about deliberation processes, an important window into how jurors come to render verdicts in Canadian trials is closed to researchers. Greater insight into jury decision-making could increase public confidence in the criminal justice system by shedding light on controversial verdicts, such as the acquittal of Saskatchewan farmer Gerald Stanley in the fatal shooting death of a young Indigenous man, Colten Boushie (see chapter 4). Greater insight into the mental health risks of jury service and more accommodations for jurors who perform such a vital service also should increase public confidence in the criminal justice system.

CRITICAL THINKING QUESTIONS

1. Do you think jury duty should be compulsory?
2. Would you want to be a juror? What factors would you consider in making your decision? How do you view jury duty – as an honour, a privilege, a responsibility? What biases might preclude your ability to consider a case fairly and without prejudice?
3. How would you propose to remove barriers to participation in jury duty so as to ensure a more representative jury?
4. Which is more important: legal proceedings remaining "secret" or a juror being able to disclose details of a trial to a mental health professional?
5. Do you think there are crimes that are too grisly to be tried before a jury of one's peers?

REFERENCES

American Psychiatric Association. (2013). *Diagnostic and statistical manual of mental disorders* (5th ed.).

American Psychological Association. (2017). *Clinical practice guidelines for the treatment of PTSD*. https://www.apa.org/ptsd-guideline/ptsd.pdf

Antonio, M. E. (2008). Stress and the capital jury: How male and female jurors react to serving on a murder trial. *Justice System Journal, 29*(3), 396–407. http://cdm16501.contentdm.oclc.org/cdm/ref/collection/criminal/id/154

Bender, J. (Director). (2006). *Karla* [Film]. MovieBank.

Blake, M., & Stebner, B. (2012, May 12). Man who abducted, raped and murdered girl, 8, on way home from school found guilty after breaking 16 of her bones and taking a hammer to her face. *Daily Mail*. https://www.dailymail.co.uk/news/article-2143331/Tori-Stafford-trial-Michael-Rafferty-guilty-murdering-grade-girl.html

Blatchford, C. (2012, May 10). Christie Blatchford: The shocking child-porn evidence the Tori Stafford jury didn't hear. *National Post*. https://nationalpost.com/opinion/tori-stafford-michael-rafferty-evidence

CBA National/ABC National. (2020, January 13). Coping with jury duty. *Canadian Bar Association*. https://nationalmagazine.ca/en-ca/articles/law/in-depth/2020/coping-with-jury-duty

Chilling Crimes. (2020, November 20). *Tori Stafford*. https://www.chillingcrimes.com/blogs/news/tori-stafford

Chopra, S. R. (2002). *Juror stress: Sources, severity, and solutions* [Unpublished doctoral dissertation]. Simon Fraser University.

Clairmont, S. (2017, March 8). Clairmont: "I can't be the only one who has suffered." Jurors seek national support. *Hamilton Spectator*. https://www.thespec.com/news/hamilton-region/2017/03/08/clairmont-i-can-t-be-the-only-one-who-has-suffered-jurors-seek-national-support.html

Cooper, M. (2019, January 3). Canadian jurors need mental health support. *LawNow Magazine*. https://www.lawnow.org/canadian-jurors-need-mental-health-support/

Hembrey, J. (2012a, May 11). What jurors at the Tori Stafford trial did not hear. *CBC News*. https://www.cbc.ca/news/canada/what-jurors-at-the-tori-stafford-trial-did-not-hear-1.1133647

Hembrey, J. (2012b, May 12). Michael Rafferty found guilty of Tori Stafford murder. *CBC News*. https://www.cbc.ca/news/canada/michael-rafferty-found-guilty-of-tori-stafford-murder-1.1230270

Hembrey, J., & Nixon, G. (2012, March 13). McClintic tells jurors about Tori's final hours. *CBC News*. https://www.cbc.ca/news/canada/mcclintic-tells-jurors-about-tori-s-final-hours-1.1203603

Housefather, A. (2018, May). *Improving support for jurors in Canada*. Report of the Standing Committee on Justice and Human Rights, 41st Parliament, 1st Session. https://www.ourcommons.ca/Content/Committee/421/JUST/Reports/RP9871696/justrp20/justrp20-e.pdf

Jaffe, P. G., Crooks, C. V., Dunford-Jackson, B. L., & Town, J. M. (2003). Vicarious trauma in judges: The personal challenge of dispensing justice. *Juvenile and Family Court Journal, 54*(4), 1–9. https://doi.org/10.1111/j.1755-6988.2003.tb00083.x

Kaplan, S. M. (1985). Death, so say we all. *Psychology Today, 19*, 48. https://doi.org/10.1203/00006450-198504000-00949

Kaplan, S. M., & Winget, C. (1992). The occupational hazards of jury duty. *Bulletin of the American Academy of Psychiatry and the Law, 20*, 325–33. https://pubmed.ncbi.nlm.nih.gov/1421562/

Krugel, L. (2018, December 30). Four things Canadians should know if they're summoned for jury duty. *Global News*. https://globalnews.ca/news/4802406/jury-duty-things-to-know-canada/

Lonergan, M., Leclerc, M.-È., Descamps, M., Pigeon, S., & Brunet, A. (2016). Prevalence and severity of trauma- and stressor-related symptoms among jurors: A review. *Journal of Criminal Justice, 47*, 51–61. https://doi.org/10.1016/j.jcrimjus.2016.07.003

Makin, K. (2002, August 14). Judges live in torment, study finds. *Globe and Mail*. http://www.fact.on.ca/news/news0208/gm020814.htm

Nasser, S. (2016, October 19). Tori Stafford murder trial juror seeks compensation, says grisly evidence traumatized her. *CBC News*. https://www.cbc.ca/news/canada/toronto/tori-stafford-murder-trial-juror-seeks-compensation-says-grisly-evidence-traumatized-her-1.3811295

Powers v. Ohio, 1991, 499 U.S. 400.

Previl, S. (2021, November 25). Canadian senator hopes for bill's fast passage to give jurors mental health support. *Global News*. https://globalnews.ca/news/8401914/jurors-mental-health-support-bill-canadian-senator-boisvenu/

Private Member Bill C-211. (2018). Royal assent – Federal framework on post-traumatic stress disorder act – Parliament of Canada. https://parl.ca/DocumentViewer/en/42-1/bill/C-211/royal-assent

R. v. Bernardo, 1995, CanLII 7434, ON SC.

R. v. Pan; R. v. Sawyer, 2001, 2 SCR 344, 2001 SCC 42.

R. v. Rafferty, 2012, ONSC 1098.

Robertson, N., Davies, G., & Nettleingham, A. (2009). Vicarious traumatisation as a consequence of jury service. *Howard Journal of Criminal Justice, 48*(1), 1–12. https://doi.org/10.1111/j.1468-2311.2008.00539.x

Shutt, S. (2015, February 2). Vicarious trauma: The cumulative effects of caring. *Canadian Lawyer*. https://www.canadianlawyermag.com/news/general/vicarious-trauma-the-cumulative-effects-of-caring/269679

Sloan, D. M., Marx, B. P., Resick, P. A., Young-McCaughan, S., Dondanville, K. A., Straud, C. L., Mintz, J., Litz, B. T., & Peterson, A. L. (2022). Effect of written exposure therapy vs cognitive processing therapy on increasing treatment efficiency among military service members with posttraumatic stress disorder. *JAMA Network Open, 5*(1), e2140911. https://doi.org/10.1001/jamanetworkopen.2021.40911

Stanton, K. (2019, May 6). Wellbeing survey of Australia's judiciary reveals risk of distress and Burnout. *Pursuit*. https://pursuit.unimelb.edu.au/articles/wellbeing-survey-of-australia-s-judiciary-reveals-risk-of-distress-and-burnout

Watkins, L. E., Sprang, K. R., & Rothbaum, B. O. (2018). Treating PTSD: A review of evidence-based psychotherapy interventions. *Frontiers in Behavioral Neuroscience, 12*. https://doi.org/10.3389/fnbeh.2018.00258

CHAPTER SIX

Médecin sans conscience? Filicide by Father

The Case of Guy Turcotte, MD

With Tamara Speth and Marie-Claire Leclerc

In February 2009, Guy Turcotte was employed as a cardiologist at the Hôtel-Dieu de Saint-Jérôme hospital alongside his wife, Isabelle Gaston, an emergency room physician. The couple had been together for ten years and had two children: Olivier (five years old) and Anne-Sophie (three years old). Although Gaston would later describe the relationship as "toxic" (i.e., marred by intimate partner violence), she considered Turcotte to be a good father and thought him incapable of harming their children (Canadian Press, 2014). Unfortunately, her confidence proved unfounded. On 21 February 2009, two police officers arrived at Turcotte's home in response to a 911 call from Turcotte's mother. Inside the home, the officers found the bodies of Olivier and Anne-Sophie Turcotte in their bedrooms, stabbed 27 and 19 times, respectively. They found Turcotte under his bed, covered in blood and vomit, claiming to have drunk windshield wiper fluid in an effort to end his life.

In July 2011, Turcotte was found not criminally responsible by reason of mental disorder (NCRMD) for the murders of his children. The verdict was heavily mediatized and received with public outrage. After 46 months in a forensic psychiatric hospital, Turcotte was released on $100,000 bail. The Crown appealed the verdict on the grounds that the trial judge had erred in law, particularly with regard to the issue of self-induced methanol intoxication as a basis for mental disorder. In November 2013, the court ordered a new trial. Turcotte surrendered into custody but was granted bail. The Turcotte case prompted the Canadian government to propose legislation for dealing with high-risk offenders found NCRMD, such as requiring longer waits between formal reviews of psychiatric status. At his second trial in 2015, Turcotte was found guilty of two counts of second-degree murder without parole eligibility for 17 years (Banerjee, 2018).

THE CRIMINAL

Guy Turcotte was born on 21 April 1972, in a suburb south of Montreal. He was the third of six children in a devout Catholic household. Reports indicate that Turcotte was small and timid as a youth, not particularly athletic or popular, had trouble fitting in, and often was the subject of teasing. Despite his awkwardness and alienation in childhood, it seems that Turcotte enjoyed a number of romantic relationships in adulthood. In 1999, Turcotte met Isabelle Gaston, who has been described as a charming and intelligent woman, full of energy. Apparently, Turcotte was attracted to Gaston immediately but was surprised that she was attracted to him. Within a couple of years, however, discord ensued. In 2001, a heated argument between the couple resulted in punches being thrown by both parties and discontinuation of the romantic relationship. The separation lasted only a few months and, shortly after reuniting, Turcotte proposed to Gaston. The couple went on to have two children: Olivier (whom Turcotte described as "his best friend") and Anne-Sophie. By all accounts, the couple's 10-year marital relationship was similarly tumultuous. Gaston later claimed that Turcotte was emotionally and psychologically abusive throughout their relationship. Despite the turmoil, it seems that Turcotte remained relatively private about his marriage. According to his older brother, Gilles, Turcotte never confided in him regarding any marital difficulties (Banerjee, 2011b).

In January 2009, Guy Turcotte discovered that his wife was involved in an extramarital affair with a family friend, Martin Huot (Feith, 2015). Apparently, the affair had started in the fall of 2008.

Huot's girlfriend at the time, Patricia Giroux, informed Turcotte of the affair by revealing emails exchanged between Gaston and Huot. Despite this revelation, Turcotte decided to proceed with a planned family vacation in Mexico. Upon returning from this vacation, however, Turcotte acquired a separate but nearby residence. Shortly thereafter, Martin Huot moved into the Gaston-Turcotte family home, which served to exacerbate the discord between the estranged couple. Nonetheless, the couple agreed to participate in a mediation process to attempt to resolve outstanding issues. By the time mediation was scheduled to begin, the children were dead.

According to his lawyer, Turcotte grew increasingly depressed in the days leading up to his offence (Canadian Press, 2015b). On 20 February 2009, one month after the couple's separation, Olivier and Anne-Sophie were staying with Turcotte in his new residence, while Gaston was out of town on a ski trip with Huot. According to his testimony at trial, Turcotte spent the evening re-reading the emails between Gaston and Huot and started contemplating suicide (Canadian Press, 2015a). Evidence presented at trial confirmed that he had been on his computer for one hour and 42 minutes between 6:27 p.m. and 8:09 p.m. on the night of the murders. Apparently, Turcotte consulted various websites related to methods of suicide and subsequently made three phone calls: one, to cancel his appointment for the final inspection of his new residence the next morning; two, to cancel the babysitter for the next day; and three, to tell his mother about the unhappiness he had experienced in his marriage.

In court, Turcotte testified that, after making the three phone calls, he began ingesting windshield wiper fluid, a substance that contains the fatal ingredient of methanol. Upon realizing that his children would find him dead, he decided to terminate their lives. Presumably due to intoxication, he claimed a "blurry recollection" of the events that followed. According to Turcotte: "He is standing in his son's room. He has a knife in his hands and stabs his son. His son cries out 'no' and moves away. He realizes that he is hurting him. He panics and [translation] 'stabs him more.' He has a similar memory with respect to his daughter. He sees himself in the bathroom. He drinks windshield washer fluid. He has blood on his hands. He has hurt his children and looks for the knife to [translation] 'stab himself in the heart,' but cannot find it." Turcotte stabbed his five-year-old son, Olivier, 27 times and his three-year-old daughter, Anne-Sophie, 19 times (*R. v. Turcotte*, 2005). The children's injuries included many defence wounds, and Turcotte later admitted that Olivier begged him to stop (Canadian Press, 2014).

Alarmed by her son's phone call, Turcotte's mother called the police. Police arrived at Turcotte's home in Piedmont, Quebec, to discover the lifeless bodies of Olivier and Anne-Sophie, and the unconscious body of Guy Turcotte under his bed. Turcotte was rushed to hospital and, on 24 February 2009, he was charged with two counts of first-degree murder (CTV Montreal, 2009). Olivier and Anne-Sophie were laid to rest on 2 March 2009.

THE TRIALS

Turcotte's first trial began in January 2011 and included testimonies from 39 witnesses, including his ex-wife Isabelle Gaston, his parents, and several mental health experts. The Crown argued that the murders had been premeditated and fueled by Turcotte's anger at his wife. The trial heard how Turcotte had emailed Gaston on the day of the killings saying, "You want war, you'll have war" (QMI Agency, 2012). Defence lawyer Pierre Poupart, on the other hand, argued that Turcotte loved his children but, at the time of the offence, had been severely distraught by his wife's infidelity and the collapse of his marriage. Turcotte himself claimed a sketchy recollection of events but denied formulating an intent to harm his children (Canadian Press, 2014). The 10-week trial ended in July 2011, when the jury reached a verdict: NCRMD (*R. v. Turcotte,* 2012). He was ordered to be held at the Institut Philippe-Pinel de Montréal, a forensic psychiatric hospital, until such time as deemed fit to be released.

Turcotte's Request for Release

Less than a year after being found NCRMD and sent to Institut Philippe-Pinel de Montréal, Turcotte applied for release. Due to the complexity of the case, a five-member (vs. the typical three-member) provincial Mental Health Review Board (Tribunal Administratif du Quebec) was convened. The two lawyers, two psychiatrists, and one social worker began hearing the case in August 2011. Turcotte maintained that he had the right to request release, according to the Canadian Charter of Rights, and asserted that he would be of more use assisting his aunt and uncle than "waste his time in prison" (*Guy Turcotte v. Her Majesty the Queen*, 2013, p. 5). In November 2011, psychiatrist Dr. Pierre Rochet stated that neither Turcotte nor his physicians could make sense of what happened at the time that he stabbed his two children to death. Dr. Rochet recommended that Turcotte remain at Pinel for another year, expressing concern that another dangerous situation could arise given that "Turcotte is someone who falls in love easily, and he has received letters from female admirers" (Postmedia News, 2011).

In March 2012, psychiatrist Dr. Louis Morissette told the board that Turcotte was an "ideal candidate to return to the community." According to Dr. Morissette, Turcotte had responded well to the antipsychotic medication and psychotherapy. He asserted that Turcotte was in remission from a major depressive disorder (MDD) with psychotic symptoms, and no longer posed a danger to the community, including his ex-wife, Gaston (*R. v. Turcotte,* 2012). Dr. Morissette testified: "He (Turcotte) is no longer the same man. He has improved everything he could improve to make sure he doesn't reoffend. He has not had any symptoms of mental illness since the fall."

In response, both the Crown and the lawyer representing the Institut Philippe-Pinel de Montréal argued that Turcotte had not adequately dealt with the rage that had played an important role in the murder of his children. The Pinel Institute's lawyer argued that Turcotte's anger and vengeance played a more significant role in his offence than what was indicated by the experts brought forward by the defence. The Crown did not believe that Turcotte had adequately paid his dues to society given the severity of his crime. Moreover, Turcotte was considered a flight risk and a continued risk to public safety. The Crown asserted that granting Turcotte's release would erode the public's trust in the efficacy of the justice system, especially given the high-profile nature of the Turcotte case, and requested that Turcotte remain at the hospital for an additional year. In June 2012, it was determined that Turcotte would be held at the psychiatric hospital for six additional months, with increased access to the community. In December 2012, it was determined that Turcotte should be granted a conditional release after spending 46 months at the Institut Philippe-Pinel de Montréal (Kelly, 2014). As part of his release, he was mandated to continue seeing a psychotherapist (i.e., psychologist, medical doctor, or psychotherapist's permit holder; Ordre des psychologues du Québec), and have no contact with Gaston. Turcotte's brother, Gilles, posted a $100,000 surety for Guy and his uncle offered his home as a residence, maintaining that his nephew could act as a helper to him and his wife.

Outside of the hearing, Turcotte's ex-wife, Isabelle Gaston, told supporters: "He was depressed during the preliminary enquiry, he was depressed during his trial, and then, miraculously, after his verdict, my goodness, he doesn't need his antidepressants anymore? He's functional? He's happy, he's got goals, he wants kids, he wants a new girlfriend?" and "I'm tired that no one sees that he is a chameleon, he changes his tune according to the situation" (CBC News, 2012).

The Crown's Appeal

In 2013, the Crown appealed the verdict in Turcotte's case and requested a new trial, claiming that NCRMD should never have been presented as an option for the jury (*Guy Turcotte v. Her Majesty the Queen*, 2013). In accordance with Section 33.1 of the Criminal Code (1985), the Crown asserted that a verdict of NCRMD should be reached only in cases where the perpetrator clearly suffered from a mental illness, and not in cases where the offender was unable to recall details of the offence due to a self-induced blackout or intoxication (Criminal Code, c. C 46, ss. 16, 33.1., 1985; Canadian Press, 2014). Furthermore, the Crown argued that the judge failed to remind jurors of their responsibility in determining whether Turcotte's intoxication was secondary to a major mental illness. "The burden of proof was on the accused to show that he was suffering from an incapacitating mental illness – distinct from the intoxication symptoms – and it was the jury's job to decide," said the Quebec Court ruling in that appeal. "But the judge did not remind jurors of that distinction" (Canadian Press, 2014). In November 2013, Turcotte turned himself in to police after a warrant was issued for his arrest and retrial. Defence lawyer Pierre Poupart's appeal to the Supreme Court of Canada to overrule the Quebec Court's decision for a new trial was refused (*Guy Turcotte v. Her Majesty the Queen*, 2018; Canadian Press, 2014).

Turcotte's Second Trial

Turcotte's second trial began in September 2015 and, by December 2015, the jury returned a verdict of guilty on both counts of second-degree murder (i.e., "non-premeditated murder"; ÉDUCALOI, 2015). Turcotte appealed the verdict but his appeal was dismissed. The jury declined the trial judge's invitation to fix the period of his ineligibility for parole. While the minimum time in prison for a verdict of second-degree murder is 10 years, the judge can make the decision to extend this time in prison up to 25 years (ÉDUCALOI, 2015). Turcotte's trial judge rendered his judgment sentencing Turcotte to the obligatory sentence of life imprisonment and fixed the period of his ineligibility for parole at 17 years (*Guy Turcotte v. Her Majesty the Queen*, 2018). See figure 6.1 for a timeline of Turcotte's major legal proceedings.

Turcotte's Appeal

Turcotte appealed the length of his parole ineligibility, claiming that 17 years was too long, given that he posed no danger to the public and that the judge failed to consider "his mental distress" at the time of the offence. Turcotte had testified that his recall of that night was sketchy (punctuated by "flashes"), having ingested windshield wiper fluid after researching ways to kill himself online. Claiming the altruistic motive of not wanting his children to find him dead (see filicide motives below), he decided to kill them instead. The Crown, however, produced evidence that he had ingested the windshield wiper fluid after killing the children. In fact, the levels of methanol in his blood suggested that the liquid was ingested shortly before being arrested in the morning following the murders (Canadian Press, 2015c). Other evidence presented at trial included testimony from a nurse with whom Turcotte had worked who said that he had asked her to give Gaston a message: "Tell her I did this to piss her off." Other aggravating factors included the gratuitous nature of the violence (i.e., the number of times he had stabbed the children) and that after the murders "he seemed more interested in securing funds to present a defence than the fate he inflicted on his two young children." The Quebec Court of Appeal rejected his appeal with Judge Allan Hilton proclaiming that "[t]he gravity of the crime is hardly in doubt.... Mr. Turcotte's degree of responsibility is complete. Obviously, he alone is responsible for the two murders." The court ruled that Turcotte's attempt to invoke the despair of his failing marriage is contradicted by evidence at the trial that he acted out of animosity toward his ex-wife in an effort to make her suffer: "Mr. Turcotte is not the first nor the last person to have lost the affections of a spouse for someone else" (Canadian Press, 2018).

CLINICAL FORENSIC PSYCHOLOGY AND GUY TURCOTTE

Filicide (i.e., the killing of one or more children by a parent, stepparent, or other parental figure) comprised 15 per cent of all murders in the United States between 1976 and 2007, with one third of victims being infants under one year of age. Slightly more than half of the filicide offenders were males with an average age of 35 years (vs. 27 years for female offenders). Most offenders and victims were White. Almost 90 per cent of victims were biological offspring, and more sons (52%) than daughters (38%). Male (vs. female) offenders were more apt to use weapons in commission of the offence (Mariano et al., 2014).

Dawson (2015) found that at least 1,612 Canadian children were killed by their parents between 1961 and 2011. Presumably, this number would include Turcotte's children. Dawson found that more men than women were accused of filicide, a difference that appeared to be increasing, and that men were more apt to be motivated by revenge or jealousy. From 1991 onward, family violence seemed to precede filicides.

Certainly, more is known about women who commit filicide (e.g., Andrea Yates) than men, such as Guy Turcotte. West (2007) found that most fathers who commit filicide are poor, unemployed, socially isolated, and at risk for suicide or attempted suicide (60%) and familicide (to kill or attempt to kill spouses; 40%–60%). Following a review of 131 maternal and paternal filicide cases described in the literature between 1951 and 1967, Resnick (1969) proposed five motive categories based on the explanation provided by the parent: altruistic ("out of love" vs. anger or hate), acutely psychotic, unwanted child, child maltreatment (consequence of abuse), and spousal revenge (i.e., deliberate attempt to make their spouse suffer). The latter was the rarest of motives and most commonly precipitated by spousal infidelity and child custody disputes (see Resnick, 2016). The prototype of spousal revenge can be found in the ancient Greek tragedy about Medea, a woman who exacts revenge on her unfaithful husband by killing their two sons, then tells him: "Thy sons are dead and gone. That will stab thy heart" (Resnick, 2016, p. 5). This is reminiscent of Turcotte saying to the emergency room nurse, "Tell her [his wife] I did this to piss her off." According to Carruthers (2016), those who engage in spousal revenge killings tend to see their own children as objects. Palermo (2002) suggested that some fathers who commit filicide may feel a sense of personal inadequacy and lack coping and effective parenting skills, all of which could fuel the anger and impulsivity more often seen in paternal (vs. maternal) filicide. In addition, intoxication more often plays a role in paternal (vs. maternal) filicide. In many respects, Turcotte fits the profile of men who commit filicide. He was 37 at the time of the offence, with young children and a history of perpetrating partner violence. His marriage had collapsed and he was not adapting well to his altered circumstances. On the other hand, Turcotte was not socially isolated, poor, or unemployed, nor was he motivated to commit his crime by some altruistic concern for his children; rather, he seemed intent on exacting revenge on his ex-wife. An examination of other possible diagnoses that might apply in this case could shed light on this "gold-collar" (i.e., young, intelligent, highly educated and specialized) killer.

POSSIBLE *DSM-5* DIAGNOSES

At his first trial, Turcotte was found NCRMD due to adjustment disorder with anxiety and depressive moods (*Guy Turcotte v. Her Majesty the Queen*, 2013). According to the fifth edition of the *Diagnostic and Statistical Manual of Mental Disorders* (*DSM-5*; American Psychiatric Association [APA], 2013), a diagnosis of adjustment disorder might apply when an individual experiences clinically significant emotional or behavioural symptoms within three months of an identifiable life stressor(s), such as marital dissolution. For a diagnosis to be made, symptoms must cause emotional distress that is disproportionate to the stressor or lead to impairment in functioning (e.g., social, occupational), and would be expected to remit within six months of the termination of the stressor. An adjustment disorder "with mixed anxiety and depressed mood" (also known as situational depression) is characterized by both predominant feelings of low moods, tearfulness, and hopelessness (i.e., depressed mood), as well as nervousness, worry, jitteriness, or fear of separation (i.e., anxiety; APA, 2013). Finally, adjustment disorder cannot simply reflect an exacerbation of a preexisting disorder nor represent normal bereavement; most importantly, the symptomatology cannot meet criteria for another mental disorder (APA, 2013). In other words, if Turcotte met diagnostic criteria for any other mental health disorder, he would not be eligible for an adjustment disorder diagnosis. This suggests that there was no evidence of a preexisting depressive condition with or without psychotic symptoms. The majority of people designated NCRMD meets diagnostic criteria for a disorder on the psychosis spectrum (Mental Health Commission of Canada, 2013). Turcotte testified that he killed his children so that they would not find him dead – a seemingly conscious decision rather than a delusional belief arising from a psychotic episode. In short, at the time that Turcotte was found NCRMD, it appears that he did not meet the standard required for such a verdict.

Reports indicate that, between January and October 2013 while residing at the Institut Philippe-Pinel de Montréal, Turcotte demonstrated a considerable decline in psychiatric symptoms (*Guy Turcotte v. Her Majesty the Queen*, 2013). By the end of October 2013, however, his symptoms of anxiety and depression increased, presumably in response to the Crown's request that the Quebec Court of Appeal order a new trial. (The Crown's request was made in September 2013 and, by November 2013, the Court of Appeal had ordered that Turcotte be retried.) By the end of November 2013, Turcotte's mental health had deteriorated to the point that he was prescribed antidepressants. Shortly thereafter, he was diagnosed with major depressive disorder (MDD) with psychotic symptoms and prescribed antipsychotic medication (*Guy Turcotte v. Her Majesty the Queen*, 2013; *R. v. Turcotte*, 2012). MDD is characterized by episodes of at least two weeks' duration and includes at least five of the following symptoms: depressed mood, markedly diminished interest or pleasure in activities, insomnia/hypersomnia, psychomotor agitation or retardation, fatigue or loss of energy, feelings of worthlessness or inappropriate guilt, diminished ability to think/concentrate, and recurrent thoughts of death.

Stressful life events are common precipitants of major depressive episodes (APA, 2013); the devolving circumstances of Turcotte's criminal defence would qualify.

Diagnoses other than adjustment disorder and MDD might explain some of Turcotte's conduct preoffence, during the offence itself, and postoffence; in particular, Cluster B personality disorders, such as borderline, narcissistic, and psychopathy (a form of character pathology associated with antisocial personality disorder). The defining features of personality disorders are enduring, pervasive, and inflexible patterns of thinking, feeling, and behaving that make it difficult for individuals to adapt to change, and lead to conflict with self and others (APA, 2013). Cluster B personality disorders are characterized by overly dramatic and erratic displays of emotions and behaviour.

Borderline personality disorder (BPD) is not uncommon amongst men who commit filicide (West et al., 2009). The defining features of BPD are impulsivity and instability in the domains of affect, interpersonal relationships, and self-image. Five or more of the nine following symptoms are required for diagnosis: profound fear of real or imagined abandonment; tumultuous interpersonal relationships which alternate between idealization and devaluation of others; instability in one's identity; impulsive and reckless behaviour (e.g., substance abuse, spending money, sexual activity); recurrent self-harm and/or suicidal behaviour, gestures, or threats; periods of intense and unstable mood (e.g., dysphoria, anxiety, irritability); subjective reports of chronic emptiness; issues with anger; and intermittent paranoid ideation or dissociation caused by stress. Some individuals with BPD may also experience psychotic-like symptoms during periods of stress, such as loss of a relationship.

Intimate partner violence (IPV) has been linked to BPD. Indeed, Dutton and others (Dutton, 1994; Dutton & Starzomski, 1993; Ross & Babcock, 2009) proposed the existence of an abusive personality type based on features of BPD: (a) a disposition to engage in intense, unstable interpersonal relationships characterized by intermittent idealization and devaluation of significant others, manipulation, and masked dependency; (b) an unstable sense of self associated with intolerance of being alone and abandonment anxiety; and (c) intense anger, demandingness, and impulsivity, usually tied to substance abuse or promiscuity; a fearful attachment style, chronic anger, and trauma symptoms. Men with this profile may become violent when they fear partner abandonment (see Cameranesi, 2016). In a review of the literature, Jackson et al. (2015) found that individuals meeting diagnostic criteria for BPD were more likely to commit seriously violent and aggressive acts of IPV. One study of men incarcerated for spousal homicide found that one third of men displayed BPD characteristics (Dixon et al., 2008). Evidence consistent with a diagnosis of BPD in Turcotte's case includes a tumultuous relationship including IPV, a need for relationships ("falls in love easily"), and an apparent sensitivity to rejection and/or abandonment, which may have fueled his spousal revenge filicide.

Narcissistic personality disorder (NPD) refers to a pervasive pattern of grandiosity and egocentrism, lack of empathy and disregard for others, and excessive need for attention and admiration. For a diagnosis of NPD to be rendered, five or more of the following nine symptoms are required: exaggerated sense of self-importance; fantasies of personal achievement (e.g., power, success, ideal love); belief that one is unique or special; excessive need for admiration; sense of entitlement to special treatment and compliance from others; exploitation of others; lack of empathy; envy of others; and arrogance. Often underlying NPD symptoms are low self-esteem and high sensitivity to criticism. Individuals with NPD can respond with rage to perceived threats to their self-worth (i.e., narcissistic insult). Interpersonal relationships are typically strained for individuals with NPD, and domestic violence has been linked to NPD (Stevens, 2014).

Research suggests that NPD as defined by the *DSM-5* (APA, 2013) is a blend of both grandiose and vulnerable narcissism, with the former more closely associated with psychopathy and the latter linked to internalizing symptoms, such as anxiety and depression (see Krusemark et al., 2018). Evidence consistent with a diagnosis of NPD in Turcotte's case includes his glaring egocentrism. For example, disregarding the advice of professionals and requesting release within one year of being found NCRMD suggests an inability to appreciate the impact of his crime on others, including his ex-wife and the general public. His assertion in court that he poses no threat to the public, resents wasting his time in prison, and would like to get on with life (resume medical practice, get married, have kids) is anathema to most people. The loss of his wife and marriage would be tantamount to narcissistic injury – a vulnerability in self-esteem that renders individuals with NPD hypersensitive to criticism or defeat (APA, 2013).

Turcotte's susceptibility to anxiety and depression suggests a vulnerable (vs. grandiose) narcissism profile. His profession may even have contributed to his narcissism. Some have suggested that narcissism can be acquired through a dysfunctional response to success based on wealth, fame, or power (Sherrill, 2001). Physicians may be prone to "medical narcissism," whereby traits of narcissism are reinforced by medical training (Banja, 2005), a defence against loss of self-esteem that makes physicians reluctant to appear uncertain, indecisive, or incorrect.

Guy Turcotte would not meet the diagnostic criteria for antisocial personality disorder (ASPD). For this diagnosis, he would have had to meet the diagnostic criteria for conduct disorder prior to age 15; that being repetitive and persistent violation of others' rights, societal norms, and rules (APA, 2013). Turcotte had no recorded history of conduct disorder or even criminal behaviour prior to his index offence. On the other hand, Turcotte does seem to display symptoms consistent with psychopathy, a form of character pathology related to ASPD but not included in the *DSM-5* (APA, 2013). Within early nomenclature (e.g., Schneider, 1923), psychopathy referred to all cases of personality disorder; it was referred to as "moral insanity" or *manie sans delire* (i.e., insanity without delusion). More recently, others (e.g., Crego & Widiger, 2015) have suggested that psychopathy is the prototypic personality disorder. Whatever the case, psychopathy has generated significantly more research attention in the past 35 years than ASPD and for good reason. It has been described as "the most dangerous and virulent constellation of personality traits that one can imagine" (Crego & Widiger, 2015, p. 10). Psychopaths are "social predators who charm, manipulate, and ruthlessly plow their way through life.... Completely lacking in conscience and feeling for others, they selfishly take what they want and do as they please, violating social norms and expectations without the slightest sense of guilt or regret" (Hare, 1993, p. xi).

Canadian psychologist Dr. Robert D. Hare summarized the research on psychopathy in 1970 and formalized a measure of psychopathy – the Psychopathy Checklist – in 1980. The *Hare Psychopathy Checklist-Revised* (*PCL-R*; Hare, 2003) consists of 20 items that assess features typical of psychopathy, including *emotional* (e.g., lack of conscience or guilt, lack of empathy, shallow affect, failure to accept responsibility for own actions), *interpersonal* (e.g., glibness/superficial charm, grandiose sense of self-worth, pathological lying, manipulation), and *behavioural* (e.g., repeated violations of social norms, disregard for laws, criminal versatility). Certainly, some of the emotional and interpersonal features (if not behavioural) seem applicable to Turcotte. For example, it is revealing that immediately prior to the offence, he had threatened his ex-wife, Isabelle Gaston, that if she wanted war, she would get one. Subsequent to the offence, he claimed to have done it to piss off Gaston. In letters to Gaston following the index offence, Turcotte displayed a seemingly emotionless and detached way of dividing the family's assets and belongings (TVA Nouvelles, 2011). Reportedly, Gaston received no money from Turcotte for the children's funerals. His disregard of professional advice in requesting release within one year of being found NCRMD for murdering his children and expressing a desire to get on with his life (i.e., resume his medical practice, find a new relationship, have more children) suggests a profound lack of shame or appreciation for the enormity of his crime – perhaps, a lack of conscience *(médecin sans conscience)*.

THE LAW

Although assessments of criminal responsibility are conducted by clinical forensic psychologists and psychiatrists (see Roesch et al., 2019; see also Pouls et al., 2022), within the context of NCRMD the term "mental disorder" is a legal concept, not a psychiatric one. The burden of proof is on the accused to prove that, at the time of the offence, they were suffering from an incapacitating mental disorder that compromised their ability to appreciate the moral wrongness (*mens rea* or guilty mind – the intention or knowledge of wrongdoing) of their criminal actions (*actus reus*). Their mental state at the time of the crime cannot have been a self-induced state caused by the consumption of a substance (e.g., drugs or alcohol) or a transitory state such as a concussion (*Cooper v. R.*, 1980).

The National Trajectory Project examined 1,800 men and women found NCRMD in Canada's three most populous provinces, British

Columbia (n = 222), Quebec (n = 1,094), and Ontario (n = 484), between May 2000 and April 2005, and were followed until December 2008 (see Crocker et al., 2015a, 2015b). Results show that the number of NCRMD decisions has increased in recent years with rates varying across the country. Decision rates are significantly higher in Turcotte's home province of Quebec (6.08 per 1,000 decisions) as compared to Ontario (0.95) or British Columbia (1.34). Quebec also is more heterogeneous with regard to index offences and diagnoses for those found NCRMD. Overall, the most common offences were those against the person (64.9%), with homicide and attempted murder making up less than 7 per cent of verdicts. Family members were the most likely victims (33.7%); children were victims in less than 3 per cent of cases. The most common disorders were psychotic spectrum (70.9%), substance use (30.8%), mood spectrum (23.2%), and personality disorders (10.6%). Approximately 29 per cent had comorbid substance use, while 9.5 per cent had comorbid personality disorder; less than half experienced delusions at the time of the offence. Relevant to Turcotte's case, suicidal ideation occurred in less than 10 per cent of cases; intoxication (alcohol and drug use) at the time of the offence was mentioned in one quarter of cases.

Turcotte was judged NCRMD based on his self-induced methanol intoxication, which presumably rendered him unable to evaluate the nature of his actions at the moment of the offence (*Guy Turcotte v. Her Majesty the Queen*, 2013). This verdict generated outrage among the general public, prompting an online petition aimed at reversing the verdict and scheduled demonstrations in 14 cities across Quebec (Nicoud, 2011). Among the protesters was Turcotte's ex-wife, Isabelle Gaston, who argued for changes to the Criminal Code. The day following Turcotte's conditional release from the Institut Philippe-Pinel de Montréal in December of 2012, the federal government released a statement that it was going to introduce new legislation impacting individuals found NCRMD for offences.

The Turcotte case was one of a number of high-profile cases, including *R. v. Vince Li* (2009) and *R. v. Schoenborn* (2010), that provided impetus for changes in federal legislation related to the management of individuals found NCRMD (Canadian Press, 2014). In 2013, the federal government tabled Bill C-54, or the Not Criminally Responsible Reform Act (Parliament of Canada, 2013). Among other things, the bill proposed that annual reviews for individuals deemed NCRMD of a violent crime could be pushed to every three years and that high-risk accused (HRA) would not be considered for release until their designation was revoked by a court. The bill was passed by the House of Commons on 18 June 2013 (Parliament of Canada, 2013) and came into effect across Canada on 11 July 2014. Members of the mental health community registered their concern about the increased restrictions.

Goossens et al. (2019) examined the HRA designation via a retrospective application of the legislative criteria to the National Trajectory Project (NTP) sample of 1,800 persons who had been found NCRMD between 2000 and 2005 in Quebec, Ontario, and British Columbia, and were followed until 2008 (see Charette et al., 2015). Results showed that an HRA designation could apply in up to 25 per cent of NCRMD cases resulting in longer supervision by a Review Board, although no evidence was shown that this subgroup represented an elevated risk of harm to others. The authors concluded that an HRA designation based largely on offence severity is unlikely to improve public safety.

SUMMARY AND CONCLUSIONS

Would Guy Turcotte have been designated HRA if his NCRMD verdict had been upheld? Perhaps, given the severity of the crime and the magnitude of the public outcry. But perhaps not, given that his mental disorder at the time of the offence (adjustment disorder with anxious and depressive symptomatology) would be considered transient and situational (distress due to marital dissolution). Moreover, Turcotte was a member of a highly respected professional group (medical doctors) accorded significant deference in our society. Media coverage at the time reminded readers of his status with headlines such as "Dr. Guy Turcotte begins telling his story on witness stand" (Banerjee, 2011a) and "Quebec cardiologist who killed his children wants to practice again" (*Toronto Star*, 2012). Turcotte's professional cloak (white coat) of respectability may have shielded him from more rigorous scrutiny and denunciation by both the public and the criminal justice system. The book *The Rich Get Richer and the Poor Get Prison: Thinking Critically about Class and Criminal Justice* (Reiman & Leighton,

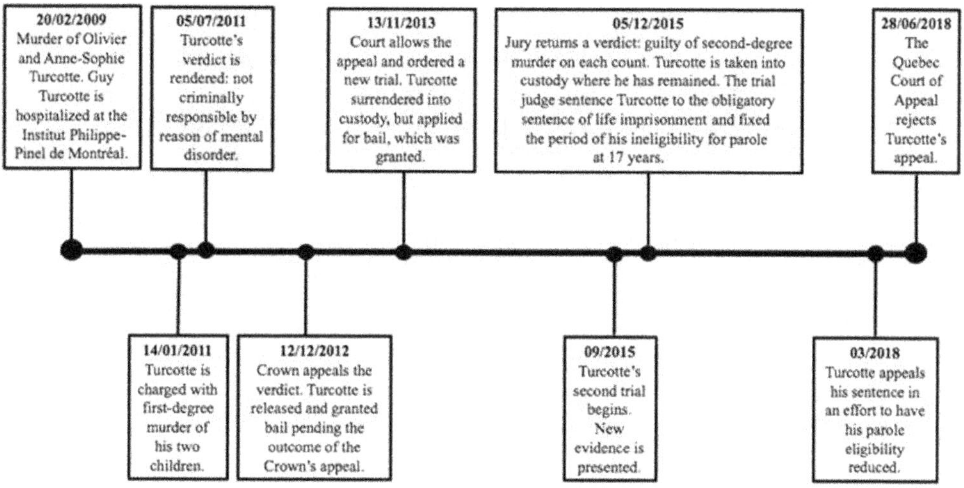

20/02/2009 Murder of Olivier and Anne-Sophie Turcotte. Guy Turcotte is hospitalized at the Institut Philippe-Pinel de Montréal.
05/07/2011 Turcotte's verdict is rendered: not criminally responsible by reason of mental disorder.
13/11/2013 Court allows the appeal and ordered a new trial. Turcotte surrendered into custody, but applied for bail, which was granted.
05/12/2015 Jury returns a verdict: guilty of second-degree murder on each count. Turcotte is taken into custody where he has remained. The trial judge sentence Turcotte to the obligatory sentence of life imprisonment and fixed the period of his ineligibility for parole at 17 years.
28/06/2018 The Quebec Court of Appeal rejects Turcotte's appeal.
14/01/2011 Turcotte is charged with first-degree murder of his two children.
12/12/2012 Crown appeals the verdict. Turcotte is released and granted bail pending the outcome of the Crown's appeal.
09/2015 Turcotte's second trial begins. New evidence is presented.
03/2018 Turcotte appeals his sentence in an effort to have his parole eligibility reduced.

Figure 6.1. Timeline of Guy Turcotte's major legal proceedings

2020) provides an impressive body of evidence of how the criminal justice system is favourably biased (more lenient) toward white-collar offenders who are less likely to serve prison sentences than poor offenders even when they have committed the same offence.

At his request for release in 2012 and again at his recent appeal in 2018 (see timeline in figure 6.1), Turcotte asserted that he did not pose a danger to the public. "I'm convinced that I am not a risk to anyone" (*Toronto Star*, 2012). Of course, anyone who perpetrates interpersonal violence on his spouse and murders his children is dangerous. Whereas it is true that he probably poses minimal risk to *most* members of the general public, his particular configuration of personality traits – features of borderline, narcissism, and psychopathy – makes him a risk to certain people, in particular, those who threaten to abandon him (e.g., Isabelle Gaston), inflict narcissistic insult or injury (e.g., social embarrassment arising from wife's infidelity), challenge his status or privilege (as husband or custodial parent), or threaten to unmask him (as a physician lacking in empathy, compassion, or remorse). This particular constellation of personality characteristics is a catalyst for violence, whether perpetrated by blue-collar, white-collar, or gold-collar criminals. Perri (2011) has worked to debunk the myth of white-collar criminals (e.g., Bernie Madoff) as being the "kinder and gentler offenders" (p. 217) by highlighting the heterogeneity of this group and the need for more attention to personality traits, such as narcissism and psychopathy. On the other hand, a logical and empirical analysis conducted by Alalehto and Azarian (2018) indicates that these two traits are neither sufficient nor necessary for white-collar criminals to resort to fatal violence. The same may be true for gold-collar offenders, highly respected professionals like Turcotte, but more research is needed before any conclusions can be drawn.

Isabelle Gaston described her former husband as a "chameleon," presumably referring to his ability to adapt his presentation to suit his audience and his personal needs. The term is commonly applied to psychopaths, whom Hervey Cleckley (1941) described as wearing a "mask of sanity." At times throughout his trials and appeals, Turcotte appeared to express remorse and shame – he claimed to be unable to look others in the eye (TVA Nouvelles, 2016) – but his behaviours always betrayed him. For example, he lied about his intoxication at the time of the offence (he ingested the windshield wiper fluid *after*, not before, the crime); ignored the advice of specialists tasked with his care and requested release from custody less than one year after being deemed NCRMD (very poor judgment if not inadequate conscience); seemed to resent wasting his time in prison (narcissism); and was eager to get on with his life and have more children (malignant egocentrism, lack of empathy). His continued attempt to blame his wife's infidelity and his failing marriage faltered at his second trial, by which time it was clear that he acted out of animosity toward his ex-wife and a burning desire to see her suffer. Spousal revenge is the rarest of motives in cases of filicide. It is the motive most apt to be fueled by anger – anger derived from feelings of powerlessness due to domestic subordination (narcissistic injury) and perceived loss of control over the relationship (loss of social power), which may be exacerbated by an external attribution bias or tendency to blame others (see Carruthers, 2016).

In an effort to make sense of spousal revenge filicide, Carruthers (2016) challenged the standard explanations for the crime as not adequately accounting for how the killer's own child can be dehumanized to the point of murder. Carruthers points out that killing one's own child violates almost universal societal norms of morality and parenting. Carruthers proposes that the perpetrators of spousal revenge filicides may reject their role as parent and actually perceive their child as an extension of the ex-partner or simply as an object.

This might explain why a parent's motivation to protect their child would not be activated when the child's welfare is in peril, such as when Olivier pleaded with his father to stop the assault.

There are many lessons to be learned from the Turcotte case including the following: risk for grievous violence crosses socioeconomic strata and professional groups; interpersonal partner violence is a risk factor for filicide (and mass killing – see chapter 10) – a risk to which spouses and police must be alert; motives matter in deliberating on these cases, especially motives fuelled by anger and revenge; such motives point to pathological personality traits (borderline, narcissism, psychopathy); personality profiling "paints the picture," especially of crimes like filicide, crimes that so defy our expectations and understanding; and personality profiling can help to elucidate subgroups within NCRMD, including HRA cases, so as to better inform risk assessment and management of individuals.

CRITICAL THINKING QUESTIONS

1. What do you think were the warning signs/risk factors that would predict Guy Turcotte to be capable of such a heinous crime?
2. Filicide is another violent crime (like spree killing) for which interpersonal violence (IPV) is a risk factor. Given that is the case, what steps should we be taking to prevent such violence?
3. Criminal profiling (i.e., offender or psychological profiling) is a process whereby a crime is analysed in an attempt to determine the offender's significant personality and demographic characteristics; in other words, to develop a "picture" of the "type" of offender (vs. specific offender) who would commit such a crime. Although considered to be a useful investigative tool by police, it continues to lack a compelling theoretical and empirical basis (see Chifflet, 2015). This case study focuses on personality profiling (per the *DSM-5*) as a way of determining whether Guy Turcotte fits the "type" of person who would commit filicide. What do you think about this approach?

REFERENCES

Alalehto, T., & Azarian, R. (2018). When white collar criminals turn to fatal violence: The impact of narcissism and psychopathy. *Journal of Investigative Psychology and Offender Profiling*, *15*(2), 215–26. https://doi.org/10.1002/jip.1503

American Psychiatric Association. (2013). *Diagnostic and statistical manual of mental disorders* (5th ed.).
Banerjee, S. (2011a, May 9). Dr. Guy Turcotte begins telling his story on witness stand. *CTV News*. https://montreal.ctvnews.ca/dr-guy-turcotte-begins-telling-his-story-on-witness-stand-1.641656
Banerjee, S. (2011b, August 4). Guy Turcotte: Des manifestations auront lieu dans 14 villes du Québec [Guy Turcotte: Demonstrations will take place in 14 cities in Quebec]. *La Presse*. https://www.lapresse.ca/actualites/justice-et-faits-divers/201108/04/01-4423555-guy-turcotte-des-manifestations-auront-lieu-dans-14-villes-duquebec.php?utm_categorieinterne=trafficdrivers&utm_contenuinterne=cyberpresse_vous_suggere_4421246_article_POS2
Banerjee, S. (2018, June 28). Quebec court rejects Guy Turcotte's bid to be eligible for parole before 17 years. *Global News*. https://globalnews.ca/news/4303173/quebec-court-rejects-guy-turcottes-bid-to-be-eligible-for-parole-before-17-years/
Banja, D. (2005). *Medical errors and medical narcissism*. Jones and Bartlett.
Cameranesi, M. (2016). Battering typologies, attachment insecurity, and personality disorders: A comprehensive literature review. *Aggression and Violent Behavior*, *28*, 29–46. https://doi.org/10.1016/j.avb.2016.03.005
Canadian Press. (2014, March 20). Guy Turcotte to be retried for 2009 murder of his two young children, Supreme Court rules. *National Post*. https://nationalpost.com/news/canada/guy-turcotte-to-be-retried-for-2009-murder-of-his-two-young-children-supreme-court-rules
Canadian Press. (2015a, October 15). Witness at Turcotte trial says accused told him his son pleaded for his life. *CBC News*. https://www.cbc.ca/news/canada/montreal/guy-turcotte-murder-trial-hears-from-witness-describing-child-s-death-1.3273619
Canadian Press. (2015b, November 4). Turcotte killed children because he was depressed: Psychiatrist. *CTV News*. https://montreal.ctvnews.ca/turcotte-killed-children-because-he-was-depressed-psychiatrist-1.2641848
Canadian Press. (2015c, November 25). Crown says Guy Turcotte drank windshield fluid after killing kids. *CTV News*. https://www.ctvnews.ca/canada/crown-says-guy-turcotte-drank-windshield-washer-fluid-after-killing-kids-1.2674248
Canadian Press. (2018, June 28). Quebec court rejects Turcotte's bid to be eligible for parole before 17 years. *Halifax City News*. https://preprod-halifax.citynews.ca/2018/06/28/quebec-court-rejects-killer-turcottes-bid-to-be-eligible-for-parole-before-17-years/
Carruthers, G. (2016). Making sense of spousal revenge filicide. *Aggression and Violent Behavior*, *29*, 30–5. https://doi.org/10.1016/j.avb.2016.05.007
CBC News. (2012, March 15). Child killer Turcotte "ideal candidate" for release: Quebecer seeks freedom after found not responsible for deaths

of 2 kids. *CBC News*. https://www.cbc.ca/news/canada/montreal/child-killer-turcotte-ideal-candidate-for-release-1.1135706

Charette, Y., Crocker, A. G., Seto, M. C., Salem, L., Nicholls, T. L., & Caulet, M. (2015). The National Trajectory Project of individuals found not criminally responsible on account of mental disorder in Canada. Part 4: Criminal recidivism. *Canadian Journal of Psychiatry*, *60*(3), 127–34. https://doi.org/10.1177/070674371506000307

Chifflet, P. (2015). Questioning the validity of criminal profiling: An evidence-based approach. *Australian & New Zealand Journal of Criminology*, *48*(2), 238–55. https://doi.org/10.1177/0004865814530732

Cleckley, H. (1941). *The mask of sanity: An attempt to clarify some issues about the so-called psychopathic personality*. C.V. Mosby Co.

Cooper v. R., 1980, 1 SCR. 1149.

Crego, C., & Widiger, T. A. (2015). Psychopathy and the *DSM*. *Journal of Personality*, *83*(6), 665–77. https://doi.org/10.1111/jopy.12115

Criminal Code of Canada. (1985). RSC, c. C-46, s. 16(1).

Crocker, A. G., Nicholls, T. L., Seto, M. C., Côté, G., Charette, Y., & Caulet, M. (2015a). The National Trajectory Project of individuals found not criminally responsible on account of mental disorder in Canada. Part 1: Context and methods. *Canadian Journal of Psychiatry*, *60*(3), 98–105. https://doi.org/10.1177/070674371506000304

Crocker, A. G., Nicholls, T. L., Seto, M. C., Charette, Y., Côté, G., & Caulet, M. (2015b). The National Trajectory Project of individuals found not criminally responsible on account of mental disorder in Canada. Part 2: The people behind the label. *Canadian Journal of Psychiatry*, *60*(3), 106–16. https://doi.org/10.1177/070674371506000305

CTV Montreal. (2009, February 24). Turcotte arraigned on first degree murder charges. *CTV Montreal*. https://montreal.ctvnews.ca/turcotte-arraigned-on-first-degree-murder-charges-1.373459

Dawson, M. (2015). Canadian trends in filicide by gender of the accused, 1961–2011. *Child Abuse & Neglect*, *47*, 162–74. https://doi.org/10.1016/j.chiabu.2015.07.010

Dixon, L., Hamilton-Giachritsis, C., & Browne, K. (2008). Classifying partner femicide. *Journal of Interpersonal Violence*, *23*(1), 74–93. https://doi.org/10.1177/0886260507307652

Dutton, D. G. (1994). Patriarchy and wife assault: The ecological fallacy. *Violence and Victims*, *9*(2), 167–82. https://doi.org/10.1891/0886-6708.9.2.167

Dutton, D. G., & Starzomski, A. J. (1993). Borderline personality in perpetrators of psychological and physical abuse. *Violence and Victims*, *8*(4), 326–37. https://doi.org/10.1891/0886-6708.8.4.327

ÉDUCALOI. (2015). Guy Turcotte guilty of second-degree murder. https://www.educaloi.qc.ca/en/news/guy-turcotte-guilty-second-degree-murder

Feith, J. (2015, December 6). Guy Turcotte found guilty of second-degree murder. *Montreal Gazette*. https://montrealgazette.com/news/guy-turcotte-found

Goossens, I., Nicholls, T. L., Charette, Y., Wilson, C. M., Seto, M. C., & Crocker, A. G. (2019). Examining the high-risk accused designation for individuals found not criminally responsible on account of mental disorder. *Canadian Psychology/Psychologie canadienne, 60*(2), 102–14. https://doi.org/10.1037/cap0000080

Guy Turcotte v. Her Majesty the Queen, 2013, The application for leave to appeal from the judgment of the Court of Appeal of Quebec (Montréal), Number 500-10-004980-114, QCCA, dated November 13, 2013.

Guy Turcotte v. Her Majesty the Queen, 2018, The application for leave to appeal from the judgment of the Court of Appeal of Quebec (Montréal), Number 500-10-006091-167, dated June 28, 2018.

Hare, R. D. (1993). *Without conscience: The disturbing world of the psychopaths among us*. Pocket Books.

Hare, R. D. (2003). *The Hare Psychopathy Checklist-Revised* (2nd ed.). Multi-Health Systems.

Jackson, M. A., Sippel, L. M., Mota, N., Whalen, D., & Schumacher, J. A. (2015). Borderline personality disorder and related constructs as risk factors for intimate partner violence perpetration. *Aggression and Violent Behavior, 24*, 95–106. https://doi.org/10.1016/j.avb.2015.04.015

Kelly, A. (2014). Former Quebec cardiologist Guy Turcotte granted bail. *Global News*. https://globalnews.ca/news/1560172/former-quebec-cardiologist-guy-turcotte-granted-bail/

Krusemark, E. A., Campbell, W. K., Crowe, M. L., & Miller, J. D. (2018). Comparing self-report measures of grandiose narcissism, vulnerable narcissism, and narcissistic personality disorder in a male offender sample. *Psychological Assessment, 30*(7), 984–90. https://doi.org/10.1037/pas0000579

Mariano, T. Y., Chan, H. C. O., & Myers, W. C. (2014). Toward a more holistic understanding of filicide: A multidisciplinary analysis of 32 years of US arrest data. *Forensic Science International, 236*, 46–53. https://doi.org/10.1016/j.forsciint.2013.12.019

Mental Health Commission of Canada. (2013). *Fact sheet about the not criminally responsible due to a mental disorder (NCRMD) population in Canada*. https://www.mentalhealthcommission.ca/sites/default/files/MHLaw_NCRMD_Fact_Sheet_FINAL_ENG_0.pdf

Nicoud, A. (2011, July 27). Affaire Guy Turcotte: Des pages et des dérapages [Guy Turcotte case: Pages and slippages]. *La Presse*. https://www.lapresse.ca/actualites/justice-et-faits-divers/201107/26/01-4421246-affaire-guy-turcotte-des-pages-et-des-derapages.php

Palermo, G. B. (2002). Murderous parents. *International Journal of Offender Therapy and Comparative Criminology*, *46*(2), 123–43. https://doi.org/10.1177/0306624X02462002

Parliament of Canada. (2013). *Bill C-54*. http://www.parl.gc.ca/About/Parliament/LegislativeSummaries/bills_ls.asp?Language=E&ls=C54&Mode=1&Parl=41&Ses=1&source=library_prb

Perri, F. (2011). White-collar criminals: The "kinder, gentler" offender? *Journal of Investigative Psychology and Offender Profiling*, *8*(3), 217–41. https://doi.org/10.1002/jip.140

Postmedia News. (2011, November 4). Doctor Guy Turcotte, who killed his son and daughter, wants to have more children. *National Post*. https://nationalpost.com/news/doctor-guy-turcotte-convicted-of-killing-his-son-and-daughter-wants-to-have-more-children

Pouls, C., Jeandarme, I., Al-Taiar, H., Bradford, J., Canton, W., Kristiansson, M., Thibaut, F., Verreyt, V., & Konrad, N. (2022). Criminal responsibility evaluations: Benchmarking in different countries. *International Journal of Law and Psychiatry*, *81*. https://doi.org/10.1016/j.ijlp.2022.101775

QMI Agency. (2012, March 15). Doctor says double child killer "ideal candidate" for release. *Toronto Sun*. https://torontosun.com/2012/03/15/doctor-says-double-child-killer-ideal-candidate-for-release/wcm/07c7f3f2-8e94-4796-a007-afe8cfd61f4a

Reiman, J., & Leighton, P. (2020). *The rich get richer and the poor get prison: Thinking critically about class and criminal justice* (12th ed.). Routledge.

Resnick, P. J. (1969). Child murder by parents: A psychiatric review of filicide. *American Journal of Psychiatry*, *126*(3), 325–34. https://doi.org/10.1176/ajp.126.3.325

Resnick, P. J. (2016). Filicide in the United States. *Indian Journal of Psychiatry*, *58*(Suppl 2), S203–S209. https://doi.org/10.4103/0019-5545.196845

Roesch, R., Kayfitz, J. H., Watt, M. C., Cooper, B. S., Guy, L. S., Hill, D., Haag, A. M., Pomichalek, M., & Kolton, D. J. C. (2019). Fitness to stand trial and criminal responsibility assessments: Advocating for changes to the Canadian criminal code. *Canadian Psychology/Psychologie canadienne*, *60*(3), 148–54. https://doi.org/10.1037/cap0000173

Ross, J. M., & Babcock, J. C. (2009). Proactive and reactive violence among intimate partner violent men diagnosed with antisocial and borderline personality disorder. *Journal of Family Violence*, *24*(8), 607–17. https://doi.org/10.1007/s10896-009-9259-y

R. v. Vince Li, 2009, https://www.documentcloud.org/documents/3458881-Manitoba-Criminal-Code-Review-Board-decision.html

R. v. Schoenborn, 2010, BCSC 220.

R. v. Turcotte, 2005, 2 SCR 519, 2005 SCC 50.

R. v. Turcotte, 2012, QCCS 5587.

Schneider, K. (1923). *Psychopathic personalities* (M. W. Hamilton, Trans.). Cassell.

Sherrill, S. (2001, December 9). Acquired situational narcissism. *New York Times*. https://www.nytimes.com/2001/12/09/magazine/the-year-in-ideas-a-to-z-acquired-situational-narcissism.html

Stevens, S. A. (2014). *Pathological narcissism as it relates to intimate partner violence*. https://www.proquest.com/openview/e573f074602437ee3b32e257b96793be/1.pdf?pq-origsite=gscholar&cbl=18750

Toronto Star. (2012, January 12). Quebec cardiologist who killed his children wants to practice again. *Toronto Star*. https://www.thestar.com/news/canada/2012/01/12/quebec_cardiologist_who_killed_his_children_wants_to_practice_again.html

TVA Nouvelles. (2011). Des lettres qui en disent long sur Turcotte [Letters that say a lot about Turcotte]. *TVA Nouvelles*. https://www.tvanouvelles.ca/2011/07/07/des-lettres-qui-en-disent-long-sur-turcott

TVA Nouvelles. (2016). 17 ans de prison pour Guy Turcotte [17 years in prison for Guy Turcotte]. *TVA Nouvelles*. https://www.tvanouvelles.ca/2016/01/15/combien-de-temps-turcotte-devra-rester-en-prison

West, S. G. (2007). An overview of filicide. *Psychiatry (Edgmont)*, *4*(2), 48–57. https://pubmed.ncbi.nlm.nih.gov/20805899/

West, S. G., Friedman, S. H., & Resnick, P. J. (2009). Fathers who kill their children: An analysis of the literature. *Journal of Forensic Sciences*, *54*(2), 463–8. https://doi.org/10.1111/j.1556-4029.2008.00964.x

CHAPTER SEVEN[1]

Partners or Pawns: The Role of Women in Co-offending Violent Couples

The Case of Karla Homolka

With Angelina MacLellan and Claire Keenan

As this case study was being written, Ghislaine Maxwell was on trial for her role (with Jeffrey Epstein) in the sexual abuse of minor girls between 1994 and 2004. On 29 December 2021, a jury in a New York federal court found 60-year-old Maxwell guilty on five of six federal charges: sex trafficking of a minor, transporting a minor with the intent to engage in criminal sexual activity, and three related counts of conspiracy. In her closing statement, the prosecutor described Maxwell as Epstein's "partner in crime," the one that lured and secured underage girls for Epstein. Maxwell's presence made the girls feel comfortable about spending time with a middle-aged man like Epstein; otherwise, it would have seemed "creepy" and "set off alarm bells." "Epstein could not have done this alone," said the prosecutor. "When that man is accompanied by a posh, smiling, respectable, age-appropriate woman, that's when everything starts to seem legitimate. And when that woman … acts like it's totally normal for that man to touch those girls, it lures them into a trap." In return for services rendered, Maxwell was able to maintain her luxurious lifestyle (Cohen, 2021).

"Partners in crime" tend to capture the public's attention and imagination. Six movies, 12 books, a documentary, and even a website are devoted to the notorious Bonnie and Clyde. Between 1932 and

1934, Bonnie Parker (aged 23) and Clyde Barrow (aged 25) committed numerous robberies and murders (possibly nine police officers and four civilians) across the Central United States before they were killed by law officers in Louisiana. The 1967 film *Bonnie and Clyde* cemented their reputation in American pop culture. In urban dictionaries, "Bonnie and Clyde" refers to "a couple who is known to do whatever it takes to be together no matter how hard it may be." Crime couples sometimes earn romantic monikers, such as "The Lonely Heart Killers" (Martha Beck and Raymond Martinez Fernandez), "The Lethal Lovers" (Gwendolyn Graham and Catherine May Wood), and "Hounds of Love" (Australia's David and Catherine Birnie). Not surprisingly, the truth about such couples is far less romantic and much more tragic than such monikers would suggest.

Canada's "Ken and Barbie Killers" or "Schoolgirl Killers" (Paul Bernardo and Karla Homolka) make every Top Ten list of partners in crime. Bernardo was the "Scarborough Rapist" for three years (1987–90), with 19 known victims (possibly 30), prior to escalating his grisly activities to include abduction, torture, rape, murder, and dismemberment alongside Homolka. The public's fascination with couples like Bonnie and Clyde or Homolka and Bernardo often has more to do with the Bonnies than the Clydes. This is because the female partner is seen as such an anomaly. Many more men than women perpetrate murder and mayhem. So what are we to think about the female partners in murderous co-offending couples? Are they heartless monsters or hapless victims under the control of a malevolent man? Are these women partners or pawns in such crimes? With these questions in mind, let's review the case of Karla Homolka.

KARLA HOMOLKA

Karla Homolka was born in Port Credit, ON, in 1970, the oldest of three girls born to Dorothy and Karel Homolka. She had two younger sisters, Lori and Tammy. Reportedly, her father was an abusive alcoholic, known to verbally assault his wife and daughters. While in high school, Homolka worked at a local animal clinic and, after graduating in 1988, she was hired as a full-time veterinary technician. In October 1987, 17-year-old Homolka attended a pet store conference in

Scarborough, ON, where she met Bernardo (then aged 23) in a hotel restaurant. By all accounts, the attraction was mutual and immediate.

Long before he met Homolka, Paul Bernardo had acquired a reputation for disturbing behaviour. He was known to be very controlling with girlfriends and inclined to degrade them in public. It seems he had developed some deviant sexual fantasies, such as creating a "virgin farm," and enjoyed forceful anal sex. His abusive conduct with women led to ever shorter relationships and dating more than one woman at the same time. Apparently, he threatened to kill girlfriends if they disclosed his treatment of them. In 1986, two women were granted restraining orders against Bernardo for making obscene phone calls to them. In 1987, Bernardo graduated from college and started work as a junior accountant for Price Waterhouse. His raping spree may have begun by May 1987. Homolka would later tell police investigators that Bernardo boasted he had raped as many as 30 women, 11 more than the 19 reported to police. She described him as "the happy rapist" (Pron, 2006).

After they met in October 1987, Bernardo would drive the 50 kilometres to Homolka's house twice a week. Apparently, it displeased him that she was not a virgin but he was prepared to overlook it as he assumed increasing power in the relationship and control over Homolka – what she thought, how she dressed, what she ate. Apparently, he often demeaned her appearance. Unlike his previous girlfriends, it seems Homolka was more submissive and accepting of his "self-improvement lists" and his increasingly deviant sexual behaviour.

By 1990, Bernardo had grown obsessed with Homolka's 15-year-old sister, Tammy. He devised a plan to rape her with Homolka's assistance, who would ensure that Tammy remained a virgin until then. "[It was] an opportunity to minimize risk, take control, and keep it all in the family," Homolka would later explain about her younger sister's rape-murder (Criminal Minds Wiki, n.d.). When a first attempt failed, the couple tried again in December 1990, two days before Christmas and following a family dinner in the Homolka home. Homolka claimed she was "gifting her sister's virginity to Paul for Christmas." After spiking Tammy's drink with sleeping pills (stolen from the vet clinic), Homolka held a rag soaked with the anaesthetic Halothane (also stolen from the vet clinic), while Bernardo raped Tammy. In the process, Tammy aspirated her own vomit and died.

The exhumation of Tammy's body in 1993 revealed that Homolka and Bernardo had placed their photo in the casket. In 1995, a graphic and disturbing video titled *Karla, Tammy and Me* revealed Homolka, dressed as Tammy, servicing Bernardo sexually and promising to find him more "virgins."

On 7 June 1991, Homolka brought home a teenager whom she had befriended at work ("Jane Doe"). She told Bernardo she had a surprise wedding gift for him. The couple's wedding was scheduled for 29 June. After consuming a drink laced with Halcion (a central nervous system depressant tranquillizer), "Jane" passed out and the couple filmed themselves as they raped her. "Jane" awoke the next day and left without realizing that she had been raped. One week later, on 15 June, Bernardo spotted 14-year-old Leslie Mahaffy locked outside her home, lured her to his car, threatened her with a knife, blindfolded her, and drove home, telling Homolka that they had "a playmate." Again, the couple videoed themselves raping and torturing the girl. When Mahaffy's blindfold slipped, they murdered her. They hid the body in the basement while they dined upstairs with the Homolka family. Later, they dismembered the body, encased the remains in concrete blocks, and disposed of them in Lake Gibson. The remains were found on 29 June, their wedding day. In August, they invited "Jane" back. They drugged her and, when she stopped breathing while being raped, Homolka called 911. When "Jane" came around, they cancelled the call (Criminal Minds Wiki, n.d.).

On 16 April 1992, 15-year-old Kristen French had just exited school when Homolka lured her to the couple's car. Homolka and Bernardo abducted, raped, and tortured the girl for the next three days. French was not blindfolded but was forced to ingest large amounts of alcohol and watch the recording of Mahaffy's rape. When she declined to be submissive to Bernardo, French was severely beaten and then strangled to death. Once again, the couple left the body in their home while they dined with the Homolkas. They later threw the remains into a ditch in Burlington, close to the cemetery where Mahaffy was buried. Shortly thereafter, Bernardo and Homolka adopted Teale as their legal name, the surname of a serial killer in the 1988 film *Criminal Law*. On 27 December 1992, Bernardo physically assaulted Homolka with a flashlight, leaving her with bruises, a broken rib, and two black eyes. When she returned to work on 4 January 1993 and tried to pass off her injuries as the result of a traffic accident, her coworkers alerted her parents and she was taken to hospital. Once there, Homolka claimed to be a battered woman and filed charges against Bernardo. Bernardo was arrested and, around the same time, body samples taken previously identified him as the Scarborough Rapist (Criminal Minds Wiki, n.d.).

Homolka moved to Brampton with her aunt and uncle and told them that Bernardo was both the Scarborough Rapist and the killer of Mahaffy and French. In February 1993, Homolka requested full immunity from prosecution in exchange for her cooperation but she was denied. Instead, she was given one week to accept a 12-year prison term for two counts of manslaughter or face charges for three murders, one of them her sister's, whose case had been reopened. Homolka accepted what the Canadian Press called the "Deal with the Devil" (Hunter, 2018). She pleaded guilty to all charges and, on 6 July 1993, was sentenced to two concurrent maximum sentences of 12 years for the manslaughter of Leslie Mahaffy and Kristen French. She divorced Bernardo in February 1994 and testified against him at his trial in 1995.

Bernardo was arrested in February 1993 and charged with dismemberment, two counts of first-degree murder, kidnapping, and aggravated sexual assault. Police searched Bernardo's home but found only one videotape, which depicted Homolka performing oral sex on an unidentified young woman. In May 1993 (prior to Homolka's trial), Bernardo's lawyer removed several videotapes that had been hidden in the bathroom ceiling and kept them a secret from prosecutors and police. That lawyer resigned in September 1994 and gave the videotapes to his former client's new lawyer, who turned the tapes over to the authorities. When investigators reviewed the videotapes, they found both Bernardo and Homolka assaulting Leslie Mahaffy and Kristen French. Homolka had received a special deal in part because she claimed Bernardo had forced her to harm the teenage girls; many who viewed the tapes thought she looked like a willing and active participant.

On 1 September 1995, Bernardo was sentenced to life in prison without parole for at least 25 years. His appeal was unsuccessful and he was subsequently designated a "dangerous offender," a designation reserved for Canada's most violent and habitual criminals and sexual predators. The designation carries an automatic indeterminate sentence of incarceration with no chance of parole for seven years. If an individual is considered to be an appropriate candidate for such a designation, meaning they have been convicted of a "Serious Personal Injury Offence" (e.g., assault causing bodily harm, aggravated sexual assault, sexual interference, unlawful confinement) and are at high risk for reoffending, a Crown attorney can request that a formal assessment be conducted. The assessment must be conducted by approved mental health experts (e.g., clinical forensic psychologists, psychiatrists) and includes an evaluation of the individual's mental health status and psychological functioning, including cognitive and memory testing. In the case of an individual who offends in a sexual manner, additional tests will be conducted to determine sexual preferences and deviant sexuality.

According to Public Safety Canada (2022), there are approximately 280 Dangerous Offenders in Canada. That number has been increasing since 1978, but use of the designation varies across provinces. For example, there are 7 Dangerous Offenders in Quebec, 11 in Nova Scotia, 21 in Alberta, 84 in British Columbia, and 126 in Ontario. More than 90 per cent of Dangerous Offenders have never been released on parole supervision. Although the designation can apply to all offenders, 85 per cent of Dangerous Offenders were sentenced for sexual assaults and 41 per cent involved pedophilia. A 2002 Correctional Service Canada (CSC) profile of 179 Dangerous Offenders shows that 85 per cent had committed sex offences, while only 3 per cent were convicted of a homicide. In cases such as Russell Williams (see chapter 9), where it is clear that he will never be considered eligible for parole (due to serving two life sentences), a Dangerous Offender assessment would be superfluous.

Homolka (a.k.a. Leanne Teale) was released from prison in July 2005. In 2007, she moved to Guadalupe, married her lawyer's brother, and had three children. After returning to the Montreal area, she was compelled to move every few years when her whereabouts would become publicly known. While Homolka has tried to have limits placed on media scrutiny, the courts (including in December 2020) have tended to agree with the Quebec Press Council that the public has a "right to know what is happening to Ms. Teale because of the nature of the crimes she committed" (Peritz & Freeze, 2005) and "[i]t is undeniable that for her entire life … Ms. Teale will have to face the postsentencing consequences of the crimes she committed which involved young women" (Ross, 2005). It is not clear why Homolka continues to use the name Teale. Presently, she is residing in Ontario.

WOMEN AND CRIME

Karla Homolka has been described as one of the most loathsome female killers in the world (Morrissey, 2006). People find it difficult to comprehend how a woman could assist someone like Bernardo in the perpetration of such heinous crimes against other women. It is not lost on people the importance of the role of the female beguiler in these cases – the woman who lures the victims by cultivating or grooming their trust and security. With Homolka, people were prepared to entertain the notion that she was an abused woman, another of Bernardo's victims, until the tapes were released. Journalist D'Arcy Jenish found that on some tapes Homolka seemed to be a "willing – even enthusiastic – participant in her future husband's fantasies" (as cited in Milhizer, 2004). Karla Homolka may be anomalous but she is not unique. To better understand women who commit crimes with male partners, we will look at the statistics for women's crimes of violence and the profile of federally sentenced women offenders. Then we will examine some possible explanations for women who are complicit in such crimes and consider if these women are partners or pawns (Correctional Service Canada, 2019; Savage, 2019).

Women account for about 25 per cent of police-reported crime in Canada (Savage, 2019). Across all crime categories, women commit fewer crimes than men (Blanchette & Brown, 2019). Women's crimes tend to include theft, impaired driving, fraud, and drug violations (Chesney-Lind & Pasko, 2013). As compared to men's, women's violent crimes tend to be less serious/less injurious, more apt to occur in private (vs. public), and directed at known victims versus strangers (Schwartz, 2013). In 2015, assault was the most common form of violent crime committed by women offenders and most (approximately 85%) knew their victims. Typically, women's violence is directed at a spouse or intimate partner (46%), and homicide is most frequently committed against either intimate partners (32%) or family members (32%) (Savage, 2019).

On any given day in Canada, women account for only 6 per cent of federally sentenced offenders (i.e., those serving sentences of more than two years). At the end of the 2017–18 fiscal year, that translated into about 1,400 federally sentenced women with roughly half held in custody and half under community supervision. Most of the women are under 35 years of age, although the proportion is higher for Indigenous women (61%) versus non-Indigenous women (42%) (Correctional Service Canada, 2021); most (60%) are serving sentences of less than five years, 20 per cent are serving five or more years, and 20 per cent are serving indeterminate (life) sentences (Correctional Service Canada, 2019). More than half are serving time for a violent offence (e.g., homicide, assault, sexual assault) and one quarter for a serious drug offence (Public Safety Canada, 2014). One third (36%) of the women will reoffend within three years of release; of those, 79 per cent have more than one conviction for an indictable offence (Correctional Service Canada, n.d.).

Most (72%) federally sentenced women lack a high school diploma, and most (77%) have children. Compared to the average Canadian, these women have a higher incidence of substance abuse and mental health problems and are more likely to have a history of physical and/or sexual abuse. Most of the women (approximately 80%) meet criteria for a mental disorder, such as substance use disorders (76%), anxiety disorders (54%), and antisocial personality disorder (49%). Substance use problems increase women's risk to commit a serious crime, to incur disciplinary offences, and to reoffend (Correctional Service Canada, 2016, 2017). Almost one third (33%) of the women have a diagnosis of borderline personality disorder (BPD) and/or posttraumatic stress disorder (PTSD) (Correctional Service Canada, 2015, 2017). Comorbid diagnoses are common among this population, including depression and self-injurious behaviour (Correctional Service Canada, 2016).

WOMEN AND CO-OFFENDING

In general, crimes committed by two or more people (co-offences; including gangs, groups, and partners) are more serious and more violent than crimes committed by a single perpetrator. Between 2008 and 2011, co-offending occurred in 11 per cent of crimes, with most (76%) involving coaccused pairs versus a group (Carrington et al., 2013). While youth (under 18 years of age) are more likely to co-offend with members of the same sex, co-offending with the opposite sex increases with age, especially among females. For example, according to Canadian statistics, women over the age of 25 are more likely than younger women to co-offend with the opposite sex (Carrington et al., 2013). Among these female co-offenders over age 25, the vast majority (70%) have offended with a member of the opposite sex (vs. same sex; Carrington et al., 2013).

Women are more likely than men to be charged as co-offenders, and about one third of police-reported co-offences include female-male dyads (Carrington et al., 2013). Older male and younger female dyads are 1.4 times more common than what was found in typical age and gender groups. Female-male (vs. same-sex) dyads are more likely in more serious/violent offences (i.e., serious drug offences, homicide, sex crimes against children; Carrington, 2016). For some female offenders, relations with older male offenders, often an intimate partner or relative, is their pathway into criminal involvement (Haynie et al., 2005). Older men may be coercive and/or exploitative of younger women (Carrington, 2016).

Comartin et al. (2018) explored coercive control in the context of women's co-offending in sex-based crimes. Research shows that most women who commit sex-based offences are *male-coerced* (see Watt, 2014). These women tend to be a passive-dependent partner in a relationship with an abusive man who abuses her own children. These women only perpetrate abuse in the presence of the male partner. The second most common type of women who commit sex-based offences are *male-accompanied.* Karla Homolka would fall within this category and, possibly, a subcategory of male-accompanied known as *rejected/revengeful.* This subcategory includes women acting with a man but motivated by jealousy and anger, such as Terri-Lynne McClintic (see chapter 5). Comartin et al.'s (2018) research showed that women co-offenders in sex-based crimes were more apt to have a history of physical, emotional, and sexual abuse, as well as intimate partner violence (IPV; i.e., intimidation, stalking, and sexual abuse), as compared to their noncoerced counterparts. DeCou et al. (2015) examined narrative themes of women who had co-offended in sex-based crimes.

Common themes included limited emotional-interpersonal support, IPV, need to please male co-offending partner, and "giving in" to the man's wishes.

CO-OFFENDING COUPLES AND MURDER

Homicide in Canada is rare, accounting for only 0.2 per cent of violent crimes – about 1.8 victims per 100,000 (David & Jaffray, 2022). Incarceration rates for homicide vary by gender: about 17 per cent of incarcerated women ($n = 210$) and 21 per cent of incarcerated men ($N = 4,410$) (Public Safety Canada, 2018).

Reports of the prevalence of women-men coaccused charged with murder are not available in Canada but, based on related statistics, we can speculate on the size of this group. For example, according to Carrington et al. (2013), police reported 80 co-offending pairs (gender not specified) charged with murder ($N = 37$) and attempted murder ($N = 43$). If one third of these cases included women-men pairs and 10 per cent resulted in a conviction (per statistics indicating that one in ten cases result in a guilty verdict), that would mean about three cases per year. This is consistent with preliminary findings from dissertation work being conducted by Dalhousie University Interdisciplinary PhD (Mental Health & Law) student Angelina MacLellan, who has identified approximately 50 such cases in the past 25 years.

Different dyad combinations express violence differently. Schwartz et al. (2015) found that the violence perpetrated by men-men dyads (vs. women-women or women-men) tends to be more instrumental (i.e., planned, premeditated) and directed at strangers (vs. acquaintances or family members), and tends to involve weapons. With women-women dyads, it depends on the crime; aggravated assaults tend to be reactive-expressive (i.e., impulsive, affect-activated), while homicides tend to be instrumental. Research (e.g., Koons-Witt & Schram, 2003) suggests that partnering with a man elevates a woman's risk to be involved in more violent crimes. Women are about three times more likely to commit murder when in the presence of one or more men than alone (Becker & McCorkel, 2011). In all likelihood, partnering elevates both women's and men's propensity for more violence. Various psychological explanations could account for this, including obedience to authority (Milgram & Gudehus, 1978) and coercive control (Stark, 2007). In the 1960s, Stanley Milgram conducted a series of experiments to test the boundaries of people's obedience to authority. Results showed that most of us, up to 65 per cent depending on the particular study, would inflict pain on others just because we were instructed to do so. Milgram's biographer and social psychology professor, Thomas Blass, claims that Milgram's studies confirmed that "[i]t is not the kind of person we are that determines how we act, but rather the kind of situation we find ourselves in" (Association for Psychological Science, 2011).

Coercive control refers to behaviours that manipulate, intimidate, humiliate, and instill fear in an intimate partner. Sociologist Evan Stark's (2007) book *Coercive Control: How Men Entrap Women in Personal Life* was instrumental in the reconceptualization of IPV. Coercive control evolves over time, and tactics can include obsessive monitoring (e.g., control, social isolation), gaslighting (e.g., mind games to make victim second-guess their sanity), low-level violence (e.g., shoving, hair-pulling), and sexual assault (e.g., nonconsensual sexual acts) (Stark & Hester, 2019). In 2015, England and Wales were the first countries to make coercive control a criminal offence with a maximum sentence of five years (Barlow et al., 2020; Home Office, 2015). To date, Canada has not followed suit (see Gill & Aspinall, 2020), although coercive control is acknowledged in other legislation (e.g., Divorce Act).

Fear, intimidation, and "love" are common themes in the narratives of female co-offenders. A study by Jones (2008) of 50 women co-offenders found that the male partner exercised a high degree of coercion (mental and physical, manipulative, or abusive). Jones's study found that women committed crimes to satisfy the male's expectation (40%; e.g., "had to stand by their man"), as "equal" partners with a man (33%) or a woman (10%), due to direct threat or use of physical violence from a male partner (12%), or "out of love" (5%). Women who reported committing a crime "out of love" were less likely to have experienced physical violence by their partner. Co-offending may serve a protective role in some relationships. One study of 37 African American women caught in coercive relationships found that the women valued their relationships more than their own safety and well-being (Richie, 1996).

Whether out of fear or "love," for many women co-offenders, committing crimes so as to avoid negative outcomes is opting for the lesser of two evils. Of course, relationships characterized by IPV, including coercive control, provide victims with few true choices (see Barlow, 2016). While both men and women can be victims, police-reported data indicate that IPV rates are significantly higher among women than men. In 2019, of the 107,810 Canadians aged 15 and over who experienced IPV, 79 per cent were women. As in previous years, 2019 rates of IPV were more than 3.5 times higher among women than among men (536 versus 149 per 100,000; Government of Canada, 2020). Self-reported data show that women (vs. men) report more physical injury (42% vs. 18%), fear for their lives (33% vs. 5%), and chronic violence (11 or more occasions of violence, 20% vs. 7%; Statistics Canada, 2019). Moreover, women are more apt to die in relationships marked by IPV. Between 2014 and 2019, there were 497 victims of intimate partner homicide and, like IPV in general, 80 per cent (400 victims) were women (Government of Canada, 2020).

CO-OFFENDING COUPLES AND THE LAW

Law, unlike psychology, sees co-offending as more clear-cut. The Criminal Code of Canada (CCC Section 21(1), 1985) clearly states: "[E]veryone is a party to an offence who actually commits it; does or omits to do anything for the purpose of aiding any person to commit it; or abets any person in committing it." Section 21(2) states that everyone is a party to an offence "[w]here two or more persons form an intention in common to carry out an unlawful purpose and to assist each other … commits an offence, each of them who knew or ought to have known that the commission of the offence would be a probable consequence of carrying out the common purpose is a party to that offence" (CCC Section 21(2), p. 38). In other words, co-offending couples are equally culpable. The principal (i.e., person who commits the offence) and the "aider/abettor" (i.e., person who assists or encourages the crime) are treated the same except that the aider/abettor doesn't require the same degree of *mens rea* (i.e., criminal intent) as the principal. A woman who assists a man in the commission of an offence, holding some knowledge that the offence will occur, will receive the same sentence as the man. If the crime is murder, the sentence will be life imprisonment.

The dynamics of a murderous woman-man partnership can be *coercive* (one partner controls the other) and/or *synergistic* (two partners truly "working together" to create an effect that exceeds the sum of the effects of each operating separately). In a national comparison done in the United States, differences between male and female co-offenders were compared through the lens of social amplification theory (Vandiver, 2010). In other words, an offender with an antisocial partner will amplify their own antisocial tendencies; thus, the seriousness of an offence increases when more than one offender becomes involved (Moffitt & Caspi, 2001). In examining co-offending rates among juveniles charged with sexual or violent offences, it was found that girls are more likely to have a co-offender and are slightly younger than their male counterparts, on average. In addition, results indicated that social amplification occurs when girls offend with a co-offender, but does not occur with male offenders (Vandiver, 2010).

"BRAINWASHING" AS A LEGAL DEFENCE IN THE KARLA HOMOLKA CASE

Legal scholar Frances Chapman (2013) argues that brainwashing could be a defence in cases like Karla Homolka's, where battered spouses commit crimes against third parties. Chapman (2013) questions whether there was a breaking point at which Homolka moved from being the battered spouse of a sexually sadistic psychopath (Bernardo) to a participant in the sexual assault, torture, and murder of young girls. Chapman (2013) cites extensively from a report by the Honourable Patrick T. Galligan who, in 1996, reviewed the circumstances surrounding the plea deal with Homolka. Galligan found considerable evidence that Homolka may have been acting involuntarily during the deaths of Mahaffy, French, and her sister Tammy. Justice Galligan questioned whether "Homolka acted with volition when she participated with Paul Bernardo in unspeakable atrocities or whether as the victim/accomplice of a psychopathic sexual sadist she acted involuntarily because she was unable to extricate herself from his complete domination and control" (Chapman, 2013, p. 63).

The Galligan Report (1996, as cited in Chapman, 2013) described how Homolka testified about the power that Bernardo exerted over her from the moment they met. According to Homolka, "[h]e just has this magnetism. It sounds stupid, but from that night I met him, I knew I would marry him. It's like, he has this power over women. He just draws them to him. It's his personality. People want to be around him" (Chapman, 2013, p. 63). Bernardo's power and control escalated over time as he would tell her what to wear, how to style her hair, where she could go. He discouraged her from associating with friends and encouraged her to drink more alcohol. He developed scripts for their sexual activity, whereby she would be made to repeat phrases such as "My name is Karla, I am 17 years old. I am your little cocksucker. I am your little cunt. I am your little slut" (Chapman, 2013, p. 64). The sex became more violent with Bernardo insisting on having anal intercourse with Homolka while she wore a dog choke collar. Approximately eight months into their relationship, Bernardo began beating Homolka. He called her his "sex slave." Homolka later described their relationship as one of "master and servant" (Chapman, 2013, p. 64).

The Galligan Report (1996, as cited in Chapman, 2013) included the results of psychological assessments of Homolka that revealed

> [f]eelings of depression, loneliness, and isolation may have typified extended periods of her life, although she is not inclined to play up these troublesome moods. Her underlying tension and emotional upset are present in disturbing mixtures of anxiety, sadness, and guilt. Her insecurity and her fear of abandonment account for what may appear to be a quiet, accepting and benign attitude towards life's difficulties.... By submerging her individuality, sabotaging opportunities, subordinating personal desires, and submitting at times to abuse and intimidation, she hopes to avoid what she fears most – total abandonment. (Chapman, 2013, p. 66)

Reportedly, expert witnesses who testified at Bernardo's trial were convinced that Homolka suffered from Battered Spouse Syndrome: "she felt totally trapped after Tammy's death and became more and more subject to Paul Bernardo's domination" (Chapman, 2013, p. 66).

Chapman (2009, 2013) argues that, through his repeated abuse and torture, Bernardo effectively "brainwashed" Homolka, an indoctrination process imposed by Bernardo whereby she was forced (violently) to adopt his rigid system of sexual and murderous proclivities that led to the rape and murder of young girls. In this way, Homolka "knew what was happening but she felt totally helpless and unable to act in her own defence or in anyone else's defence. She was ... paralyzed with fear and in that state she became obedient and self-serving" (2009, p. 278). One of the psychological experts who assessed Homolka prior to the plea bargain compared her experience with Bernardo to that of a "concentration camp survivor" who was subject to a horrible situation in which she had to act in unfathomable ways to preserve herself. This is reminiscent of the circumstances of *Sonderkommando* – death camp prisoners who were forced to assist with the disposal of gas chamber victims during the Holocaust. For more information on *Sonderkommando,* see Filip Müller's (1979) book *Eyewitness Auschwitz: Three Years in the Gas Chambers.*

Psychiatric reports on Homolka concluded that she showed no signs of a psychotic disorder or personality disorder (e.g., such as BPD) or anything that would qualify her to be found not criminally responsible due to a mental disorder (NCRMD; see chapter 6). Experts seemed to agree that she met the criteria for severe posttraumatic stress disorder (Chapman, 2009, p. 294; see PTSD; see chapter 5): "suffers from and requires treatment for the effects of extremely severe prolonged exposure to her husband's sadistic acts and the ominous atmosphere he created" (Chapman, 2009, p. 296). Experts noted that Homolka had a history of adopting passive behaviour as a coping mechanism and found no evidence that she would act aggressively on impulse. Nor did she seem to have "masochistic tendencies in terms of finding pleasure by being hurt herself nor her observing the suffering of others" (p. 291). It was generally agreed that she was intimidated by Bernardo; her autonomy and morality were eroded over time and a series of experiences with escalating deviance and depravity, climaxing with the death of her sister Tammy. After that, Homolka may have believed herself trapped and fending for survival. While she may have been a victim and in need of psychological treatment, her psychological state did not excuse her culpability for the crimes.

"BRAINWASHING" AS A MENTAL DISORDER

In the fifth edition of the *Diagnostic and Statistical Manual of Mental Disorders* (American Psychiatric Association, 2013), brainwashing is included in the category of Other Specified Dissociative Disorder. This category is reserved for symptom presentations that cause clinically significant distress or impairment in functioning but do not meet the criteria for any specific dissociative disorder, such as Dissociative Identity Disorder, Dissociative Amnesia, or Depersonalization/Derealization Disorder (pp. 306–7). In common with all dissociative disorders, symptoms usually appear after exposure to trauma and include embarrassment or confusion about symptoms, and the desire to hide them. One type of "other specified" presentation involves identity disturbance due to prolonged and intense coercive persuasion. Coercive persuasion can include brainwashing, thought reform, indoctrination while captive, torture, long-term political imprisonment, and recruitment by sects/cults or by terror organizations. Individuals who have been subjected to intense coercive persuasion may present with prolonged changes in, or conscious questioning of, their identity.

Coercive persuasion was first studied among North American war prisoners in the Korean War (Palacio et al., 2019). It is one explanation (along with Domestic Stockholm Syndrome, Paradoxical Adaptation to Domestic Violence Syndrome, and Cycle of Violence) proposed to explain some of the changes in psychological functioning described in people who have suffered long-term traumatic events. Being subjected to physical or psychological pressure for a protracted period of time can trigger dissociative symptoms, such as amnesia, emotional detachment and numbness, and depersonalization. In some cases, coercive persuasion can result in behavioural regression, diminished cognitive flexibility, and profound alterations in beliefs, values, attitudes, and sense of self (see Palacio et al., 2019).

Boulette and Andersen (1985) compiled a list of 10 coercive strategies, specifically tied to gender violence, that seem to apply in the Karla Homolka case: (a) use of dominance strategies from the beginning of the relationship that the woman justifies as adequate for a strong-willed man, (b) isolation or entrapment, (c) escalation of fear, (d) guilt inducement, (e) fixed expressions of love, (f) loyalty toward the aggressor, (g) promotion of helplessness or invalidity, (h) pathological expressions of jealousy, (i) intermittent reinforcement through hope-inducing behaviours, and (j) mandatory requirement of secrecy. The combination of these control strategies, applied over time, could cause the victim to develop a progressive state of emotional confusion, distorted thoughts, and inaction that hamper her ability to abandon the established relationship with the abusive partner. Apparently, Homolka felt powerless against Bernardo from the night they met. Theirs was a "master and servant" relationship; she was his "sex slave." As the relationship evolved and especially following Tammy's death, Homolka was "paralyzed with fear," increasingly unable to act in her own best interests. Their co-offending rendered her complicit and ensured her silence.

SUMMARY AND CONCLUSIONS

Karla Homolka may have appeared to be different from many of the women with whom she served prison time. She had no prior criminal history, a demonstrated employment record, no children, and a good education. Her crime, of course, was heinous. Thirty years later, Homolka's role in the crime remains contentious. Was she a willing conspirator in the seduction and torture of girls or a young woman ensnared by the Machiavellian charm and control of Paul Bernardo? Was she coerced into conduct she would never have committed of her own volition – a partner or a pawn in one of Canada's most notorious crimes?

People struggle to view Homolka as a victim. At the very least, she seemed to be a woman who was willing to sacrifice others (including her younger sister) to save herself. On the other hand, substantive evidence presented in the Galligan Report (1996, as cited in Chapman, 2013) offers insight into some of the psychological factors that might account for Homolka's apparent ruthlessness. These factors include a history of passive submission to authority (perhaps linked to growing up with an abusive father), Bernardo's considerable skills at manipulation and coercive control, and the traumatizing effects of her situation and her own actions. "Moral injuries" can result from having witnessed or perpetrated actions that go against one's values and moral beliefs and can produce feelings of profound guilt, shame, disgust, and anger (see van Reekum & Watt, 2019). In addition, legal scholars like Frances Chapman provide a compelling argument for brainwashing as an explanation in this case.

Certainly, Homolka's case is fraught with contradictions. To her credit, she testified against Bernardo, thereby ensuring that his fate was sealed. On the other hand, she secured herself a sweet deal for a coaccused and secured it knowing that tapes could provide incriminating evidence. It is difficult to know how much blame Homolka should be apportioned – how much agency (rational choice) does a person possess under conditions of coerced control? Barlow (2015) would advise that we avoid overly simplistic characterizations, such as bad woman, sexual deviant, or "other" (i.e., evil or nonhuman), and instead consider how agency and coercion are interconnected within the context of unhealthy relationships. All relationships have interdynamic forces at play in balancing levels of individuality, autonomy, power, and control. Relationships like Homolka and Bernardo's are complicated – the older, sexually deviant, and violent man ensnares a younger, attractive female partner. She becomes the beguiler (the "lure") in his predatory scheme; her complicity ensures her loyalty.

"What does it matter who is to blame? My story is a Love Story … but only those tortured with love, can understand what I mean.… In the History of the World, how many crimes have been attributed to Love?" said Martha Beck, one of the Lonely Heart Killers, in her last words before being executed on 8 May 1951 (Mcdonell-Parry, 2016). She and Raymond Martinez Fernandez are thought to have murdered as many as 20 women between 1947 and 1949; each was convicted of three murders. Theirs was no love story, nor was Homolka and Bernardo's. These are tragedies writ large with innocent victims sacrificed to satisfy the deplorable needs of others.

CRITICAL THINKING QUESTIONS

1. In considering the case of Karla Homolka, do you see her as Bernardo's partner or pawn in crime?
2. Given its derivation and encumbrance to her efforts to live out of the public eye, why do you think Homolka has continued to use the name Teale?

3. Do you agree with the Quebec Press Council that the public has a "right to know what is happening to Ms. Teale because of the nature of the crimes she committed"? Should Homolka continue to face the consequences of her crimes, postincarceration, or should she be allowed more privacy in her current life?
4. Should co-offending couples be treated as being equally culpable? In other words, should the "aider/abettor" be held to the same degree of responsibility and, thus, the same sentence as the principal offender?

NOTE

1. This case study benefited from the contribution of legal scholar Dr. Frances Chapman, Professor in the Faculty of Law at Lakehead University.

REFERENCES

American Psychiatric Association. (2013). *Diagnostic and statistical manual of mental disorders* (5th ed.). https://doi.org/10.1176/appi.books.9780890425596

Association for Psychological Science. (2011, August 24). 50th anniversary of Stanley Milgram's obedience experiments. https://www.psychologicalscience.org/news/releases/50th-anniversary-of-stanley-milgrams-obedience-experiments.html

Barlow, C. (2015). Silencing the other: Gendered representations of co-accused women offenders. *Howard Journal of Criminal Justice, 54*(5), 469–88. https://doi.org/10.1111/hojo.12145

Barlow, C. (2016). *Coercion and women co-offenders: A gendered pathway into crime*. Policy Press.

Barlow, C., Johnson, K., Walklate, S., & Humphreys, L. (2020). Putting coercive control into practice: Problems and possibilities, *British Journal of Criminology, 60*(1), 160–79. https://doi.org/10.1093/bjc/azz041

Becker, S., & McCorkel, J. A. (2011). The gender of criminal opportunity: The impact of men co-offenders on women's crime. *Feminist Criminology, 6*(2), 79–110. https://doi.org/10.1177/1557085110396501

Blanchette, K. D., & Brown, S. L. (2019). Female offenders. In R.D. Morgan (Ed.), *The SAGE encyclopedia of criminal psychology* (pp. 490–5). SAGE Publications.

Boulette, T. S., & Andersen, S. M. (1985). Mind control and the battering of women. *Community Mental Health Journal, 21*(2), 109–18. https://doi.org/10.1007/BF00754370

Carrington, P. J. (2016). Gender and age segregation and stratification in criminal collaborations. *Journal of Quantitative Criminology, 32*(4), 613–49. https://doi.org/10.1007/s10940-015-9269-2

Carrington, P. J., Brennan, S., Matarazzo, A., & Radulescu, M. (2013, November 19). Co-offending in Canada, 2011. *Juristat*. https://www150.statcan.gc.ca/n1/pub/85-002-x/2013001/article/11856-eng.pdf

Chapman, F. E. (2009). Intangible captivity: The potential for a new Canadian criminal defence of brainwashing and its implications for the battered woman [Unpublished master's thesis]. York University.

Chapman, F. E. (2013). Intangible captivity: The potential for a new Canadian criminal defense of brainwashing and its implications for the battered woman. *Berkeley Journal of Gender, Law & Justice*, *28*(1), 30–76. https://ssrn.com/abstract=2467087

Chesney-Lind, M., & Pasko, L. (2013). *The female offender: Girls, women, and crime* (3rd ed.). SAGE Publications.

Cohen, L. (2021, December 20). Ghislaine Maxwell was Epstein's "partner in crime," prosecutor says. *Global News*. https://globalnews.ca/news/8463485/ghislaine-maxwell-complicit-prosecutor-closing-arguments/

Comartin, E. B., Burgess-Proctor, A., Kubiak, S., & Kernsmith, P. (2018). Factors related to co-offending and coerced offending among female sex offenders: The role of childhood and adult trauma histories. *Violence and Victims*, *33*(1), 53–74. https://doi.org/10.1891/0886-6708.33.1.53

Correctional Service Canada. (2002). *A profile of federal offenders designated as dangerous offenders or serving long-term supervision orders*. https://www.csc-scc.gc.ca/research/r125-eng.shtml

Correctional Service Canada. (2019, May 16). Statistics and research on women offenders. https://www.csc-scc.gc.ca/women/002002-0008-en.shtml

Correctional Service Canada. (2019). Women offenders. https://www.csc-scc.gc.ca/publications/005007-3012-en.shtml

Correctional Service Canada. (2021). Age structure of women in federal custody: 2009–10 and 2019–20. https://www.csc-scc.gc.ca/research/005008-rib-21-09-en.shtml

Correctional Service Canada. (n.d.). Forum on corrections research. https://www.csc-scc.gc.ca/research/forum/e053/e053e-eng.shtml

Criminal Code of Canada. (1985). R.S.C., c. C-46, s. 16(1).

Criminal Minds Wiki. (n.d.). Paul Bernardo and Karla Homolka. https://criminalminds.fandom.com/wiki/Paul_Bernardo_and_Karla_Homolka

David, J.-D., & Jaffray, B. (2022, November 21). Homicide in Canada, 2021. *Statistics Canada*. https://www150.statcan.gc.ca/n1/pub/85-002-x/2022001/article/00015-eng.htm

DeCou, C. R., Cole, T. T., Rowland, S. E., Kaplan, S. P., & Lynch, S. M. (2015). An ecological process model of female sex offending: The role of victimization, psychological distress, and life stressors. *Sexual Abuse*, *27*(3), 302–23. https://doi.org/10.1177/1079063214556359

Gill, C., & Aspinall, M. (2020). Understanding coercive control in the context of intimate partner violence in Canada: How to address the issue through the criminal justice system. https://www.victimsfirst.gc.ca/res/cor/UCC-CCC/index.html

Government of Canada. (2020). *Fact sheet: Intimate partner violence*. Women-gender-equality.canada.ca/en/gender-based-violence/intimate-partner-violence.html

Haynie, D. L., Giordano, P. C., Manning, W. D., & Longmore, M. A. (2005). Adolescent romantic relationships and delinquency involvement. *Criminology, 43*(1), 177–210. https://doi.org/10.1111/j.0011-1348.2005.00006.x

Home Office. (2015). *Statutory guidance framework: Controlling or coercive behaviour in an intimate or family relationship*. https://www.gov.uk/government/publications/statutory-guidance-framework-controlling-or-coercive-behaviour-in-an-intimate-or-family-relationship

Hunter, B. (2018, June 28). Deal with the devil: 25 years since Karla Homolka skated. *Toronto Sun*. https://torontosun.com/news/local-news/deal-with-the-devil-25-years-since-karla-homolka-skated

Jones, S. (2008). Partners in crime: A study of the relationship between woman offenders and their co-defendants. *Criminology & Criminal Justice, 8*(2), 147–64. https://doi.org/10.1177/1748895808088992

Koons-Witt, B. A., & Schram, P. J. (2003). The prevalence and nature of violent offending by females. *Journal of Criminal Justice, 31*(4), 361–71. https://doi.org/10.1016/S0047-2352(03)00028-X

Mcdonell-Parry, A. (2016, June 17). Beyond Bonnie and Clyde: 10 infamous crime spree couples. *Rolling Stone*. https://www.rollingstone.com/tv-movies/tv-movie-lists/beyond-bonnie-and-clyde-10-infamous-crime-spree-couples-22210/joseph-and-jenny-carrier-16170/

Milgram, S., & Gudehus, C. (1978). *Obedience to authority*. Ziff-Davis.

Milhizer, E. R. (2004). Justification and excuse: What they were, what they are, and what they ought to be. *St. John's Law Review, 78*(3), 725–896. https://scholarship.law.stjohns.edu/cgi/viewcontent.cgi?referer=&httpsredir=1&article=1300&context=lawreview

Moffitt, T. E., & Caspi, A. (2001). Childhood predictors differentiate life-course persistent and adolescence-limited antisocial pathways among males and females. *Development and Psychopathology, 13*(2), 355–75. https://doi.org/10.1017/S0954579401002097

Morrissey, B. (2006). "Dealing with the devil": Karla Homolka and the absence of feminist criticism. In A. Burfoot & S. Lord (Eds.), *Killing women: The visual culture of gender and violence* (pp. 83–103). Wilfrid Laurier University Press.

Müller, F. (1979). *Eyewitness Auschwitz: Three years in the gas chambers*. Published in association with the United States Holocaust Memorial Museum.

Palacio, A. F. C., Fuente, E. D., del Castillo, R. P., & Usaola, C. P. (2019). Intimate partner violence against women: Impact on mental health. In M. Sáenz-Herrero (Ed.), *Psychopathology in women: Incorporating gender perspective into descriptive psychopathology* (pp. 55–80). Springer Nature. https://doi.org/10.1007/978-3-030-15179-9_3

Peritz, I., & Freeze, C. (2005, June 30). Attempt to muzzle media fails. *Globe and Mail*. https://www.theglobeandmail.com/news/national/attempt-to-muzzle-media-fails/article983032/

Pron, N. (2006, February 21). Bernardo admits more rapes. *Toronto Star*. https://canadiancrc.com/newspaper_articles/Tor_Star_Bernardo_admits_more_rapes_21FEB06.aspx

Public Safety Canada. (2014). Research results: Women offenders. https://www.csc-scc.gc.ca/publications/005007-3014-eng.shtml#_ftn4

Public Safety Canada. (2018). *2018 corrections and conditional release statistical overview*. https://www.publicsafety.gc.ca/cnt/rsrcs/pblctns/ccrso-2018/index-en.aspx#sectionc15

Public Safety Canada. (2022). High-risk offenders – A handbook for criminal justice professionals. https://www.publicsafety.gc.ca/cnt/rsrcs/pblctns/hghrsk-ffndrs-hndb/index-en.aspx

Richie, B. (1996). *Compelled to crime: The gender entrapment of battered black women*. Psychology Press.

Ross, S. (2020, December 15). Karla Homolka, after moving again near Montreal, can't expect privacy: Quebec press council. *CTV News*. https://montreal.ctvnews.ca/karla-homolka-after-moving-again-near-montreal-can-t-expect-privacy-quebec-press-council-1.5232444

Savage, L. (2019, January 10). Female offenders in Canada, 2017. *Statistics Canada*. https://www150.statcan.gc.ca/n1/pub/85-002-x/2019001/article/00001-eng.htm

Schwartz, J. (2013). A "new" female offender or increasing social control of women's behaviour? Cross-national evidence. *Feminist Studies, 39*(3), 790–821. https://doi.org/10.1353/fem.2013.0031

Schwartz, J., Conover-Williams, M., & Clemons, K. (2015). Thirty years of sex stratification in violent crime partnerships and groups. *Feminist Criminology, 10*(1), 60–91. https://doi.org/10.1177/1557085114536765

Stark, E. (2007). *Coercive control: How men entrap women in personal life*. Oxford University Press.

Stark, E., & Hester, M. (2019). Coercive control: Update and review. *Violence against Women, 25*(1), 81–104. https://doi.org/10.1177/1077801218816191

Vandiver, D. (2010). Assessing gender differences and co-offending patterns of a predominantly "male-oriented" crime: A comparison of a cross-national sample of juvenile boys and girls arrested for a sexual offense. *Violence and Victims, 25*(2), 243–64. https://doi.org/10.1891/0886-6708.25.2.243

van Reekum, E. A., & Watt, M. C. (2019). A pilot study of interpersonal process group therapy for PTSD in Canadian veterans. *Journal of Military, Veteran and Family Health, 5*(2), 147–58. https://doi.org/10.3138/jmvfh.2018-0001

Watt, M. C. (2014). *Explorations in forensic psychology: Cases in criminal and abnormal behaviour*. Nelson Education.

CHAPTER EIGHT

Mad, Bad, and/or Sad? Homicide in Custody

The Case of Ashley Smith

With Jessica Doyle and C.K. MacLean

All the force in the world could not make her healthy or obedient.

– Globe & Mail *Editorial, November 2012*

Name of Deceased: Ashley Smith
Date and Time of Death: October 19, 2007 at 8:10 a.m.
Place of Death: St. Mary's General Hospital in Kitchener
Cause of Death: Ligature strangulation and positional asphyxia
By what means: Homicide

– Coroner's Inquest Touching the Death of Ashley Smith (Correctional Service Canada, 2014)

Between 2001 and 2011, 530 incarcerated Canadians died in federal custody. Two thirds died due to natural causes, another 17.4 per cent of deaths (92 deaths) were attributed to suicide, and 5.5 per cent of deaths (29 deaths) were considered homicides (Correctional Service Canada [CSC], 2016). While 2007 marked the fewest annual deaths in custody (*N* = 40), one death was deemed to be, a homicide which was not committed by an inmate. The death of 19-year-old Ashley Smith led to a Coroner's Inquest and 104 recommendations that would essentially transform the CSC.

ASHLEY SMITH

The video presented in court is time stamped 6:27:26 p.m., 12 April 2007. Nineteen-year-old Ashley Smith is being transported by plane from the Regional Psychiatric Centre (RPC) in Saskatoon, SK, to the Institut Philippe-Pinel, a psychiatric centre in Montreal, QC. In a scene reminiscent of *Silence of the Lambs*, Ashley's head is covered with a black mesh-and-canvas spit hood, which is tied around her neck; her wrists are bound together with duct tape and her forearms are shackled to the armrests. Constrained as if straitjacketed, Ashley sits in her own feces. Flash forward three months, and seven Joliette correctional officers in black helmets, gas masks, and hazmat-type suits pin Ashley to a metal gurney so that a nurse can inject her with antipsychotic drugs. "You have to cooperate," the nurse tells a seemingly compliant Ashley. "You have no choice." This scene repeats itself five times within seven hours. Flash forward another three months to 19 October 2007, and Ashley is face down on the floor of her solitary confinement cell in Grand Valley Institution for Women (Kitchener, ON), having strangled herself to death with a piece of cloth. Correctional officers have watched her die – obeying orders not to intervene unless she stops breathing lest they reinforce "attention seeking behaviour." While the video images of Ashley Smith constrained and dying scream out that many things went wrong in this case, we will focus on one element – the distinction between mental and behavioural disorders, a distinction that may have rendered a deadly difference (see Zlomislic, 2012, for video).

The following timeline of events in Ashley Smith's life is derived from CBC's Fifth Estate's (2010) *Timeline: The Life and Death of Ashley Smith* and Correctional Investigator Howard Sapers's (2008) report, *A Preventable Death.*

Ashley Smith was born on 29 January 1988, and grew up in Moncton, NB. Little is known about her biological history as she was adopted at age five by Coralee Smith and Herbert Gober. Reportedly, she enjoyed a "normal" childhood but began to "act out" (i.e., defiant, disruptive, disobedient) when she was 13 or 14 (Fifth Estate, 2010). By the time she was 15, she had been in and out of youth court 14 times for various minor offences including trespassing and causing a disturbance. Her parents hired a psychologist, who concluded there was no evidence of mental illness, just behavioural problems. A youth worker was assigned, and efforts were made to support Ashley in half-days in school (Grade 8), along with interventions for oppositional and impulsive behaviour. Her performance in school continued to deteriorate, and her youth worker consulted a psychologist who offered a diagnostic impression that Ashley showed signs of non-learning verbal difficulties that "may relate to some neurological deficits." Behaviour modification was recommended. In March 2003, 15-year-old Ashley is admitted to the Pierre Caissie Centre for a 34-day assessment. Psychological and psychiatric assessments indicated that Ashley had a learning disorder, attention deficit hyperactivity disorder (ADHD), borderline personality disorder (BPD), and traits of narcissistic personality disorder (NPD). She was discharged early, after only seven days, due to difficulties interacting with peers and staff. Reportedly, she was "intimidating, rude, demanding and verbally aggressive." Police were called twice because she assaulted staff. Correctional Investigator Howard Sapers (2008) maintains that this was the missed opportunity. According to Sapers (2008): "This discharge may have been premature and could possibly have been the key missed opportunity to assist this young girl and her family long before she entered the criminal justice system."

Next, Ashley is admitted to the New Brunswick Youth Centre (NBYC) in Miramichi, NB. Within a couple of weeks, she incurred over 30 institutional charges for refusing staff orders, being aggressive, and threatening self-harm. Over the next three years, Ashley orbited in and out of NBYC five times and accrued 800 documented incidents. Each time, according to the Ombudsman & Child and Youth Advocate (2008), Bernard Richard, she "pushed the staff of the youth centre to their limits." Ashley's conduct at NBYC often led to being placed in restraints and/or secured in the Therapeutic Quiet unit, essentially a segregation cell measuring 9 x 6 feet and 7.5 feet high. Efforts to maintain Ashley in the community, between stints in NBYC, met with limited success. Between 2003 and 2006, 150 incident reports recounted Ashley's efforts to self-harm, many of which would foreshadow her actions on 19 October 2007. See the postscript for an excerpt from Ashley's journal in September 2006.

In 2005, Ashley undergoes a judge-ordered psychiatric assessment at Restigouche Hospital. According to the Ombudsman report, a psychiatrist at Restigouche Hospital determined that "Ms. Smith clearly understands her responsibilities and their consequences and can control her actions when she chooses to." The assessment-informed assumption that Ashley's destructive behaviour was entirely of her own volition resulted in an extra 180 days in custody. **29 January 2006**: Ashley Smith turns 18 – the age of majority. Legally, she is an adult and, in July 2006, the superintendent of NBYC applies under the Youth Criminal Justice Act to have her transferred to an adult facility. **September 2006**: Ashley hires a lawyer to fight the transfer to an adult prison. In an affidavit Ashley states she can't control her outbursts: "Although I know that my record looks bad, I would never intentionally hurt anyone. I am really scared about the thought of going to an adult facility with dangerous people. It has occupied my mind for a long time. I have wanted to behave to ensure that I would not ever go to adult and was sure that I would succeed." **28 September 2006**: Ashley expresses her fear about the pending court date in her diary. "I don't know what to feel. I'm f***ing scared about what's going to happen. Sometimes I think it would just be easier to give up." A month before Ashley is transferred, she attempts to self-harm 16 times. **5 October 2006**: Ashley is transferred to Saint John Regional Correctional Centre (SJRCC), where she is held in segregation for most of the 26 days she is there. **24 October 2006**: Ashley appears in adult court. She is given an adult sentence for criminal charges laid while she was still a youth at NBYC. She is given 348 days extra on top of the 1,455 days she is already serving. Because her sentence duration exceeds two years, she is ordered to serve its remainder in a federal institution. **31 October 2006**: Ashley Smith is involuntarily transferred to the Nova Institution for Women in Nova Scotia. This is a federal institution. **December 2006**: Ashley is sent to the Women's Unit at CSC's Prairie Regional Psychiatric Centre (RPC) in Saskatoon for diagnostic clarification and to develop a treatment plan. She is moved from RPC for her own safety. A guard is charged with assault. **April 2007**: Ashley is voluntarily transferred to the Institut Philippe-Pinel de Montréal (Pinel) for treatment, but she withdraws from treatment there. According to Correctional Investigator Howard Sapers, this starts a long sequence of "highly inappropriate, unnecessary and unlawful transfers between CSC facilities." **21 May 2007**: Ashley is transferred to Grand Valley Institution, in Kitchener, ON. **27 June 2007**: Ashley is transferred to Joliette Institution in Quebec. **26 July 2007**: Ashley is transferred back to Nova Institution in Truro, NS. **31 August 2007**: Ashley is transferred back to Grand Valley Institution for Women in Kitchener, ON. **24 September 2007**: Ashley is visited by Kim Pate of the Canadian Association of Elizabeth Fry Societies. Ashley wanted Pate to file a complaint on her behalf since she was not allowed to have a pen or paper for security reasons. The complaint is not read until after her death. **9 October 2007**: A Use-of-Force training session is held by Ken Allen at Grand Valley Institution. Sources told CBC's The Fifth Estate that it was to deal with the high number of use-of-force incidents with inmate Ashley Smith. **16 October 2009**: The Fifth Estate learned that three days before her death Ashley asked to go to a psychiatric hospital. She told correctional staff that she would take medication and stop choking herself. There were no beds available at the hospital. **17 October 2007**: According to Sapers's report (2008), a few days before her death, an institutional psychologist recognized "that Ashley's mental health had further deteriorated. She was allowed out of her cell for brief periods in an attempt to establish meaningful interaction with staff." **18 October 2007**: According to the Correctional Investigator, Ashley was placed on 24-hour suicide watch under direct staff observation. There was confusion regarding Ashley's risk for suicide. **19 October 2007**: A few hours before her death, Ashley told a correctional officer that she wanted to die. Correctional officers discover Ashley with a ligature around her neck in the early morning of 19 October. According to the Correctional Investigator, "correctional staff failed to respond immediately to this medical emergency" (Sapers, 2008). Sources told The Fifth Estate that, when Ashley was applying ligatures, guards were instructed not to enter her cell if she was still breathing. At 6:57 a.m., a guard removes the ligature from her neck. By 7:10 a.m. correctional officers and a nurse perform CPR. By 8:10 a.m., Ashley is pronounced dead.

By the time she died on 19 October 2007, 19-year-old Ashley Smith had endured over 1,000 hours in segregation interspersed with use-of-force episodes that included tasers and pepper spray. During her 11 months in federal custody, she had been transferred a total of 17 times among eight different institutions since, by law, she could not be held longer than 60 days in segregation in any one facility (see table 8.1). Following two inquests into the circumstances of her death, the

Table 8.1. Timeline of days Ashley Smith spent in custody at various institutions across Canada, including date of birth and death

Place	DoB – Moncton, NB	Nova	RPC	Pinel	GVI	STPH	GVI	GVH	JI	Nova	CNSCF	Nova	GVI	GVH	GVI	GVH	GVI	DoD – GVI
Date	Jan. 29, 1988	Oct. 31, 2006	Dec. 20, 2006	Apr. 12, 2007	May 10, 2007	June 11, 2007	June 19, 2007	June 26, 2007	June 27, 2007	July 26, 2007	Aug. 24, 2007	Aug. 27, 2007	Aug. 31, 2007	Sept. 6, 2007	Sept. 6, 2007	Sept. 21, 2007	Sept. 21, 2007	Oct. 19, 2007
Days in Custody	–		60	110	30	30	8	1	8	30	28	3	7	1	15	1	49	–

Note: DoB = Date of Birth. Nova = Nova Institution for Women. RPC = Regional Psychiatric Centre. Pinel = Institut Philippe-Pinel de Montréal. GVI = Grand Valley Institution for Women. STPH = St. Thomas Psychiatric Hospital. GVH = Grand River Hospital. JI = Joliette Institution. CNSCF = Central Nova Correctional Facility. DoD = Date of Death.
Source: Fifth Estate (2010).

coroner's jury returned a verdict of homicide on 19 December 2013, claiming that the actions of others contributed to her death. The jury offered 104 recommendations for ways in which CSC could better serve women and inmates suffering from mental illness. The jury also recommended that indefinite solitary confinement be banned. In the aftermath of Smith's death, CSC introduced mental health screening for all federal inmates and, as of December 2019, inmates in Canada's federal prisons can no longer be legally held in solitary confinement for longer than 15 days or more than 20 hours per day. Administrative segregation has been replaced by "structured intervention units," the operation and efficacy of which are currently under review (see Sprott and Doob, 2021).

BEHAVIOURALLY DISORDERED?

According to the fifth edition of the *Diagnostic and Statistical Manual of Mental Disorders* (*DSM-5*), a mental disorder is "a syndrome [i.e., symptoms that tend to coalesce] characterized by clinically significant disturbance in cognition, emotional regulation, or behaviour that reflects a dysfunction in the psychological, biological, or developmental processes underlying mental functioning" (American Psychiatric Association [APA], 2013, p. 20). A diagnosis of a disorder requires a careful assessment – file review, clinical interview, administration of actuarial measures, consultation with collateral sources if available – by a licensed clinical psychologist or psychiatrist. If the assessment data indicate that the pattern of presenting symptoms is consistent with the diagnostic criteria for a specific mental disorder outlined in the *DSM-5*, then a diagnosis may be assigned. A diagnosis is intended to have clinical utility, meaning that it "should help clinicians to determine prognosis, treatment plans, and potential treatment outcomes" (APA, 2013, p. 20). Whether the patient requires treatment depends on their symptom severity, symptom salience (e.g., suicidal ideation), patient distress, and/or functional impairment.

Throughout Ashley's life, and especially during her time in custody, a critical question seems to have persisted: Was she mentally ill or behaviourally disordered? The critical distinction was whether her actions were beyond her control or of her own volition. The former would guide one approach to care and treatment; the latter would suggest a different approach (e.g., behavioural modification). The distinction arises from a commonly held view that some mental disorders (e.g., anxiety, depression, schizophrenia) are largely governed by biological and psychological factors, while those with a manifest behavioural component are governed more by environmental factors (e.g., learning). Over the course of her short life, most of Ashley's diagnoses fell within the latter group, which includes *DSM-5* categories of Neurodevelopmental – attention deficit hyperactivity disorder (ADHD) and specific learning disorder (SLD); Personality – borderline personality disorder (BPD) and antisocial personality disorder (ASPD); and Disruptive, Impulse-Control, and Conduct – oppositional defiant disorder (ODD) and conduct disorder (CD). While disorders such as anxiety, depression, and schizophrenia spectrum are considered mental disorders with a behavioural component, disorders such as ADHD, ODD, and CD are recognized more by disruptive behaviours (actions) than mental features (e.g., cognitions, perceptions). See table 8.2 for an outline of the main features of each disorder.

SELF-CONTROL

The distinction between mental and behavioural disorders hinges largely on the word "self-control." For example, the category of "Disruptive, Impulse-Control, and Conduct Disorders" includes conditions (e.g., ODD, CD) that are characterized by problems in the "self-control of emotions and behaviors" (APA, 2013, p. 462). Of course, the construct of self-control figures prominently in theories of crime as well as mental health. Indeed, one of the most influential theories in criminology – Gottfredson and Hirschi's (1990) General Theory of Crime – asserts that one's propensity for crime is largely a function of individual differences in self-control. Self-control is considered to be largely shaped by parenting practices, well ingrained by age eight, and defined by the degree to which a person is "vulnerable to the temptations of the moment" (Gottfredson & Hirschi, 1990, p. 87). Low self-control is seen to be characterized by low gratification delay, preference for physical (vs. cognitive) activities and simple (vs. complex) tasks, self-centredness or insensitivity to others, high

Table 8.2. Key characteristics of Ashley Smith's possible and diagnosed disorders and fatality rates

Category		Key Characteristics of Disorder	Prevalence General Population[a]	Prevalence Correctional Population
Neurodevelopmental	ADHD	Persistent pattern of severe inattention and/or marked hyperactivity-impulsivity that impacts functioning or development	5%	16.5%[b]
	ASD	Persistent deficits in social behaviour and social communication; rigid/ritualistic/repetitive behaviours	1%	9%[c]
	SLD	Significant deficits in ability to learn and apply specific academic skills despite targeted intervention	5%–15%	38%[d]
	ND-PAE	Various developmental disabilities related to neurocognition, self-regulation, and adaptive functioning, following in utero exposure to alcohol	Unknown; ~2%–5% rate of disorders related to PAE	Unknown; 23.3% rate for FASDs[e]
Disruptive, impulse control, & conduct	ODD	Persistent pattern of frequent defiant behaviour, irritability, and vindictiveness that is developmentally inappropriate and negatively affects functioning	1%–11%	12.3%[f]
	CD	Persistent behavioural pattern including repetitive violation of rights of others/societal norms and involving aggression, deceitfulness, and destruction of property	2%–10%	59%[g]
Personality disorders	ASPD	Pervasive pattern of disregard for and violation of other/society; impulsivity, aggressiveness, irresponsibility, and lacking remorse; history of CD	0.2%–3.3%	49.4%[h]
	BPD	Pervasive pattern of instability in emotions, identity, and relationships; marked impulsivity and recklessness; typically, recurrent suicidality and/or self-injurious behaviour	1.6%–5.9%	33.3%[h]
Depressive disorders	DMDD	Severe and recurring temper outbursts (verbal or behavioural) that are significantly longer or more intense than warranted by situation and developmentally inappropriate	2%–5%	Unknown
Deaths in federal custody, 2008–2017[i]		*N* = 554		
Suicide rate		14.6%	11.5/100,000	55/100,000
Homicide rate		3.4%	1.8/100,000	13.0/100,000

Note: ADHD= Attention Deficit Hyperactivity Disorder. ASD = Autism Spectrum Disorder. SLD = Specific Learning Disorder. ND-PAE = Neurodevelopmental-Prenatal Alcohol Exposure. ODD = Oppositional Defiant Disorder. CD = Conduct Disorder. ASPD = Antisocial Personality Disorder. BPD = Borderline Personality Disorder. DMDD = Disruptive Mood Dysregulation Disorder. FASDs = Fetal Alcohol Spectrum Disorders.

[a] DSM-5 (APA, 2013). [b] Usher et al. (2013). [c] Young et al. (2018). [d] Shelton (2006). [e] Fast et al. (1999). [f] Baglivio et al. (2017). [g] Beaudy et al. (2021). [h] Brown et al. (2018).
[i] Adult Correctional Services Survey, Canadian Centre for Justice and Community Safety Statistics, Statistics Canada.

risk-taking, and low tolerance for frustration. Individuals with low self-control are considered more apt to respond to conflict in a physical rather than verbal manner (see DeLisi et al., 2018, p. 54). Although popular among American criminologists, Gottfredson and Hirschi's theory has been widely criticized for being definitionally flawed, tautological, paternalistic, parent-blaming, and unable to explain racial and/or gender differences in crime. Moreover, the theory is superseded by advances in psychology and neuroscience.

Today, self-control is understood to be part of a larger self-regulation system that falls within the domain of executive functions. Executive functions include cognitive abilities (e.g., working memory, inhibitory control, cognitive flexibility, planning, reasoning, and problem solving) that enable us to achieve goals, adapt to new situations, and manage social interactions. Self-regulation allows us to formulate goals and monitor discrepancies between our current and desired end-state; self-control is what we do to move toward the desired end state. For example, we exercise self-control to prevent or override undesirable/unwanted/maladaptive thoughts, emotions, and behaviours in the face of temptations and impulses (see Gillebaart, 2018).

Multiple brain regions are involved in self-control, but the prefrontal cortex (PFC) appears to play a critical role. The PFC is one of the last brain regions to reach maturity. Indeed, it may not reach full maturation until age 25, which explains why self-control can follow a slow developmental time course (Gillebaart, 2018). The slow development of the PFC allows for greater neural plasticity and environmental impact, both positive and negative. For example, prenatal exposure to toxic substances (e.g., alcohol or opioids; see Beauchamp et al., 2020) or emotional turbulence (e.g., maternal depression and/or anxiety; Warnock et al., 2016) can disrupt the development of self-regulatory processes. Postnatally, adverse childhood experiences have been linked to poor self-control and subsequent maladaptive outcomes (see Berkman et al., 2012). Reports indicate that Ashley Smith's adoptive parents were strong advocates for their daughter both in life and since her death. On the other hand, little is known about Ashley's prenatal development. Prenatal exposure to alcohol could have increased her risk for fetal alcohol spectrum disorders (FASDs). Nor do we know Ashley's genetic history. A recent meta-analysis conducted by Willems et al. (2019) that included 31 studies with more than 30,000 twins, published between 1997 and 2018, reported a heritability estimate of 60 per cent for self-control, with no variation across gender or age. Of course, we also don't fully understand the potential traumatizing impact of repeated incarceration, use of force, and segregation on a "child."

In short, blaming Ashley for not exercising more self-control was neither fair nor effective in changing her "end-state." It seems likely that Ashley would have failed the "marshmallow test" of self-control. Walter Mischel, an Austrian-American psychologist based at Stanford University, launched a series of studies in the 1960s whereby preschool children were given the choice between one reward (e.g., one marshmallow to be eaten immediately) or a larger reward (e.g., two marshmallows for which they would have to wait – alone, for up to 20 minutes). Years later, Mischel and his team followed up with the preschoolers and found that those children who were able to wait for the second marshmallow generally fared better in life. In an interview for his 2015 book, *The Marshmallow Test*, Mischel explained that many factors can influence a child's (or an adult's) decision to delay gratification, such as trust in or obedience to authority figures, cognitive fatigue, distraction, and emotional dysregulation. He compares self-control to a muscle that requires training and practice. Mischel welcomes the burgeoning research on executive functioning and many breakthroughs in neuroscience that advance our understanding of how the brain works to exercise self-control (see Urist, 2014).

COMORBIDITY AMONG MENTAL DISORDERS

We have learned a lot since Mischel's original study. We now know that the inability to delay gratification (inhibit impulses) is neither a character flaw nor a parenting failure. Moreover, the distinction between mental and behavioural disorders, whether it hinges on self-control or not, is increasingly anachronistic. Advances in neuroscience and genetics challenge our current conceptualization of mental disorders as independent entities. In practice, the lines are more blurred with high rates of comorbidity (co-occurrence of disorders). Indeed, comorbidity is the rule rather than the exception. Epidemiological studies show that, among individuals with a diagnosis within the past year, almost half have one (22%) or more (23%) additional diagnoses. In a survey of adolescents 13 to 17 years of age, Kessler et al. (2012) reported that 27.9 per cent of respondents met criteria for two or more disorders. Community-based surveys have found that, among respondents with at least one mental disorder, about half have one or more additional lifetime diagnoses (see Plana-Ripoll, 2019). Comorbidity rates are high both *within* categories (e.g., neurodevelopmental) where, for example, approximately 30 per cent with a specific learning disorder (SLD) also have ADHD; and *between* categories, where one third to one half of children with ADHD or oppositional defiant disorder (ODD) (two different categories) also meet the criteria for the other (Harvey et al., 2016).

ADHD was one diagnosis assigned to Ashley Smith. It is a good example of a clinically heterogeneous condition that is typically complicated by extensive comorbid conditions. See Gnanavel et al. (2019) for a good summary of this literature, some of which is outlined below. ADHD is highly comorbid with other neurodevelopmental disorders, including autism spectrum disorder (ASD). A 2016 study of American children diagnosed with ASD found the rate of comorbidity with ADHD was 42 per cent and the rate of comorbidity with both ADHD and SLDs was 17 per cent for a total comorbidity rate of 59 per cent. Other reports of comorbidity between ADHD and SLD have ranged from 10 per cent to 92 per cent, which probably reflects differences in diagnostic standards. One study found the prevalence of ADHD in Tourette's syndrome (tic disorder) to be 55 per cent.

ADHD is highly comorbid with both *internalizing* (e.g., mood, anxiety) and *externalizing* disorders (e.g., ODD, CD). The prevalence of major depression in youth with ADHD has been found to range from 12 per cent to 50 per cent, which is five time higher than in youth without ADHD. The prevalence of anxiety symptoms in ADHD patients has been found to range from 15 per cent to 35 per cent. Research has demonstrated that 30–50 per cent of children with ADHD meet full criteria for ODD and conduct disorder (CD). The high comorbidity rate is thought to be attributable to shared genetic origin. Longitudinal studies indicate that the correspondence between the two disorders increases with age and that ADHD-like traits may exacerbate externalizing tendencies from adolescence into adulthood. The combined impact of ADHD and ODD/CD can be profound, significantly increasing the risk for poor academic performance, misuse of drugs, antisocial personality disorder, and criminal conduct. Individuals with ADHD, ODD, or CD also are at greater risk for Intermittent Explosive Disorder (IED), which is characterized by aggression, anger, and impulsivity. One diagnosis that was not available to Ashley Smith but may have applied is Disruptive Mood Dysregulation Disorder (DMDD), a new addition to the Depressive Disorders category of the *DSM-5*. The core feature of DMDD is chronic, severe, persistent irritability that is marked by angry mood and temper outbursts. It has been suggested that DMDD may actually capture the presence of ODD/CD with ADHD or perhaps anxiety (see Gnanavel et al., 2019).

Recently, Plana-Ripoll et al. (2019) published findings from a population-based cohort study of almost six million Danish citizens and 83.9 million person-years to create a comprehensive map of pairwise comorbidity within mental disorders. Four surprising findings emerged: (a) Comorbidity was pervasive across all pairs of disorders. In essence, every single mental disorder predisposed the patient to every other mental disorder; (b) Although the rate of a subsequent disorder was higher in the first six months post-onset of a prior disorder, the risk stabilized at an elevated rate; (c) Pairwise comorbidity was bidirectional; and (d) Certain pairs of disorders had substantial absolute risk. For example, results showed that among individuals who developed a mood disorder before 20 years of age, 40 per cent of the men and 50 per cent of the women would subsequently develop a neurotic (anxiety or stress-related) disorder within the next 15 years. Caspi et al. (2014) evinced that psychiatric disorders are accounted for by three continua: Internalizing, Externalizing, and Thought Problems spectra; however, all psychiatric disorders considered were better explained by one General Psychopathology factor. These findings provide further evidence that the key to understanding mental disorders will be found in their roots (what they have in common) versus their branches (where they diverge).

One thing that various mental disorders seem to share is a common architecture – underlying latent constructs that cut across diagnostic boundaries. Examples of such transdiagnostic factors are rumination, neuroticism (negative affectivity), anxiety sensitivity (AS; of arousal-related somatic sensations) and, in the case of disorders like ADHD, CD, or ODD, externalizing (vs. internalizing) factors such as emotional/behavioural dysregulation. Transdiagnostic factors offer new ways of conceptualizing and treating mental disorders. For example, they help to explain why certain psychopharmacological agents (e.g., selective serotonin reuptake inhibitors) and particular psychotherapeutic approaches (e.g., cognitive behavioural therapy or CBT) show efficacy across disorders (e.g., anxiety, depression, trauma). High AS, for example, is a known risk factor for anxiety, mood, substance use, and trauma disorders (Olatunji & Wolitzky-Taylor, 2009). CBT specifically designed to reduce AS has been found to yield benefits across all of these disorders (Taylor, 2019). Research into transdiagnostic factors complements research focused on biological substrates of behaviour, such as that being conducted by the US National Institute of Mental Health's Research Domain Criteria (RDoC). While some suggest that we are rapidly moving away from "categorical diagnoses derived from patient interviews" (Kreuger & Eaton, 2015, p. 29), others (e.g., Clark et al., 2017, p. 74) remind us that mental disorders reflect the influence of multiple factors – "from neurons to neighbourhoods" – "and no one level of analysis has causal primacy over the other."

SUMMARY AND CONCLUSIONS

What does all this mean for Ashley Smith? What are the lessons that Ashley can teach us? The case of Ashley Smith serves as a cautionary tale – reminding us of how little we know about mental illness and how little we have advanced in treating conduct that confounds us. We have a long history of questionable practices in "treating" behavioural disorders – trephination, insulin shock therapy, transorbital and chemical (Thorazine) lobotomies, and indiscriminate electroconvulsive therapy (ECT). The images of officers forcibly restraining Ashley, while a nurse injects her with antipsychotic medication, hearken back to obsolescent practices from our ignominious past. People thought they knew what was "wrong" with Ashley and thought they knew how to manage her "behaviour," but you only need to look at the picture of this young girl straitjacketed, hooded, and duct-taped to know that something/many things went sorely wrong with her case.

Assessment, diagnosis, and treatment are important for psychologists and psychiatrists in conceptualizing cases and planning treatment. Categorization of mental disorders (i.e., diagnoses) is necessary for better understanding, for easier communication, and for clinical decision-making. At the same time, we must resist the lure of reification (i.e., treating as if concrete or immutable) and the illusion that all disorders are distinct (e.g., behavioural vs. mental). In correctional environments, the management of complex mental health cases often falls to frontline staff who have minimal mental health training and rely on professionals for guidance and direction. Correctional officers at Grand Valley Institution were directed by administrators (vs. intervention staff) not to enter Ashley's cell unless she stopped breathing. The thinking was that staff needed to be careful not to reinforce (reward) her "attention seeking behaviour," behaviour commonly viewed as "manipulative," with secondary gain for the inmate but against the objectives of correctional staff. According to Marsha Linehan (1993), "it is a logical error to assume that if a behaviour has a particular effect, the actor has therefore engaged in the behaviour in order to bring about the effect. The labelling of suicidal behaviour as manipulative, in the absence of an assessment of the actual intent of the behaviour, can have extremely deleterious effects" (p. 61).

What if Ashley had been understood to have had one or more serious mental disorders that constrained her ability to manage her cognitions, emotions, behaviours, and choices? Would the outcome have been different? Across sites and throughout her incarceration, it seems that many custodial staff were effectively blinkered by Ashley's behaviour, losing sight, in the process, of the young girl within. Mental disorders versus behavioural disorders are a distinction without an essential difference; however, for Ashley Smith, the distinction made a big difference and effectively compromised her care and her life.

The adage "Insanity is doing the same thing over and over again and expecting different results" (apocryphally attributed to Albert Einstein) essentially captures the treatment of Ashley Smith. "All the force in the world could not make her [Ashley] healthy or obedient" (*Globe and Mail* editorial, 2012). Of course, we have known for years (centuries) that trying to force behavioural change via physical might or chemical manipulation has limited value and great potential for harm. In a correctional facility, such actions can have a brutalizing effect on the environment – on both staff and other inmates. For all concerned, we must do better, especially for those who are most vulnerable – those with complex mental health needs – cases marked by high comorbidity; deficits in cognitive, intellectual, affective, and/or behavioural functioning; personality and addiction problems; emotional dysregulation and self-injurious behaviour; possible brain injury. Such cases are challenging, and they tend to elicit a negative response from the environment. They require more resources (time, energy, services), more professional skills and ingenuity. Paradoxically, the more complex the case, the more simplified and individualized should be the approach (empathy, respect, authenticity) within an evidence-based format (e.g., cognitive behavioural therapy). "It is much more important to know what kind of person has a disease than what kind of disease a person has" (author unknown).

POSTSCRIPT

September 2006

Ashley's daily battle with staff at NBYC is wearing her down. Ashley's journal entry from 4 September 2006 reflects her desperation:

> If I die then I will never have to worry about upsetting my Mom again.... It would have been nice today to stick my head in the lawn mower blade. F***, I really did have to hold back the urge. Maybe the next time I will give it a try. Most people are scared to die. It can't be any worse then living a life like mine. Being dead I think would just suit me fine. I wonder when the best time to do it would be. I'm not going to get locked because then I'm back on checks and they will expect me to act up then. I will call my Mom before bed and have one more chat. Somehow I have to let her know that none of this is her fault. I don't know why I'm like I am but I know she didn't do it to me. People say there is nothing wrong with me. Honestly I think they need to f***off because they don't know what goes on in my head. When I use to try to hang myself I was just messing around trying to make them care and pay attention. Now it's different. I want them to f***off and leave me alone. It's no longer a joke. It kind of scares [me] to think that

> they might catch me before it's done and then I will be a vegetable for the rest of my life. That's why the most important thing right now is to stay unlocked so they don't think anything is up. It's over. Maybe I will use a brand new pair of socks. Fresh for me. No I don't f***ing deserve a new pair of socks. I will use the old dirty ugly ones. Ha Ha that kind of explains me. Dirty and ugly. Two peas in a pot [*sic*]. F*** THIS WORLD!!! Ha Ha. When [name omitted] told me she took me off fifteen minute checks I almost s**t myself. Can she help me anymore. I should ask her for a razor blade. Maybe she will give me that to [*sic*]. Joke of the day. Ashley Smith is no longer on checks. 12345 what the F*** is the point of being alive.... I can't have another apartment visit because I'm f***ing DEAD! I want to die. I went to court yesterday and I thought he was going to send me to adult! Time is running out. My chances are getting fewer and fewer. F***. I give up! I'm done trying.

CRITICAL THINKING QUESTIONS

1. Based on the case information presented in this chapter, were Ashley's concerns primarily related to that of a mental or a behavioural disorder? Is this distinction important? If so, how is it important for Ashley's case?
2. Self-control (or lack thereof) seems to figure prominently in Ashley's presentation. Would Ashley's trajectory through the mental health and criminal justice systems have differed had she been understood to have deficits in self-control, regardless of diagnoses?
3. Is prison the right place for the Ashley Smiths of the world? For that matter, are prisons the right place for anyone? What are the alternatives to prison for individuals like Ashley Smith, whose behaviour brings them into conflict with the law? What are the alternative to prisons generally?

REFERENCES

American Psychiatric Association. (2013). *Diagnostic and statistical manual of mental disorders* (5th ed.).

Beauchamp, K. G., Lowe, J., Schrader, R. M., Shrestha, S., Aragón, C., Moss, N., Stephen, J. M., & Bakhireva, L. N. (2020). Self-regulation and emotional reactivity in infants with prenatal exposure to opioids and alcohol. *Early Human Development*, *148*. https://doi.org/10.1016/j.earlhumdev.2020.105119

Berkman, E. T., Graham, A. M., & Fisher, P. A. (2012). Training self-control: A domain-general translational neuroscience approach. *Child Development Perspectives*, *6*(4), 374–84. https://doi.org/10.1111/j.1750-8606.2012.00248.x

Caspi, A., Houts, R. M., Belsky, D. W., Goldman-Mellor, S. J., Harrington, H., Israel, S., Meier, M. H., Ramrakha, S., Shalev, I., Poulton, R., & Moffitt, T. E. (2014). The p factor: One general psychopathology factor in the structure of psychiatric disorders? *Clinical Psychological Science: A Journal of the Association for Psychological Science*, *2*(2), 119–37. https://doi.org/10.1177/2167702613497473

Clark, L. A., Cuthbert, B., Lewis-Fernández, R., Narrow, W. E., & Reed, G. M. (2017). Three approaches to understanding and classifying mental disorder: ICD-11, *DSM-5*, and the National Institute of Mental Health's Research Domain Criteria (RDoC). *Psychological Science in the Public Interest*, *18*(2), 72–145. https://doi.org/10.1177/1529100617727266

Correctional Service Canada. (2014). *Coroner's inquest touching the death of Ashley Smith*. https://www.csc-scc.gc.ca/publications/005007-9009-eng.shtml

Correctional Service Canada. (2016, March 14). Priority: Deaths in custody. *Office of the Correctional Investigator*. https://www.oci-bec.gc.ca/cnt/priorities-priorites/deaths-deces-eng.aspx

DeLisi, M., Tostlebe, J., Burgason, K., Heirigs, M., & Vaughn, M. (2018). Self-control versus psychopathy: A head-to-head test of general theories of antisociality. *Youth Violence and Juvenile Justice*, *16*(1), 53–76. https://doi.org/10.1177/1541204016682998

Fifth Estate. (2010, November 12). *Timeline: The life & death of Ashley Smith*. https://www.cbc.ca/fifth/2010-2011/behindthewall/timeline.html

Gillebaart, M. (2018). The "operational" definition of self-control. *Frontiers in Psychology*, *9*. https://doi.org/10.3389/fpsyg.2018.01231

Globe and Mail. (2012, November 1). Editorial: Degrading videos show the futility of criminalizing Ashley Smith. *Globe and Mail*. https://www.theglobeandmail.com/opinion/editorials/degrading-videos-show-the-futility-of-criminalizing-ashley-smith/article4831974/

Gnanavel, S., Sharma, P., Kaushal, P., & Hussain, S. (2019). Attention deficit hyperactivity disorder and comorbidity: A review of literature. *World Journal of Clinical Cases*, *7*(17), 2420–6. https://doi.org/10.12998/wjcc.v7.i17.2420

Gottfredson, M. R., & Hirschi, T. (1990). *A general theory of crime*. Stanford University Press.

Harvey, E. A., Breaux, R. P., & Lugo-Candelas, C. I. (2016). Early development of comorbidity between symptoms of attention-deficit/hyperactivity disorder (ADHD) and oppositional defiant disorder (ODD). *Journal of Abnormal Psychology*, *125*(2), 154–67. https://doi.org/10.1037/abn0000090

Kessler, R. C., Petukhova, M., Sampson, N. A., Zaslavsky, A. M., & Wittchen, H.-U. (2012). Twelve-month and lifetime prevalence and lifetime morbid risk of anxiety and mood disorders in the United States. *International Journal of Methods in Psychiatric Research*, *21*(3), 169–84. https://doi.org/10.1002/mpr.1359

Kreuger, R. F., & Eaton, N. R. (2015). Transdiagnostic factors of mental disorders. *World Psychiatry*, *14*(1), 27–9. https://doi.org/10.1002/wps.20175

Linehan, M. M. (1993). *Cognitive-behavioral treatment of borderline personality disorder*. Guilford Press.

Mischel, W. (2015). *The marshmallow test: Mastering self-control*. Little, Brown and Company.

Olatunji, B. O., & Wolitzky-Taylor, K. B. (2009). Anxiety sensitivity and the anxiety disorders: A meta-analytic review and synthesis. *Psychological Bulletin*, *135*(6), 974–99. https://doi.org/10.1037/a0017428

Ombudsman and Child and Youth Advocate. (2008). *The Ashley Smith report*. https://www.ombudnb.ca/site/images/PDFs/AshleySmith-e.pdf

Plana-Ripoll, O., Pedersen, C. B., Holtz, Y., Benros, M. E., Dalsgaard, S., de Jonge, P., Fan, C. C., Degenhardt, L., Ganna, A., Greve, A. N., Gunn, J., Iburg, K. M., Kessing, L. V., Lee, B. K., Lim, C. C., Mors, O., Nordentoft, M., Prior, A., Roest, A. M., … McGrath, J. J. (2019). Exploring comorbidity within mental disorders among a Danish national population. *JAMA Psychiatry*, *76*(3), 259–70. https://doi.org/10.1001/jamapsychiatry.2018.3658

Sapers, H. (2008). *A preventable death*. Correctional Service Canada. https://www.oci-bec.gc.ca/cnt/rpt/pdf/oth-aut/oth-aut20080620-eng.pdf

Sprott, J. B., & Doob, A. N. (2021, February 23). *Solitary confinement, torture, and Canada's structured intervention units*. https://www.crimsl.utoronto.ca/sites/www.crimsl.utoronto.ca/files/Torture%20Solitary%20SIUs%20%28Sprott%20Doob%2023%20Feb%202021%29.pdf

Taylor, S. (2019). Treating anxiety sensitivity in adults with anxiety and related disorders. In J. A. J. Smits, M. W. Otto, M. B. Powers, & S. O. Baird (Eds.), *The clinician's guide to anxiety sensitivity treatment and assessment* (pp. 55–75). Elsevier Academic Press. https://doi.org/10.1016/B978-0-12-813495-5.00004-8

Urist, J. (2014, September 24). What the marshmallow test really teaches about self-control. *Atlantic*. https://www.theatlantic.com/health/archive/2014/09/what-the-marshmallow-test-really-teaches-about-self-control/380673/

Warnock, F. F., Craig, K. D., Bakeman, R., Castral, T., & Mirlashari, J. (2016). The relationship of prenatal maternal depression or anxiety to maternal caregiving behavior and infant behavior self-regulation during infant heel lance: An ethological time-based study of behavior. *BMC Pregnancy and Childbirth*, *16*(1), 264. https://doi.org/10.1186/s12884-016-1050-5

Willems, W. E., Boesen, N., Li, J., Finkenauer, C., & Bartels, M. (2019). The heritability of self-control: A meta-analysis. *Neuroscience and Biobehavioral Reviews, 100*, 324–34. https://doi.org/10.1016/j.neubiorev.2019.02.012

Zlomislic, D. (2012, November 1). Shocking Ashley Smith video revealed. *Toronto Star*. https://www.thestar.com/news/gta/2012/11/01/shocking_ashley_smith_video_revealed.html

CHAPTER NINE

Great White Sharks and Black Widow Spiders: Two Unlikely Serial Killers

The Cases of Russell Williams and Melissa Shephard

With Jessica Doyle and C.K. MacLean

> They [sharks] lurk out of sight to observe their prey, hunting strategically and learning from previous attempts.
>
> – *Martin et al. (2009)*

> Escape from the black widow spider
> is a miracle as great as art.
> what a web she can weave
> slowly drawing you to her
> she'll embrace you
> then when she's satisfied
> she'll kill you
> still in her embrace
> and suck the blood from you.
>
> – *Charles Bukowski (1977)*

The term "serial killer" often is attributed to FBI Agent Robert Ressler in the 1970s, but credit may more rightly be due Ernst Gennat (1880–1939), chief inspector of the Berlin criminal police (see Babylon Berlin Series, n.d.). Gennat was a man ahead of his time. Besides establishing the first homicide division, which boasted a 95 per cent clearance rate, Gennat introduced the "Murder Car" (a mobile crime scene lab), the "Central Murder Index" (a documentation of various crimes), and the protocol for what is now known as criminal profiling. In a 1930 publication, he coined the term "Serienmörder" (serial killer). Reputedly, Gennat solved almost 300 homicides, including the Butcher of Hanover (Fritz Haarmann) and Vampire of Düsseldorf (Peter Kürten) cases. It seems he was well-suited to his vocation – thorough in approach, dogged in pursuit, with excellent powers of observation and memory, and a "knack" (psychological insight) for dealing with criminals. Gennat's reputation succeeds him as a recurring character in Philip Kerr novels, the Netflix series *Babylon Berlin* (based on Volker Kutscher books), and as a model for detective Karl Lohmann in the films *M* (1931) and *The Testament of Dr. Mabuse* (1933).

The FBI defines "serial killing" as a series of two or more murders, committed as separate events, typically by one offender acting alone (Morton, 2005). It has been suggested that "multiple-event killer" might be a more accurate term given that many cases in the Radford University/FGCU Serial Killer Database (i.e., the most comprehensive worldwide database; Aamodt et al., 2020) are characterized by perpetrators who committed several murders over a long period of time though not necessarily in a series. As of June 2020, the database contains information on 5,334 serial killers and 14,759 victims since 1900, two thirds (68%) of whom are from the United States. The only other countries for which data are available on at least 100 serial killers include England (176), Japan (137), South Africa (123), India (121), and Canada (119). Interestingly, Canada is one of six countries that have the highest percentages of serial killers relative to their populations; the others are the United States, Australia, England, Scotland, and Austria (Aamodt et al., 2020).

Serial killers seem to be a vanishing breed or, at least, a diminishing breed worldwide. In the United States, the number of serial killers peaked at 823 in the 1980s; in Canada, the numbers peaked at 25 between 2000 and 2009. In both countries, the numbers have declined each decade since. The decline has been attributed to advancements in technology, which have improved investigative and reporting practices (e.g., fraud detection) and reduced opportunities for serial killers due to longer prison sentences and fewer easy targets (e.g., hitchhikers; see Aamodt et al., 2020).

Across all time periods, approximately 11 per cent of serial killers have been women. While the percentage has decreased over time, the male-to-female ratio has increased significantly. Whereas females accounted for 38 per cent of serial killers in the 1900s, by the 2000s they accounted for less than 10 per cent (see Aamodt, 2016). The increasing ratio likely reflects the different motivations, modus operandi, and victim choices of male and female serial killers. Females are more likely to kill family members (57%), with poison (53%) or by shooting (20%); their motivation is primarily for financial gain (69%) or out of anger (18%). Males, on the other hand, are more apt to kill strangers (43%) by shooting (36%) or strangling their victims (15%) and are significantly more inclined to torture, mutilate postmortem, and engage in overkill, necrophilia, or vampirism. Males' motivations are primarily for financial gain (29%), enjoyment-rape (27%), anger (18%), or multiple motives (12%). Males' preferred targets are females, whereas females are more inclined to kill both males and females, as well as infants and children (see Aamodt et al., 2020).

Since the beginning of record keeping, serial killers have been more apt to be White (about 50%) than Black (40%), Hispanic (7%), Asian (1%), or Indigenous (1%). The average ages for onset and cessation of serial killing were 28 and 33 years, respectively, although there is a broad age range. The database cites the youngest serial killer as being 6 years of age and the oldest as 72 years of age (Aamodt et al., 2020). Female serial killers have tended to be older (on average by four years) than male serial killers at the start of their series. Serial killers motivated by enjoyment and who committed rape were the oldest at the start of their series (29 years old), whereas serial killers motivated by gang or organized crime related activity were the youngest at the start of their series (24 years old). Generally speaking, the higher the number of kills, the older the serial killer was at the start of their series (Aamodt et al., 2020).

TYPOLOGIES OF MALE SERIAL KILLERS

Typologies of serial killers have been constructed in an effort to identify homogeneous groups or clusters based on offender behaviour, motivation, modus operandi, and victim targets. No typology escapes criticism, least of all the organized-disorganized-mixed trichotomy in the FBI's *Crime Classification Manual* (see Douglas et al., 1992). Readers are encouraged to consult Canter et al. (2004) for a good critique of this typology. Notwithstanding the criticism, this is one of the most widely used typologies for male serial killers and is pertinent to the discussion of Leary et al.'s (2019) research described below. Analysis of victim and crime scene characteristics, along with other forensic evidence, can indicate whether a murder was planned, victim targeted, and conduct controlled (i.e., organized) versus more spontaneous, reckless, and disordered (disorganized), or a mixture of the two. Whereas an organized serial killer may appear socially competent, meticulous, methodical, efficient, and intelligent, a disorganized serial killer may demonstrate poor verbal and social skills, cognitive deficits in planning and execution, and less intelligence. Mixed cases tend to defy these categorical boundaries and may present with features of both (Sellbom & Drislane, 2021). Given both the persistent myth that serial killers are highly intelligent ("evil geniuses") and the paucity of research in this area, Leary et al. (2019) examined intelligence levels in a subset (n = 303) of the Radford University/FGCU Serial Killer Database for whom IQ scores were publicly available – not a random sample. Leary et al. (2019) sought to determine if there was an association between IQ level (high vs. low) and modus operandi (organized vs. disorganized). Findings showed that, on average, this sample of serial killers had lower IQ scores (IQ = 93) than the general population (IQ = 100). On the other hand, the sample included significantly more extreme or infrequent scores than is typically found within a normal distribution. For example, serial killers were five times more likely to have a Very Superior IQ (>130) than the general population (46/303, or 15.2%, vs. 2.2% of a normal distribution) and seven times more likely to have an extremely low IQ (<70) (32/303, or 10.6%, vs. 2.2% of a normal distribution). Overall, higher IQs were associated with organized crime scene characteristics and motivated by enjoyment with or without rape; lower IQs were associated with disorganized crime scene characteristics and motivated by financial gain. In addition, those who enjoyed killing but did not rape had higher IQs than those who enjoyed killing and did rape. Leary et al. (2019) suggested that highly intelligent, organized serial killers resemble criminal psychopaths.

SERIAL KILLERS AND PSYCHOPATHS

People often confuse serial killers and psychopaths. Not all serial killers are psychopaths, and most psychopaths are not serial killers. A psychopath is a person with a specific type of antisocial personality disorder (ASPD) commonly associated with crime and violence. ASPD is characterized by persistent ways of thinking and acting that violate social norms and infringe on the rights of others. Symptoms of ASPD include chronic deceitfulness, impulsivity, recklessness, aggressiveness, irresponsibility, and remorselessness. Despite being recognized in the scientific literature since the 1800s, psychopathy has not been recognized as a clinical diagnosis by the American Psychiatric Association (APA). In the fifth edition of the *Diagnostic and Statistical Manual of Mental Disorders* (*DSM-5*; APA, 2013), however, it is now considered a "specifier" or distinct variant of ASPD. With the alternative model of personality disorders, a clinician can now specify whether the individual meets the criteria for ASPD "with psychopathic traits" (APA, 2013, p. 765). The defining features of psychopathy are low levels of anxiousness and fear of consequences, coupled with high levels of attention seeking, assertiveness, and dominance. While 75–80 per cent of the incarcerated male population would meet the criteria for ASPD, a substantially smaller proportion (15%–20%) would meet the criteria for psychopathy (see Hare, 2003). Psychopathy also must be distinguished from "psychosis," which refers to a major mental disorder characterized by hallucinations, delusions, and thought disorder.

The most frequently used and validated diagnostic tool for assessing psychopathy is the Hare Psychopathy Checklist-Revised (PCL-R; Hare, 2003). As measured by the 20-item PCL-R, psychopathy is a constellation of emotional, interpersonal, and behavioural characteristics. The *emotional* characteristics include shallow affect, lack of conscience or sense of guilt, lack of empathy, failure to accept responsibility for own actions, and egocentricity ("malignant narcissism"). The *interpersonal* characteristics include glibness/superficial charm, grandiose sense of self-worth, pathological lying, and manipulation. The *behavioural* characteristics include poor behavioural controls, repeated violations of social norms, disregard for the law, and criminal versatility. The PCL-R is a semistructured interview designed for use by specially trained clinical forensic psychologists. Using postinterview and file review (including collateral source information), each of the 20 items is scored as 0 (*no evidence for feature*), 1 (*maybe*), or 2 (*evidence for feature*). PCL-R total scores can range from 0 to 40, with scores above 30 typically considered to be indicative of psychopathy. Some countries (e.g., United Kingdom, Scandinavia) employ a lower threshold of 25 (Wynn et al., 2012). Using a cut-off of 30, it has been estimated that about 1 per cent of the general non-offender population would meet the threshold for psychopathy; the average PCL-R score is less than five. Among offender populations, about 15 per cent of males and 10 per cent of females would meet criteria for psychopathy (Babiak & Hare, 2006).

Fox and DeLisi (2018) examined the psychopathy-homicide nexus by conducting a meta-analysis of 22 studies with more than 2,600 homicide offenders (not serial killers) in six countries. Results showed that the average PCL-R score for this sample was 21.1, with scores ranging from 9.4 to 31.5, indicating that all homicide offenders scored higher than the non-offending average and most could be considered at least "moderately" psychopathic. Using a cut-off score of 30, 27.8 per cent met criteria for psychopathy; with a cut-off score of 25, 34.4 per cent met criteria for psychopathy. In other words, about one quarter to one third of homicide offenders could be considered psychopaths. More violent and extreme forms of homicide were associated with higher psychopathy scores, and murders involving sexual and/or sadistic elements were associated with higher average psychopathy scores than less heinous forms of murder. Fox and DeLisi (2018) concluded that psychopathic traits are "a significant risk factor for various forms of lethal violence" (p. 76), and the more extreme the violence, the stronger the relationship between psychopathy and homicide. Hence, while not all murderers are psychopaths and not all psychopaths are murderers, psychopaths commit a disproportionate number of murders and murderers seem to have unusually high levels of psychopathic traits. Perhaps this is not surprising given that features of psychopathy (i.e., callousness, coldness, recklessness, criminal lifestyle) are conducive to committing callous crimes. Lack of empathy would be especially conducive to a person's willingness to inflict pain and suffering, such as in committing a series of sadistic murders (i.e., serial killing). Indeed, Stone (2001) found that 86.5 per cent of serial killers met PCL-R criteria for psychopathy.

GENDER DIFFERENCES IN PSYCHOPATHY

Generally speaking, women report lower PCL-R scores than men, and there are fewer female (vs. male) psychopaths. Kennealy et al. (2007) found that a PCL-R cutoff score of 27 in female offenders was comparable to a score of 30 in male offenders. These findings probably reflect women's lower propensity (vis-à-vis men) for criminal and antisocial behaviour (i.e., the behavioural characteristics of psychopathy). In 2000, Grann compared the PCL-R scores of 36 matched pairs of female and male violent offenders in Sweden and found that men were almost three times more likely to meet the criteria for psychopathy than women (31% vs. 11%). Men scored relatively higher on the "callous/lack of empathy" and "juvenile delinquency" items, whereas women scored relatively higher on the "promiscuous sexual behaviour" item (Grann, 2000). Some studies (e.g., Salekin et al., 1997; Warren et al., 2003) have reported higher rates of psychopathy among female offenders (17% and 16%, respectively, vs. 11%) but they are still lower than rates for men. A more recent study found similar rates of psychopathy for males (20.8%) and females (19.3%) in a sample of forensic psychiatric patients (de Vogel & Lancel, 2016). Males (vs. females) with psychopathy were less likely to commit fraud and offend in response to relational frustration (de Vogel & Lancel, 2016).

In the *DSM-5* (APA, 2013), the psychopathy specifier for ASPD refers to "primary" psychopathy (idiopathic) versus secondary psychopathy. Substantial research with incarcerated males supports this bifurcation (see Porter, 1996). Whereas both primary and secondary psychopathy include high levels of antisocial and criminal behaviour, the two differ in key features. While primary psychopaths typically lack empathy and guilt, appearing callous, cold, and lacking in anxiety, secondary psychopaths may present with high levels of anxiety and emotional distress, hostility, aggression, and impulsive behaviour due to environmental stressors and trauma (see Hicks et al., 2010). Whereas primary psychopathy seems to reflect deficits in self-regulation, such as innate fearlessness and attentional difficulties, which may lead to the development of manipulative and callous traits, secondary psychopathy seems to reflect deficits in emotion regulation arising in response to environmental stressors (e.g., intimate partner violence, low socioeconomic status). Indeed, secondary psychopathy in both men and women has been compared to Borderline Personality Disorder (BPD). BPD is characterized by a pervasive pattern of instability in interpersonal relationships, self-image, mood, and behaviour, with features including extreme negative affect and impulsivity; reactive anger, aggression, and violence; substance abuse; trauma history and PTSD; and suicidal behaviour (see Hicks et al., 2010). Most people diagnosed with BPD are female (80%), and most people diagnosed with ASPD are male (80%). Among incarcerated women, the prevalence of BPD is estimated to be as high as 20 per cent versus 2 per cent in the general non-offender population (Leschied, 2011). There are many possible reasons for such gender disparities. They may reflect implicit bias in the theoretical construction of the disorders, whereby gender-specific characteristics are associated with specific disorders, or gender bias on the part of assessors. The diagnostic criteria may be insufficiently sensitive or they may be true gender differences.

TYPOLOGIES OF FEMALE SERIAL KILLERS

Females don't fit tidily into typologies designed for male serial killers. Kelleher and Kelleher (1998) developed a motivation-based typology based on 50 American female serial killers operating since 1900. "Black Widows" (from the venomous spider known to kill vulnerable mates) represented 26 per cent of their sample, second only to "team killers" who operate with a partner (28%). Kelleher and Kelleher (1998) defined "Black Widows" as females who "systematically murder multiple spouses, partners, other family members, or individuals outside of the family with whom [they have] developed a personal relationship" (p. 19). Regardless of type, the women's preferred weapons of choice were poison (38%), suffocation (18%), lethal injection (12%), shooting (10%), and strangulation (4%). Female (vs. male) serial killers were more "successful," careful, precise, methodical, and subtle in the commission of their crimes. Their success derived from their ability to evade capture twice as long (i.e., an average of 8 years) as males, possibly a reflection of their more covert and subtle methodology (e.g., poison), as well as gender disparities in the criminal justice system. For example, females (vs. males) are significantly more apt to avoid charges and convictions, and twice as likely to avoid incarceration (and execution) if convicted (see Starr, 2012). Newton and French (2008) posited that the absence of sexual motives may account for why female serial killers so often "fly under the radar" where police and journalists are concerned (p. 44).

A recent study by Harrison et al. (2019) compared the behaviours and crimes of female and male serial killers from an evolutionary perspective. They tested a "hunter-gatherer" model of serial murder, proposing that differences between male and female serial killers may be by-products of ancestral tendencies in division of labour. Using a mass media method to collect archival data, they obtained information on 55 male and 55 female serial killers, matched for age of first murder, who committed their crimes in the US between 1856 and 2009. As predicted, males more frequently stalked and "hunted" victims, targeting strangers across dispersed areas, in pursuit of sexual pleasure, power, and thrill (hedonistic motivation). By comparison, females more frequently "gathered" their victims, targeting people who were familiar and in close proximity, in pursuit of profit and resources (e.g., Black Widows). Most males (68%) were single; most females (57%) were in a relationship. For males, the most common method of killing was asphyxiation (47%); for females, poisoning (47%). Twice as many males (vs. females) received the death penalty for their crimes (55% vs. 24%, respectively). In cases where a sobriquet had been assigned by law enforcement, the media, or the public (n = 47), female nicknames seemed more benign and more frequently (73.3%) conveyed the gender of the serial killer (e.g., "Jolly Jane," "Tiger Woman," "Death Row Granny"). Male nicknames more often conveyed the brutality of the crime and the modus operandi (e.g., "The Kansas City Strangler," "The Serial Slasher," "The Tourniquet Killer") than did women's (78.1% vs. 53.3%), although the difference was not significant.

TWO UNLIKELY SERIAL KILLERS

Given what we know from research on serial killers, do most serial killers fit this typology? Two relatively recent Canadian cases suggest that typologies are not as cleanly cut as one might hope. Next, we will review the cases of two unlikely serial killers who, in some ways, defy the stereotype of serial killer but in other ways fit their sex-specific

Figure 9.1. Research shows that sharks resemble serial killers in that they hunt strategically within familiar territory; stalk their victims; target vulnerable prey when unexpected; and hone their skills via experience. Sharks, however, kill to survive.

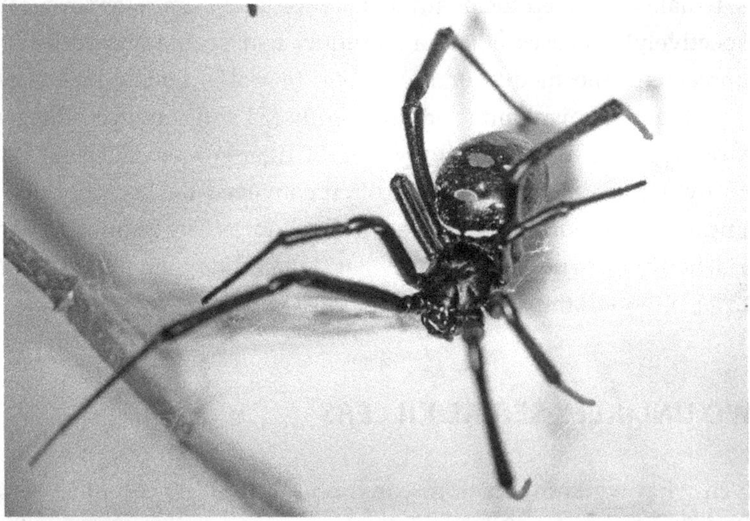

Figure 9.2. Melissa Shephard is a prototypical Black Widow serial killer: a woman who systematically targets vulnerable intimate partners and poisons them for profit. Like her spider namesake, she kills weaker or weakened individuals.

typologies. We can consider which one is more dangerous – the great white shark (see figure 9.1) or the black widow spider (see figure 9.2).

Unlikely Serial Killer #1: Russell Williams

Russell Williams was born in England in 1963, the elder of two boys. His family moved to Canada in 1968, when his father accepted a position as a metallurgist at Chalk River Laboratories in Ontario. His parents, Nonie and Dave Williams, befriended another couple, Jerry and Lynn Sovkas and, within two years, the couples had switched partners. The new family unit (Nonie, Jerry, Russell, and his brother) moved to Scarborough, ON. Reportedly, Williams was a well-behaved, shy, and polite child, who grew into a reliable, self-disciplined, and fastidious teenager (Appleby, 2011). He attended Upper Canada College (UCC), an elite boarding school in Toronto, where he participated in sports, drama, and music. In 1982, he began studies in politics and economics at the University of Toronto's Scarborough campus; he learned to fly at a local municipal airport, and established an intimate relationship with a young woman from Japan. Apparently, when the relationship ended after four years, Williams was quite distressed and withdrew from others and from dating for a number of years. He was a big fan of the movie *Top Gun* and watched it so often that his friend, Jeff Farquhar, grew concerned that he was living out a fantasy based on the Tom Cruise character to win the girl back. Although Williams was known to be private and seemingly lonely, he acquired a reputation for being a prankster – someone inclined to hide in closets and catch his unsuspecting roommates off-guard. With these pranks, Williams seems to have honed his skills in delivering the element of surprise and in the stealthy assembling and disassembling of door locks.

In 1987, Williams enrolled in the Canadian Forces. He received his flying wings in 1990, served as a flying instructor for two years, and was promoted to captain in 1991, the same year he married Mary-Elizabeth Harriman. After a brief posting in Nova Scotia, he was transferred to Ottawa, where he transported high-ranking government officials and foreign dignitaries, such as Queen Elizabeth II, the prime minister, and the governor general of Canada. He was promoted to major in 1994 and obtained a Master of Defence Studies from the Royal Military College in 2004. In June 2004, he was promoted to lieutenant-colonel and, in July, he was appointed commanding officer of CFB Trenton, ON. Following a brief stint in Dubai, United Arab Emirates, he returned to Canada in 2006. At this point, Williams and his wife spent their weekends together in Ottawa but, during the week, Williams lived alone 200 kilometres away in their Tweed, ON, cottage. In 2009, Williams was promoted to colonel. He was viewed as a model military man, a "shining bright star," whose 23-year career trajectory had been rapid and faultless. One year later, he was a convicted serial killer and sadistic sexual predator, sentenced to two concurrent life sentences without parole eligibility for 25 years. Williams's fall from grace rocked the military and shocked the country.

How could such an accomplished military man, in his mid-40s, happily married for 18 years, with no criminal record, suddenly embark on such a heinous crime spree? It appears that Williams began breaking into homes near his Tweed cottage in 2007 and near his Ottawa home in 2008. He would scope out nearby houses and, if no one was home, would enter and steal girls' and women's underwear and other personal items (e.g., bathing suits, family photos, personal items). In the home of one 12-year-old girl, he spent almost three hours taking pictures of himself posing in her underwear, standing in front of a mirror with a pink piece of clothing draped across his erect penis, or lying on the bed masturbating. In the home of a 15-year-old girl, he laid on her bed, masturbating and holding her stuffed bear. In one house, he left a note on the computer ("merci").

Williams's deviant behaviour escalated rapidly. In July 2009, he disrobed and masturbated while watching an unsuspecting woman prepare to take a shower. He then entered through the window and stole a pair of her underwear. After 62 successful break-and-enters, Williams graduated to sexual assault in September 2009. His first victim ("Jane Doe") testified that she was asleep in her Tweed home with her infant daughter when a man broke in, bound and blindfolded her, fondled her breasts, and took pictures of her while she was naked. He remained in the home for two hours, all the while reassuring her that he would not harm her or her baby. A few hours later, he was planning an upcoming charity event with members of the Criminal Intelligence Service of Ontario.

Two weeks later, Williams assaulted Laurie Massicotte in her home. He had surreptitiously visited her home on previous occasions and stolen pieces of lingerie. Massicotte awoke to someone punching her in the head. She was then blindfolded, restrained, and forced to assume pornographic poses while Williams took pictures. He was more concerned with getting pictures than with raping her. At one point in the three hours of terror, Williams apologized to Massicotte for punching her in the head and allowed her to take some aspirin (Appleby, 2011).

In November 2009, Williams stalked and killed 37-year-old Corporal Marie-France Comeau, a military flight attendant based at CFB Trenton, ON. Comeau discovered him hiding in the basement of her home, which he had scouted out in advance. Williams struck Comeau repeatedly with a flashlight and, despite a valiant effort to defend herself, Comeau was eventually subdued and her face wrapped in duct tape. For two hours, Williams repeatedly raped, tortured, and tormented Comeau while videotaping his exploits. Despite her desperate pleas for mercy, Williams sealed the one remaining air hole in the duct tape and watched her die. He then cleaned up the scene and went to work.

In late January 2010, Williams broke into the home of 27-year-old Jessica Lloyd, a resident of Belleville, a community near Tweed. Again, Williams had conducted a reconnaissance mission to the home in advance. He blindfolded Lloyd with duct tape and bound her hands with rope. For three hours, he sexually assaulted her, including forcing her to perform fellatio. Then, he took her to his cottage in Tweed where the torture continued for another 21 hours. After reassuring her that he would not kill her, he clubbed her with his flashlight and strangled her to death. Again, Williams's video documented his exploits. He left her body in the garage and went to work. He disposed of the body three days later. It would not be found until after his arrest.

On 7 February 2010, Williams was interrogated for 10 hours by the Ottawa police. After being presented with the evidence (matching tire treads and footprints), he confessed and provided details of all his crimes – the murders, sexual assaults, and 82 fetish break-ins and burglaries. He directed police to his stockpile of mementos (lingerie) and thousands of images hidden inside his Ottawa home and cottage in Tweed – all neatly stored, catalogued, and concealed. He revealed the whereabouts of Jessica Lloyd's body. On 18 October 2010, Williams pleaded guilty to all charges before the Ontario Superior Court of Justice. As a condition of his plea bargain, evidence of child pornography was not included in the charges. According to some accounts, Williams appeared remorseful for his crimes. In handwritten letters, he offered his apologies to his victims and his wife: "Dearest Mary-Elizabeth, I love you, Sweet [illegible]. I am so sorry for having hurt you like this. I know you'll take good care of sweet Rosie [their cat]. I love you, Russ" (Appleby, 2011, p. 226). See the postscript for Williams's statement in court.

Unlikely Serial Killer #2: Melissa Shephard

> These are the quiet killers. They are every bit as lethal as male serial murderers, but we are seldom aware that they are in our midst because of the low visibility of their killing.
>
> *– Hickey (2016, p. 308)*

Melissa Shephard was born in New Brunswick on 16 May 1935 (Fifth Estate, 2012). At age 17, she met and married Russell Shephard with whom she had two children. Her criminal career seems to have begun in 1970. Between 1970 and 1985, she incurred numerous charges for crimes largely characterized by deceit and duplicity, such as false pretences (9 times), forgery (11 times), uttering threats (9 times), fraud (8 times), and personation with intent. In 1988, Shephard, 53 years old at the time, met widower Gordon Stewart (aged 41), who was selling some real estate. Shephard approached him about buying the property and the two began a romantic relationship the same day. She told Stewart that she was separated from her husband. By 1991, when Shephard killed him with a car, Stewart was bankrupt and despondent. Shephard claimed self-defence, alleging that Stewart was an abusive alcoholic who had sexually assaulted her. Evidence, including her own conduct and the testimony of eyewitnesses, told a different story. For one thing, Shephard had not reported Stewart's death until three hours later and only after she had changed her clothes. Toxicology reports revealed the presence of alcohol and nonprescribed benzodiazepines (Valium and Restoril) in his system, a mixture deemed sufficient to kill. Two eyewitnesses claimed to have witnessed Shephard hitting Stewart with the car, reversing and backing over him. Notwithstanding, Shephard applied for Stewart's benefits from the Department of National Defence and Canada Pension Plan.

In May 1992, Shephard was convicted of manslaughter and sentenced to six years in the Kingston Prison for Women (P4W). While incarcerated, Shephard revealed considerable skill at refurbishing her reputation. Indeed, she reinvented herself as a victim versus a perpetrator. She formed a support group for women and participated in a documentary on battered woman syndrome titled "When Women Kill." Following her release in March 1994, she received government start-up funds to establish a telephone support service called "Project Another Chance," a service designed for women in prison and on parole. In 1997, she published an article, *Prison for Women's Invisible Minority*, about the plight of battered women who are convicted for killing their abuser.

In April 2000, Shephard (then aged 66) met Robert Friedrich (aged 83) at a Christian retreat in Ontario. Friedrich was a retired engineer who had recently lost his wife. Following the retreat, Shephard wrote to Friedrich, including a photo and telling him, "God wants us to be married." One month later, she travelled to Florida to meet him and, within three days, the two were engaged. They married a month later in June 2000. Friedrich's family soon grew concerned about his health (and suspicious of his new bride) due to his repeated hospitalizations. Police records later confirmed that Shephard had procured multiple prescriptions for lorazepam from various physicians. In 2002, Friedrich changed his will to make Shephard the sole beneficiary of all his assets ($100,000). By December of that year, Friedrich was dead of an apparent cardiac arrest. Friedrich's family were unequivocal in holding Shephard responsible, alleging she had abused and murdered their loved one. No autopsy was conducted, and cremation prevented a proper investigation; no charges were laid. Reportedly, "the widow Shephard" continued to receive Friedrich's social security cheques long after his death (Fifth Estate, 2012).

In November 2004, while the RCMP was preparing to charge Shephard for Old Age Security fraud, she was meeting her new romantic interest and prey. Alexander Strategos (aged 73) was a divorced and retired tax collector. The two met online via AmericanSinglesDating .com. Shephard had been trolling the site for a few months and connected with as many as 20 men from across North America. Strategos was physically disabled with diabetes and was seeking a caring woman who would procure groceries and prepare meals. They met in person on 5 November 2004. Shephard moved in that same day, and that night, Strategos was taken to hospital after falling and hitting his head. Over the next two months, Strategos would be hospitalized eight times for similar falls, episodes of confusion, and incoherent speech. At first, his family members were not alarmed, given his history of strokes. After three months of Shephard's "caretaking" (including bedtime feedings of ice cream), Strategos was confined to a nursing home, having signed over power of attorney to Shephard. Not one to waste time, she promptly took over his condominium and emptied his bank accounts. When medical tests revealed the presence of unprescribed drugs (Xanax and Valium) in Strategos's system, police were called. In January 2005, Shephard was arrested and charged with exploitation of the elderly, theft, and forgery. A search of the condominium revealed a suitcase full of pills and Strategos's internet homepage converted to a Christian singles site. She was already trolling for her next victim. In March 2005, Shephard pleaded guilty to seven charges including grand theft and forgery, but not attempted murder. She served five years in a Florida jail and, upon release, was deported to Canada. All things considered (i.e., her extensive criminal history including conviction for manslaughter), this was a rather fortuitous outcome for Melissa Shephard.

After returning to Canada, Shephard faced charges for defrauding the government of over $30,000 for using two different social insurance numbers under the names Melissa Shephard and Melissa Stewart. The charges were later dropped and, in a media interview, Shephard claimed she would "try to behave myself" (Fifth Estate, 2012). In 2011, Shephard (aged 76) assumed residence in a seniors' complex in Nova Scotia where she met widower Fred Weeks (aged 75). In September 2012, the two got married and left for their honeymoon in Newfoundland. Three days into their honeymoon, Weeks fell ill and was taken to hospital. Upon admission, benzodiazepines (not prescribed) were detected in his system and police were notified. Court documents later revealed that police seized two purses containing several bags and bottles of prescription drugs, as well as a handwritten note about the immediate need to get the power of attorney from Melissa Weeks's home in New Glasgow (*Toronto Star*, 2012). Mr. Weeks later claimed little recollection of events following their wedding.

Shephard was arrested on 1 October 2012, and charged with attempted murder and administering a noxious substance. She pleaded guilty to the lesser charges of administering a noxious substance and failing to provide the necessaries of life, but not attempted murder. She was sentenced to three and a half years in prison. The sentencing judge issued the caution that "[p]eople who have contact with this lady should be careful" (CBC News, 2013). She was released in 2016 on several strict conditions, including not to access the internet, which she breached almost monthly for the first six months of her release.

It is difficult to read the Shephard case and not be struck by her repeated good fortune in eluding capture and more severe sanctions. Why such leniency by the criminal justice system? Scott (2005) contends that female (vs. male) serial killers are more apt to "get away with murder" because they are perceived to be more vulnerable and less dangerous – the "gentler sex." Unlike their male counterparts, female serial killers rarely use knives, guns, or other weapons, opting instead for more subtle and covert methods, such as poison or withdrawal of medical assistance. Of course, the "gentler" touch of female serial killers matters little to their prey. The men who fell victim to Melissa Shephard were seeking a companion and caregiver. Caregiving is the traditional domain of females. While a male caregiver might elicit more scepticism, a female would engender more trust. Shephard's last victim, Fred Weeks, was aware of his new bride's history but, as one neighbour suggested, he chose to "live dangerously," clearly underestimating her potential to do harm (see Watt, 2014).

SIMILARITIES AND DIFFERENCES

How similar and different are Russell Williams and Melissa Shephard to each other and how typical are each of their gender type of serial killer? In table 9.1, we have compared Williams and Shephard on a number of variables for which there is research evidence relevant to serial killers.

SUMMARY AND CONCLUSIONS

In his 2011 book, Timothy Appleby describes Russell Williams as "a new kind of monster." At first blush, Williams does appear to be an anomaly – a married man in his mid-40s with a distinguished military

Table 9.1. Similarities and differences between Williams and Shephard

	Russell Williams	Melissa Shephard
Targeted murder victim	Stranger (86%)	Someone familiar (91%) Intimate partners (27%)
Sex profile of victims	Only female (49%)	Only male (20%)
Age of victims	Young adults (49%)	Older adults (49%)
Motive	Sexual, power, thrill (75%)	Financial (52%)
Stalked victim	Yes (65%)	**Yes (4%)**
Murders across provinces/ countries	No (60%)	**Canada & US (18%)**
Education	**University or more (27%)**	High School or less (46%)
IQ level	**High (15%)**	Average (50%)
Occupation	Military personnel[a]	N/A
In a relationship	Yes (32%)	Yes (57%)
Psychopathy[b]	[c]	Psychopathy
Method of killing	Asphyxiation (47%)	Poisoning (47%)
Criminal history	**3–4 years**	**40+ years**
Killing span	**3 months (Mean = 8.69 years)**	**22 years (Mean = 7.78 years)**
Number of victims	2 (Mean = 8.55)	2 (Mean = 6.02)
Type	Organized	Black Widow
Evolutionary type	Hunter	Gatherer
Judicial disposition	Life (55%)	<6 years (64%)
Nickname conveys gender	N/A	*Internet Black Widow* (74%)

Bolded highlights indicate notable differences from the literature.

Note: Percentages in brackets are comparisons with male and female serial killers generally, and are derived from Harrison et al. (2019), Leary et al. (2019), and Aamodt et al. (2020).

[a]In their book *Murder in Plain English*, Arntfield and Denesi (2017) list common occupations of male serial killers. According to their analysis, the top three professional/government serial killer occupations are police/security official, military personnel, and religious official. No percentages are provided.

[b]Stone (2001) found that 86.5 per cent of serial killers met the PCL-R criteria for psychopathy, and another 9 per cent presented with some psychopathic traits. Fox and DeLisi (2018) found that psychopathy levels did not differ between sadistic murderer offenders and serial homicide offenders (both meeting criteria for psychopathy, as measured by the PCL-R).

[c]Russell Williams might not meet the threshold for a diagnosis of psychopathy. His lack of criminal history or socially deviant lifestyle, lack of impulsivity or irresponsibility, and capacity for remorse and guilt (albeit questionable and limited, perhaps) would argue against the diagnosis. On the other hand, his callous disregard for his victims is consistent with psychopathy. See Watt (2014) for a broader discussion of Williams's mental disorder profile.

career. As indicated in table 9.1, his high education and IQ levels, limited criminal history, and abbreviated killing span distinguish Williams from many male serial killers. By many other indicators, however, he appears quite typical of male serial killers, especially highly intelligent, well-organized serial killers. He acts like a "hunter," stalking his victims, catching them unaware, is impelled by hedonistic motivations (sex, power, thrill), and asphyxiates his victims. Williams would not meet the PCL-R threshold for psychopathy, based on antisocial lifestyle factors, but personality traits like lack of empathy and malignant narcissism would elevate his score. What triggered the rapid escalation of Williams's sexually sadistic and murderous behaviour in his mid-40s remains a bit of a mystery. Put another way, what led to his loss of control over the impulses and urges that would have long predated his acting upon them?

Unlike Williams, Melissa Shephard is a prototype for Black Widow serial killers, especially those of the psychopathic type. She acts like a "gatherer" who targets intimate partners and poisons them for profit. Her playbook is methodical and predictable: meet, marry, (steal) money, and murder. Like her spider namesake, she kills weaker or weakened individuals. What makes Shephard an unlikely serial killer is her age. Like Williams, her killing career began later in life although, unlike Williams, she has a long criminal history. Other atypical features of the Shephard case include how she stalked her victims, not in a stealthy but overt way, and how she committed her murderous exploits across borders, outside familiar territory. Of course, when home is your territory for killing, as is the case with Black Widows, territorial boundaries are moot. Shephard is opportunistic and exhibits many of the traits consistent with psychopathy – shallow affect, lack of conscience or sense of guilt, lack of empathy, failure to accept responsibility for own actions, pathological lying, manipulation, disregard for the law, and criminal versatility. Indeed, her pre- and post-offence conduct suggests that she is incorrigible. In all likelihood, only increasing age and debilitation will impede her long-term, well-ingrained pattern of criminal behaviour.

When asked what is most surprising about serial killers, Mike Aamodt replied that it is their variety – so many different types and no one-size-fits-all profile (Justice Clearinghouse, 2018). Leary et al.'s (2019) study of IQ levels in serial killers supports Aamodt's supposition with more extreme IQ scores in each tail of the Gaussian distribution. Researchers from outside of psychology also are intrigued by serial killers. For example, Canadians R.A. Martin (zoology) and Kim Rossmo (criminology and geospatial intelligence), along with South African N. Hammerschlag (who studied at the University of Toronto and now is a marine and atmospheric scientist at the University of Miami), have explored the similarities between great white sharks and serial killers. In a 2009 article published in the *Journal of Zoology*, they reported on their findings from data on 340 predatory interactions between great white sharks and seals. They had investigated the spatial patterns of shark attacks and shark search behaviour. In doing so, they applied geographic profiling – an investigative methodology developed by Rossmo for analysing serial crime. Indeed, Rossmo's analysis of missing sex trade workers in Vancouver was instrumental in the arrest and conviction of Robert "Willie" Pickton in 2002. Martin et al. (2009) discovered that sharks' predatory behaviour was not dissimilar to that of serial killers. Sharks hunt strategically. Where they kill is not random but adheres to territorial boundaries. To maximize efficiency, they stalk their victims, lurking out of sight, neither too close to nor too far away from base. They target vulnerable prey (e.g., young, alone) when light is low so as not to be observed. Sharks typically strike from below (element of surprise) when no competing sharks are in their territory. Older sharks are more successful (stealthier) than younger, smaller sharks, indicating that they learn from experience and hone their hunting technique over time. In Martin et al. (2009), Hammerschlag points out that, if sharks were random, opportunistic killers, they would wait until seals congregated in an area, an approach that is not advisable for either sharks or humans. There is a key difference between sharks and human serial killers, however: sharks kill to survive, to benefit their species; humans kill for thrills.

POSTSCRIPT

Russell Williams: "Your Honour. I stand before you indescribably ashamed. I know the crimes I have committed have traumatized many people. The family and friends of Marie-France Comeau and Jessica Lloyd in particular have suffered and continue to suffer profound, desperate pain and sorrow as a result of what I've done. My assaults of Ms. [name redacted because of publication ban] and Ms. Massicotte have caused them to suffer terribly as well. Numerous victims of the break and enters I have committed have been very seriously distressed as a result of my having so invaded their most intimate privacy. My family, your honour, has been irreparably damaged. The understandable hatred that was expressed yesterday and that has been palpable throughout the week has me recognize that most will find it impossible to accept, but the fact is, I deeply regret what I have done and the harm I know I have caused to many. I committed despicable crimes, your Honour, and in the process betrayed my family, my friends and colleagues and the Canadian Forces" (McArthur & Freeze, 2010).

CRITICAL THINKING QUESTIONS

1. Who do you think is more dangerous – the great white shark (Williams) or the black widow spider (Shephard)?
2. Not all serial killers are psychopaths, and not all psychopaths commit serial homicides. Can a compelling case be made for characterizing Williams and Shephard as psychopaths? What additional factors might have contributed to Williams's and Shephard's late start in their respective, but similarly heinous, criminal behaviours?
3. Like all forms of psychopathology, psychopathy can be conceptualized along a dimension (as opposed to a category). What are the benefits of characterizing psychopathy as a dimension rather than a qualitatively distinct construct? Might Williams's and Shephard's danger have been more readily acknowledged if using a dimensional approach?
4. The marked difference in the criminal justice system's response to Williams's and Shephard's crimes is undeniable. Does this difference represent differential reactions to crimes of a sexual nature, or to crimes committed by males versus females?

REFERENCES

Aamodt, M. (2016, September 4). *Serial killer statistics*. Radford University. http://maamodt.asp.radford.edu/Serial%20Killer%20Information%20Center/Serial%20Killer%20Statistics.pdf

Aamodt, M. G., Leary, T., & Southard, L. (2020). *Radford/FGCU annual report on serial killer statistics: 2020*. Radford University.

American Psychiatric Association. (2013). *Diagnostic and statistical manual of mental disorders* (5th ed.).

Appleby, T. (2011). *A new kind of monster: The secret life and chilling crimes of Colonel Russell Williams.* Vintage Canada.

Arntfield, M., & Denesi, M. (2017). *Murder in plain English.* Prometheus.

Babiak, P., & Hare, R. D. (2006). *Snakes in suits: When psychopaths go to work.* Harper Collins.

Babylon Berlin Series. (n.d.). *Chief inspector Gennat, of the Berlin Police.* http://babylon-berlin-series.blogspot.com/2020/03/chief-inspector-gennat-of-berlin-police.html

Bukowski, C. (1977). *Love is a dog from hell.* Ecco.

Canter, D. V., Laurence, J. A., Alison, E., & Wentink, N. (2004). The organized/disorganized typology of serial murder: Myth or model? *Psychology, Public Policy, and Law, 10*(3), 293–320. https://doi.org/10.1037/1076-8971.10.3.293

CBC News. (2013, June 11). Internet black widow sentenced to 3 ½ years in jail. *CBC News.* https://www.cbc.ca/news/canada/nova-scotia/internet-black-widow-sentenced-to-3-years-in-jail-1.1324946

de Vogel, V., & Lancel, M. (2016). Gender differences in the assessment and manifestation of psychopathy: Results from a multicenter study in forensic psychiatric patients. *International Journal of Forensic Mental Health, 15*(1), 97–110. https://doi.org/10.1080/14999013.2016.1138173

Douglas, J. E., Burgess, A. W., Burgess, A. G., & Ressler, R. K. (1992). *Crime classification manual: A standard system for investigating and classifying violent crime.* Simon and Schuster.

Fifth Estate. (2012, October 5). *Melissa Ann Shepard: Internet Black Widow.* https://www.dailymotion.com/video/x6g0fuf

Fox, B., & DeLisi, M. (2018). Psychopathic killers: A meta-analytic review of the psychopathy-homicide nexus. *Aggression and Violent Behavior, 44,* 67–79. https://doi.org/10.1016/j.avb.2018.11.005

Grann, M. (2000). The PCL-R and gender. *European Journal of Psychological Assessment, 16*(3), 147–9. https://doi.org/10.1027//1015-5759.16.3.147

Hare, R. D. (2003). *Manual for the Hare Psychopathy Checklist-Revised* (2nd ed.). Multi-Health Systems.

Harrison, M. A., Hughes, S. M., & Gott, A. J. (2019). Sex differences in serial killers. *Evolutionary Behavioral Sciences, 13*(4), 295–310. https://doi.org/10.1037/ebs0000157

Hickey, E. W. (2016). *Serial murderers and their victims* (7th ed.). Cengage Learning.

Hicks, B. M., Vaidyanathan, U., & Patrick, C. J. (2010). Validating female psychopathy subtypes: Differences in personality, antisocial and violent behavior, substance abuse, trauma, and mental health. *Personality Disorders: Theory, Research, and Treatment, 1*(1), 38–57. https://doi.org/10.1037/a0018135

Justice Clearinghouse. (2018, March 20). *Serial murder – Separating fact from fiction: An interview with Dr. Michael Aamodt*. https://www.justiceclearinghouse.com/resource/serial-murder-separating-fact-fiction-interview-dr-michael-aamodt/

Kelleher, M. D., & Kelleher, C. L. (1998). *Murder most rare: The female serial killer.* Praeger/Greenwood.

Kennealy, P. J., Hickes, B. M., & Patrick, C. J. (2007). Validity of factors of the Psychopathy Checklist-Revised in female prisoners. *Assessment, 14*(4), 323–40. https://doi.org/10.1177/1073191107305882

Leary, T., Southard, L., & Aamodt, M. (2019). Serial killers and intelligence levels: Variability, patterns, and motivations to kill. *North American Journal of Psychology, 21*(4), 787–800. link.gale.com/apps/doc/A610419152/AONE?u=googlescholar&sid=googleScholar&xid=f08f6792

Leschied, A. W. (2011). *The treatment of incarcerated mentally disordered women offenders: A synthesis of current research*. Public Safety Canada.

Martin, R. A., Rossmo, D. K., & Hammerschlag, N. (2009). Hunting patterns and geographic profiling of white shark predation. *Journal of Zoology, 279*(2), 111–18. https://doi.org/10.1111/j.1469-7998.2009.00586.x

McArthur, G., & Freeze, C. (2010, April 17). Colonel Russell Williams: The making of a mystery man. *Globe and Mail*. https://www.theglobeandmail.com/news/national/colonel-russell-williams-the-making-of-a-mystery-man/article4390081/

Morton, R. J. (Ed.). (2005). *Serial murder: Multi-disciplinary perspectives for investigators*. Behavioral Analysis Unit-2, National Center for the Analysis of Violent Crime. https://www.ojp.gov/ncjrs/virtual-library/abstracts/serial-murder-multi-disciplinary-perspectives-investigators

Newton, M., & French, J. L. (2008). *Criminal investigations: Serial killers.* Chelsea House Infobase Publishing.

Porter, S. (1996). Without conscience or without active conscience? The etiology of psychopathy revisited. *Aggression and Violent Behavior, 1*(2), 179–89. https://doi.org/10.1016/1359-1789(95)00010-0

Salekin, R. T., Rogers, R., & Sewell, K. W. (1997). Construct validity of psychopathy in a female offender sample: A multitrait-multimethod evaluation. *Journal of Abnormal Psychology, 106*(4), 576–85. https://doi.org/10.1037/0021-843X.106.4.576

Scott, H. (2005). *The female serial murderer: A sociological study of homicide and the "gentler sex."* Edwin Mellen.

Sellbom, M., & Drislane, L. A. (2021). The classification of psychopathy. *Aggression and Violent Behavior, 59*. https://doi.org/10.1016/j.avb.2020.101473

Starr, S. B. (2012, August 29). Estimating gender disparities in federal criminal cases. *University of Michigan Law and Economics Research Paper, No. 12-018*. https://doi.org/10.2139/ssrn.2144002

Stone, M. H. (2001). Serial sexual homicide: Biological, psychological, and sociological aspects. *Journal of Personality Disorders, 15*(1), 1–18. https://doi.org/10.1521/pedi.15.1.1.18646

Toronto Star. (2012, October 17). Nova Scotia man who wed 'Black Widow' says marriage not registered. https://www.thestar.com/news/canada/2012/10/17/nova_scotia_man_who_wed_black_widow_says_marriage_not_registered.html

Warren, J. I., Burnette, M. L., South, S. C., Chauhan, P., Bale, R., Friend, R., & Van Patten, I. (2003). Psychopathy in women: Structural modeling and comorbidity. *International Journal of Law and Psychiatry, 26*(3), 223–42. https://doi.org/10.1016/S0160-2527(03)00034-7

Watt, M. C. (2014). *Explorations in forensic psychology: Cases in criminal and abnormal behaviour*. Nelson Education.

Wynn, R., Hoiseth, M. H., & Pettersen, G. (2012). Psychopathy in women: Theoretical and clinical perspectives. *International Journal of Women's Health, 4*, 257–63. https://doi.org/10.2147/IJWH.S25518

CHAPTER TEN

April Is the Cruelest Month: Spree Killing in the Midst of a Pandemic

The Case of Gabriel Wortman

With Jessica Doyle and Laura MacKay

April is the cruelest month, breeding
Lilacs out of the dead land, mixing
Memory and desire, stirring
Dull roots with spring rain

– *T.S. Eliot, "The Wasteland"*

American poet T.S. Eliot penned the line "April is the cruelest month" while recuperating from the 1918 pandemic. The line was meant to suggest that with April comes the dissonance between the promise of renewal and the present reality. In the spring of 2020, Gabriel Wortman may have been "mixing / Memory and desire" (past and future) when he embarked on his murderous rampage. In his wake would lay unimaginable waste. In the span of 13 April hours, Wortman wreaked carnage across seven rural communities and 100+ kilometres of a small Canadian province, a province already reeling from the impact of the COVID-19 pandemic. By 18 April 2020, Nova Scotia (pop. approximately one million) had lost seven people to a deadly virus; by noon the next day, it had lost three times that number to deadly violence.

The 22 murders committed by Wortman marked the deadliest spree killing in Canadian history and added Nova Scotia to locations with similar tragedies committed in the middle of the "cruelest month." For example, in 1993, 19 April marked the fiery end to a 51-day siege of the Branch Davidian compound in Waco, Texas, and its leader, David Koresh. In 1995, 19 April marked the truck bombing of a federal building in Oklahoma City that killed 168 people and injured more than 680 others, an act perpetrated by Timothy McVeigh and Terry Nichols. In 1999, 20 April marked the murders, by Eric Harris and Dylan Klebold, of 12 students and 1 teacher at Columbine High School in Colorado. In 2007, 16 April marked the deadliest school shooting in United States history when Seung-Hui Cho shot and killed 32 people and wounded 17 others at Virginia Polytechnic Institute and State University in Blacksburg, Virginia (see Raquel, 2021).

WHAT HAPPENED ON 18–19 APRIL 2020?

The province of Nova Scotia (see figure 10.1) clings to the mainland of North America by a narrow strip of land called the Isthmus of Chignecto. Approximately 100 kilometres south of the isthmus is the small coastal community of Portapique, home to about 100 year-round residents and twice as many summer residents. Gabriel Wortman, a prosperous denturist from the larger metropolitan area of Halifax-Dartmouth, was a summer resident who maintained two large properties in Portapique. When the province declared a state of emergency on 22 March 2020, due to the COVID-19 pandemic, Wortman was required to cease operation of his two denture clinics in Halifax-Dartmouth and he began to spend more time in Portapique.

The chronology of events outlined below has been gleaned from media reports and highly redacted police warrants and undertakings. As this chapter is being written, an independent public enquiry – the Mass Casualty Commission – is examining what happened on 18–19 April 2020, and is expected to release findings and recommendations by 30 March 2023. It is hoped that the enquiry will elucidate some of the many questions that remain outstanding about this tragedy.

On the night of Saturday, 18 April 2020, Gabriel Wortman (aged 51) and his girlfriend, Lisa Banfield (aged 51), were at their residence at 123 Orchard Beach Drive ("the warehouse") in Portapique, NS. They were celebrating their 19th anniversary, drinking and video chatting

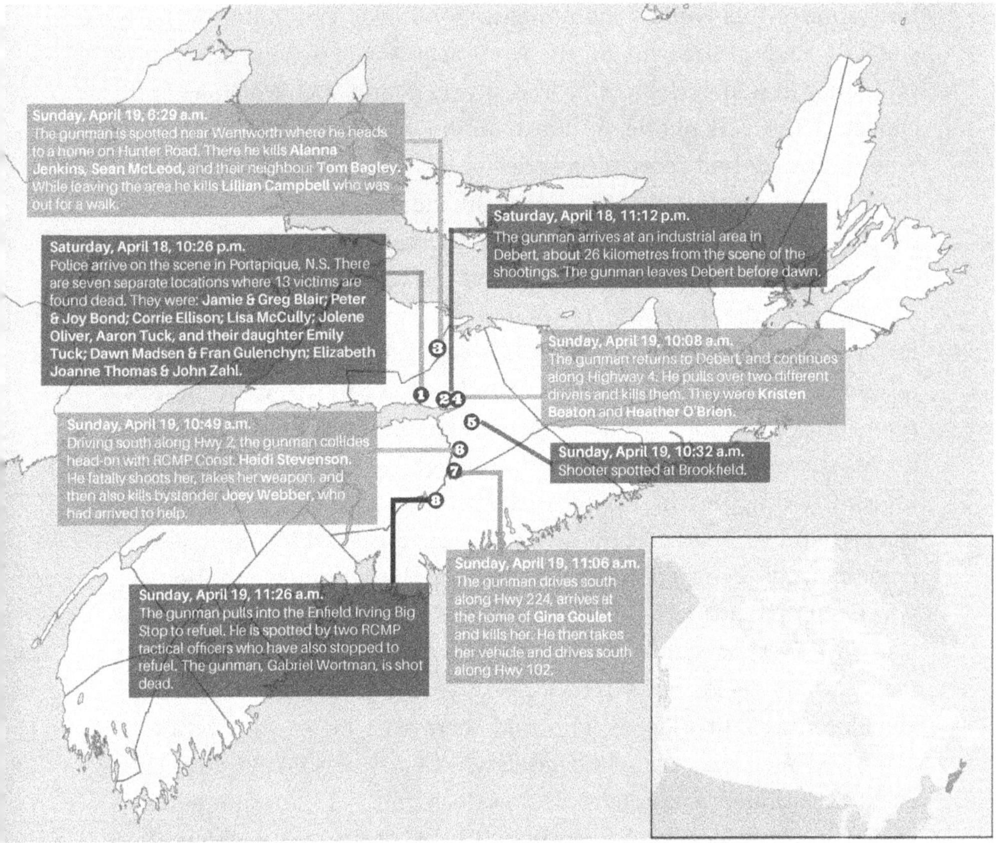

Sunday, April 19, 6:29 a.m.
The gunman is spotted near Wentworth where he heads to a home on Hunter Road. There he kills Alanna Jenkins, Sean McLeod, and their neighbour Tom Bagley. While leaving the area he kills Lillian Campbell who was out for a walk.
Saturday, April 18, 10:26 p.m.
Police arrive on the scene in Portapique, N.S. There are seven separate locations where 13 victims are found dead. They were: Jamie & Greg Blair; Peter & Joy Bond; Corrie Ellison; Lisa McCully; Jolene Oliver, Aaron Tuck, and their daughter Emily Tuck; Dawn Madsen & Fran Gulenchyn; Elizabeth Joanne Thomas & John Zahl.
Saturday, April 18, 11:12 p.m.
The gunman arrives at an industrial area in Debert, about 26 kilometres from the scene of the shootings. The gunman leaves Debert before dawn.
Sunday, April 19, 10:08 a.m.
The gunman returns to Debert and continues along Highway 4. He pulls over two different drivers and kills them. They were Kristen Beaton and Heather O'Brien.
Sunday, April 19, 10:49 a.m.
Driving south along Hwy 2, the gunman collides head-on with RCMP Const. Heidi Stevenson. He fatally shoots her, takes her weapon, and then also kills bystander Joey Webber, who had arrived to help.
Sunday, April 19, 10:32 a.m.
Shooter spotted at Brookfield.
Sunday, April 19, 11:06 a.m.
The gunman drives south along Hwy 224, arrives at the home of Gina Goulet and kills her. He then takes her vehicle and drives south along Hwy 102.
Sunday, April 19, 11:26 a.m.
The gunman pulls into the Enfield Irving Big Stop to refuel. He is spotted by two RCMP tactical officers who have also stopped to refuel. The gunman, Gabriel Wortman, is shot dead.
1
2
3
4
5
6
7
8

Figure 10.1. In the span of 13 hours in April 2020, Gabriel Wortman wreaked carnage across seven rural communities and 100+ kilometres of Nova Scotia. In the end, 22 people lay dead.
Picture courtesy of Ryanne Chisholm.

with friends, and discussing the prospect of confirming their commitment in the upcoming year. Around 8 p.m., Banfield texted a picture of the "happy" couple. Soon after, an argument ensued, which quickly escalated to Wortman assaulting Banfield and handcuffing her inside one of the four decommissioned police cars that he owned. Banfield managed to escape to the woods where she remained until early the next morning (the 19th), when she appeared at the home of Portapique resident Leon Joudrey, who called 911.

Banfield told RCMP officers that Wortman had "poured gasoline all inside the cottage" (200 Portapique Beach Road) and the "warehouse," as well as the remaining vehicles. She reported that she saw several firearms on the front seat of the decommissioned police car in which she had been restrained, and that Wortman had smashed her cell phone. While Banfield had been hiding in the woods, RCMP had received a series of 911 calls about shootings in the Portapique area. RCMP arrived in the area around 10:30 p.m. on that Saturday night to encounter several houses on fire. Confusion reigned supreme as police and area residents struggled to comprehend the mayhem. Two individuals who drove to the area to inspect the fires noticed a "police car" parked in the driveway of one of the burning buildings. The "police car" drew up beside them. Thinking the "police officer" wanted to talk to them, the driver started to roll down his window but then noticed the "police officer" had a firearm aimed at them. Fortunately, the occupants ducked and escaped certain death, although one later found a bullet embedded in his coat. They told police they thought the shooter was Gabriel Wortman.

As the RCMP began searching the area, they discovered a deceased male and female in one house and, next door, a deceased female. They encountered Clint Ellison, who told them that he and his brother, Cory, had been walking on the beach when Cory was fatally shot. The RCMP continued to discover deceased victims – 13 Portapique residents, in total, including a family with a 17-year-old daughter. The carnage continued the following day, when nine others were murdered, including an RCMP officer, two VON nurses, an elementary school teacher, two correctional managers, business people, and a fellow denturist. Some of the victims were known to Wortman; others were simply in the wrong place at the wrong time.

Reports (e.g., search warrants) describe one witness's account of the murder of RCMP Constable Heidi Stevenson on Sunday morning. The witness reported hearing a popping sound that turned out to be gunfire. The witness saw "two Mountie cars smashed together" – Wortman's decommissioned police car and Stevenson's cruiser – and a "bald man was doing a lot of gunfire." The witness "thought the bald guy was a Mountie because you could see the shirt.... But it seemed funny ... that the bald man would be shooting at a Mountie." The witness dialed 911 and then saw a grey SUV pull up near the two smashed police cruisers and a man get out to offer assistance. That man, Joseph

Webber, was shot dead. The "bald man" then opened the trunk of the fake police car, set it on fire, pulled items out of both his car and Stevenson's cruiser, climbed into Webber's SUV, and fled the scene.

Wortman's spree finally ended when police serendipitously discovered him procuring gas in Enfield, NS, and shot and killed him. In his vehicle, police found two loaded semi-automatic rifles, two loaded handguns, and Stevenson's Smith & Wesson 9-mm service pistol. It was later revealed that Wortman never had a firearms licence.

WHO WERE THE VICTIMS?

Wortman's victims included neighbours (12), acquaintances (3), random strangers (6), and police officers (1); 14 were female (including one teenager) and 8 were male. The neighbours included Jamie and Greg Blair, Peter and Joy Bond, Dawn and Frank Gulenchyn, Elizabeth and John Thomas, Jolene Oliver and Aaron Tuck and their 17-year-old daughter, Emily. Some people – Cory Ellison and Lisa McCully – were killed when responding to the fires at their neighbours' homes. Two of the female victims – Kristen Beaton and Heather O'Brien – were VON nurses on their way to work in separate vehicles. Lillian Hyslop was out for her morning walk. Alanna Jenkins and Sean McLeod were correctional managers with Correctional Service Canada and casual acquaintances of Wortman. Reports indicate that Wortman killed their two dogs and remained at the site for three hours. Alanna and Sean's good friend and neighbour, Tom Bagley, was shot while responding to their house fire. Wortman also shot Gina Goulet's German Shepherd dog; Goulet was someone he knew through her work as a denturist. RCMP Constable Heidi Stevenson died in the line of duty while trying to stop Wortman; Joey Webber died trying to offer her assistance. Apparently, Jamie and Greg Blair hosted the online gathering that Wortman and Banfield joined on 18 April, where the couple's dispute may have begun.

Many of Wortman's relationships, including with family and neighbours, were marked by conflict and often revolved around contentious property disputes. At the time of the shooting, he owned six properties in Nova Scotia, including three in Portapique. A fourth Portapique property had triggered a rancorous dispute with his uncle,

Glynn Wortman, and ultimately was purchased by Lisa McCully, one of his 22 victims. It seems that Wortman would try to purchase his neighbours' properties and, when they declined, he would become irate. His tendency to harbour grudges meant that the disputes seldom were resolved. Elizabeth and John Thomas purchased their Portapique home from a couple, one of whom was Brenda Forbes, who had been harassed and intimidated by Wortman for years. This dispute arose when Brenda reported Wortman to police for domestic violence after Lisa Banfield had arrived at the Forbes's home begging for help but too scared to report him. Wortman confronted Brenda about her intrusion into his life and then would drive by and stare at her house. Brenda attributed the death of one of their pets to Wortman. She contends that Wortman's actions compelled them to sell their home and leave the area. When Elizabeth and John Thomas bought the house, they were not aware that Wortman wanted to buy the Forbes's property. On 18 April 2020, Wortman set ablaze all the properties that he owned and had coveted as if to say that if he couldn't have them, no one would.

WHAT DO WE KNOW ABOUT SPREE KILLERS AND KILLINGS?

The FBI defines spree killing as the murder of two or more people in a short span of time with no "cooling off" period (see Morton, 2005). A recent book, *Spree Killers: Practical Classifications for Law Enforcement and Criminology* (Safaric and Ramsland, 2020), explains the history of the term "spree" and how it has long been a "muddled concept" (p. xviii) with varying definitions and poor delineation from serial and mass murder. Safaric and Ramsland (2020) offer a number of distinctions (see table 10.1).

Unlike Mellor (2013), who essentially conflates mass and spree killing by using the term "rampage," Safaric and Ramsland (2020) provide a compelling rationale for retaining the three distinct categories of multicide (multiple murder). They argue that "even if differences are subtle, they can be important for intervention, investigative management, and risk evaluation" (p. 15). Safaric and Ramsland (2020) analysed data on 359 cases involving 419 killers across 43 countries

Table 10.1. Three major multicide categories

Mass Murder	Spree Killing	Serial Killers
4+ fatalities One basic locale Short-lived incident	3+ murders 2+ locations Murders occur fairly close in times Key precipitating incident fuels continuing need to kill	2+ murders 2+ separate incidents

Table 10.2. Four of the seven main categories of spree killers

	Anger & Revenge	Deadly Desperation	Mental Illness	Mixed Multicides
Prevalence	110/359 30.6%	26/359 7.2%	42/359 11.7%	26/359 7.2%
Victims	Targeted & random-opportunistic	Random & targeted	Random (vs. targeted)	Spree/Mass crossover
Essence	Know who they want to kill but generalized need to act out or punish	Seem to "snap"; Grudge = trigger? "Nothing to lose" Must keep moving until stopped ~1:3 die	Reactive (vs. planned) ~31% suicide incl. suicide by cop	72% suicidal
Examples	Paul Devoe III	Jean-Claude Romand	Ernst August Wagner	Martin Bryant (see below)

and proposed seven main categories of spree killers. These included anger and revenge, mission, desperation, mental illness, robbery and thrill, movement in tight locations, and mixed multicides (spree crossovers). Across categories, perpetrators are almost exclusively White males operating alone. Of their seven categories, the four described in table 10.2 seem most relevant to Wortman; of these four, sample cases from Deadly Desperation and Mixed Multicides seem particularly fitting.

In 2007, Paul Devoe III (aged 43) killed six people over the course of two days while travelling between Texas and New York; his spree was triggered by a verbal altercation with an ex-girlfriend. In 1913, Ernst August Wagner killed 14 people (including his wife and 4 children) and wounded 11 in one day before being beaten unconscious by German villagers. Wagner had a history of depression as a boy and, as an adult, developed paranoia. In January 1993, 38-year-old Jean-Claude Romand killed his wife, children, and parents. Eighteen years earlier, Romand had dropped out of medical school and, to spare himself the humiliation of failure, he created a persona as a successful medical professional and researcher for the World Health Organization. He maintained the elaborate ruse and also devised an investment fraud. When his father-in-law grew suspicious in 1988, he "accidentally" fell to his death. Four years later, everyone (mistress, friends, associates) was growing suspicious. To save himself from exposure as a personal fraud (rather than for criminal fraud), he murdered six people. Like Romand, Wortman may have shared the fundamental narcissistic fear of exposure. Wortman has been described as a man with many secrets and parallel lives, including in his love life. Apparently, he used false IDs and fake names, made illegal secret purchases of RCMP uniforms, and drove illegal unregistered road-ready replica RCMP cars. He also purchased illegal unregistered guns and ammunition. Secret lives can be hard to maintain.

Focusing on Canadian multiple murderers, Lee Mellor's 2013 book, *Rampage*, proposed a preliminary typology of spree killers (N = 12) with four categories: Utilitarian (natural-born killer, n = 4), Exterminator (mission killer, n = 3), Signature (resembles a serial killer, n = 3), and Marauder (n = 0); two were unclassified. At the time, Mellor cited no Canadian examples of Marauder. The typology is preliminary, and the sample size is too small to draw grand conclusions. While Wortman resembles the Utilitarian insofar as his spree seemed to be the actions of an angry and arrogant man who "uses violent means to solve a situation that causes frustration to his inflated ego" (Mellor, 2013), he seems quite unlike the examples Mellor cites for this category – Gregory McMaster (in 1978) and Jesse Imeson (in 2007). In some ways, Wortman seems more like the Marauder. According to Mellor (2013), characteristics of Marauders include usually single; student, unemployed, or employed in menial work; lack social skills; shunned for being "weird"; not psychopathic; no pattern of substance misuse; no history of suicide attempts, although more than half commit suicide or suicide-by-cop at the end of the spree; their spree killing does not always have a triggering event but often involves vehicles and firearms; initial victims are known and later victims are selected at random; no sexual assault or signature at crime scene; usually does not spend time with victims; possible motivations include psychosis or other severe mental health problems, including anger and revenge; warning signs include mental health deterioration, obsession with firearms, and nonserious criminal history.

Given that no Canadian cases fit this category, Mellor (2013) cites a number of international examples of Marauders: Mark O. Barton (GA), Derrick Bird (UK), Michael Ryan (UK), Maksim Gelman (NY), Michael McLendon (AL), and Martin Bryant (AU). Like serial killers (see chapter 9), spree killers are a diverse group, so it is unlikely to find two with identical features. Wortman seems to share some characteristics with Martin Bryant, who perpetrated one of the world's deadliest shooting sprees, in Port Arthur, Tasmania, in April 1996, killing 35 people and injuring 23 others. Bryant was subsequently diagnosed with conduct disorder, attention deficit hyperactivity disorder, and autism spectrum disorder. Wortman's academic and professional success, however, suggests a much higher IQ than Bryant's, which was assessed as being 66.

Although not specific to spree killing, Duwe (2004) contends that mass and serial murderers are equally common. While serial killers are not noted for their suicidal tendencies, Duwe (2004) found that almost one third (29%) of 909 mass murderers between 1909 and 1999 either killed themselves after the murders or were killed by police, also known as "suicide by cop" or "suicide by proxy" (see Duwe, 2009; Edelstein, 2014). Adam Lankford's research (2015) shows that a shooter's likelihood of committing suicide or suicide by cop is 1.16 times higher for each additional victim, after controlling for the shooter's age and sex. Lankford suggests that those with the most rage toward others (and the most victims) also would feel the most guilt and shame about their crimes; they would therefore be more likely to engage in "self-punishment" (suicide). Besides killing more victims, those who arm themselves with more weapons may be fueled by a greater sense of "injustice" and hopelessness. For each additional weapon that a rampage killer brings to the crime scene, their likelihood of dying is 1.76 times higher. Lankford (2015) posits that those who target random victims in open spaces may be the most universally hopeless. Committing a murderous rampage against random victims in open venues suggests a response to failures of social control at a societal (vs. more localized) level (Capellan, 2016).

WHAT DO WE KNOW ABOUT GABRIEL WORTMAN?

> The mind of the murderer is a complex mechanism which requires a great deal of unraveling to give us an idea of what leads a person to commit murder.
>
> – *Podolsky (1954)*

Psychosocial History

Wortman was born on 5 July 1968, to Paul (b. 1946) and Evelyn (Scott) Wortman (b. < 1946). It is not clear if he was born in Moncton, NB, Stoney Creek, ON, or possibly Cleveland, OH. We do know that he was living in Fitchburg, MA, at age 20 months when his brother was born on 28 March 1970, and then relinquished for adoption. The circumstances of the adoption are described in an article published in the *Spencer New Leader* (see Franco, 2010). The article recounts the twists and turns by which the Wortmans were reunited with their second son, Jeff Samuelson, on his 40th birthday celebration. As the story goes, the Wortmans were married with a 20-month-old son (Gabriel) and living in Fitchburg at the time of Samuelson's birth. It seems the pregnancy was unexpected, and the couple decided that they could not financially support a second child. In the article, Evelyn Wortman recalls crying and having a nurse ask her if she wanted to keep him, assuring her they could help her. "But I knew in my heart that I had to let him go." Apparently, she used a false name when arranging the adoption "because she was scared about the situation." The false name made it difficult for Jeff Samuelson (and his wife Robin) to find his birth parents. Paul and Evelyn first started searching for their relinquished son in 1994. Interestingly, the article mentions that Gabriel was not present for the reunion and that "family members said they agreed it would be best if the two met on a separate occasion." Some have proposed a causal connection between Gabriel Wortman expressing (to his Uncle Glynn) a desire to kill his parents and his parents' reunion with his brother. Apparently, Jeff Samuelson is a carpenter by trade and independent contractor. There exist at least two YouTube videos detailing his work in restoring and raising up a bell tower in the historical district of his hometown, North Brookfield, MA, and featuring his wife (see Rad-X Pictures, n.d.-a, n.d.-b).

Gabriel Wortman was raised as an only child within a large extended family. His father, Paul, was the second of five sons born to Stan and Doris (Scott) Wortman, in Moncton, NB. The other sons in order were Neil (PhD education, lives in Sackville, NB, with his wife, Annette), Alan Ross (retired RCMP, lives in Ottawa, ON), Glynn (lives in a Moncton nursing home), and Chris (retired RCMP, lives in Chilliwack, BC). Gabriel's grandmother, Doris (Scott) Wortman, hailed from Stratford, ON. Apparently, Gabriel attended his Uncle Chris's RCMP graduation in 1982. Paul and Evelyn Wortman married in December 1967 and, sometime around 1968–9, moved to Fitchburg, MA. It is not clear what prompted the move although, at the time, Fitchburg was the headquarters for Assumption Life, one of Moncton's biggest employers. It seems the couple (or at least Paul) moved around a bit in those years and also lived in Cleveland, OH, and Phoenix, AZ.

By May 1974, Paul and Evelyn were back in Canada and living in Riverview, NB, where Gabriel attended Riverview High School. His 1986 yearbook entry describes him as being most likely seen performing wheelies on his dirt bike and skiing with friends. According to the entry, he didn't like the cold weather or English class, and "Gabe's future may include being an RCMP officer." The latter was perhaps not surprising, given that two of his paternal uncles were active Royal Canadian Mounted Police officers. Between 1987 and 1991, Wortman attended the University of New Brunswick (UNB) in Fredericton where he studied to be a mortician and reportedly earned "UNB's asshole loser of the year award." Fellow UNB student, Candy Palmater (recently deceased Canadian lawyer, comedian, broadcaster), claimed that people at UNB were not nice to Wortman and that "he was the brunt of everybody's jokes." She says she befriended him because he "needed a friend" even though "most of my friends didn't like him." According to Palmater, "Gabriel always had a sadness about him, but I was so shocked to hear that he'd hurt other people" (Canadian Press, 2020).

Following graduation from UNB, it seems that Wortman completed a mortician's course at the Nova Scotia Community College in Kentville (1993–5). In the aftermath of the spree killing, it was reported that, by 1995, Gabriel Wortman had completed an 18-month mortician course but had not become licensed and his records had been transferred back to New Brunswick. Donnie Walker, of Walkers

Funeral Home in Dartmouth, NS, told the media that he remembers employing Wortman as a mortician assistant in the mid-1990s. A former girlfriend shared on social media that she remembered him holding down two jobs at the same time: mortician and denturist. It is not entirely clear how Wortman transitioned from a middle-class mortician assistant in the mid-1990s to a licensed dental health professional, prosperous entrepreneur, and multiple property owner by 2001. Wortman seems to have embraced his career as a denturist. He operated two denture clinics in the Halifax Regional Municipality – the Atlantic Denture Clinic in Dartmouth, NS, and one in the Halifax area. By 2001, court records show that he was living in the rooms above his denturist clinic at 193 Portland Street, Dartmouth, which would remain his main residence until he died in April 2020. Sometime around 2002–4, Wortman started buying up properties in Portapique, NS. He would spend more and more time in Portapique as years went on. His uncle, Glynn Wortman, purchased property next door in 2010.

Relationship History

In the aftermath of the spree killing, a former girlfriend of Wortman's shared a story with the media: "When I heard his name and saw his face on TV my heart sunk to my feet." Explaining that "I got chills thinking what, why would he kill all those people? He was a good person, he worked hard, people liked him, it just makes no sense, I can't believe he did what he did." She said that during their year and a half together, "I saw no guns, there was no aggression or violence." She said, "The only time I ever saw him really mad or angry, was when we broke up and I moved to western Canada," adding, "We had talked about getting married, having kids, he wanted me to work at his denture clinic." She continued, "I was young (22) and wasn't ready to settle down." Talking through tears, she said, "It is like yesterday, I remember what he told me, when I broke up with him and that I was leaving the province." Explaining that it gave her chills thinking about it, she added, "He was angry at me, he told me that I was making a huge mistake … that one day I would regret that I could have had all of this" (Braid, 2020).

Between 1996 and 2001, Gabriel Wortman was married to Corinna B. Kincaid, and owned a house in Dartmouth and a residence at Lawrencetown Beach, NS. One blog site (40 Gallons and a Mule, 2020) claims that Kincaid was familiar with Wortman's penchant to guard his "toys" and to intimidate children who ventured too close to his front door. Lisa Banfield also was married between 1996 and 2001 to a man named Mike Wagner. At some point, Wortman and Banfield met, divorced their spouses, and proceeded to work and live together until 18 April 2020 (40 Gallons and a Mule, 2020). Various reports attest to the relationship being marked by intimate partner violence (IPV). Brenda Forbes, a former neighbour of Wortman's, claims that she and her husband "weren't even in that house for a year when (Wortman's partner) ran over to my house one day saying that (he) was beating her up and she was scared. She wanted to hide somewhere because he had blocked her car with his truck so she couldn't get out. But she managed to get away from the house." Forbes told her there were services for women experiencing domestic violence, but the woman refused, claiming that Wortman would kill her. Forbes reported Wortman's interpersonal violence and cache of firearms to the RCMP in 2013. Apparently, she told police about other reports that Gabriel Wortman had held Banfield down and beaten her behind one of the properties he owned in Portapique (Tutton & McKenzie-Sutter, 2020). Forbes claimed that the RCMP told her their hands were tied unless Banfield reported the abuse. Forbes maintained that Banfield would never do that. "(He) had her under his thumb." On another occasion, after Forbes told Banfield that Wortman had other women over when she was working in the city, Banfield apparently confronted him. Wortman then dragged Banfield to Forbes's door and, when Forbes told him she was only telling the truth, he dragged Banfield away again. After that, every day for four days, Wortman would stop his truck outside Forbes's house and get out and stare at the house for about 30 minutes. When Forbes's husband returned from a work trip to Africa, she was adamant that they had to move. In 2014 they moved to Halifax but, because Forbes still did not feel safe, they moved out west three years later. Like Brenda Forbes, Aaron Tuck, another neighbour, had expressed concerns about Wortman, especially about his extensive collection of four police cruisers and a number of firearms. He even expressed his concerns to Wortman.

Banfield had been named executor to Wortman's will and sole heir to his assets, which included homes worth $712,000 and personal belongings worth $500,000. His four-page handwritten will, dated 2011, outlined his wishes to be buried quietly at the cemetery in Portapique, NS, "in a Hudson Bay blanket" with no service, obituary, or public notice. Banfield renounced the will, saying they had never been married (see Tutton & McKenzie-Sutter, May 12, 2020).

Criminal History

Although Wortman had no formal criminal record, he had a long criminal history – violence (domestic and other), criminal associates, and criminal activities. Indeed, it appears that he straddled the line between legal and illegal for most of his life. Table 10.3 shows a timeline of some of Wortman's noteworthy conflicts and criminal activities, some of which are documented formally and some of which are more anecdotal. The timeline demonstrates a pattern of violence and antisocial conduct going back 20 years but does not include allegations related to gun and other contraband smuggling.

Mental Health History

Wortman's mental health history is not known, and his mental status in April 2020 can only be inferred from witness reports. Many witnesses described Wortman to police as abusive, controlling, vengeful, and increasingly paranoid in the days leading up to the spree. COVID-19 lockdown meant his clinics were closed and he would have more time on his hands to drink and to ruminate – indeed, more time to refine his ruminations and for his paranoia to blossom. The lockdown also increased victims' vulnerability in that most Nova Scotians were sheltering in place from a virus – "sitting ducks" for a violent rampage.

It seems alcohol was a factor in many of the incidents recounted above. Wortman's father, Paul, has claimed that his son was a heavy drinker. For a busy man known to struggle with alcohol misuse, the loss of routine, work, and income would have had a destabilizing influence. According to RCMP Superintendent Darren Campbell (see McMillan, 2020), people close to Wortman claimed that he was very concerned about COVID-19. Campbell claimed there were no

Table 10.3. Timeline of Wortman's conflicts and criminal activities

DATE	INCIDENT
2000s	Firearms licence revoked for nine months. Dispute with Halifax Regional Municipality over signage for his business.
29 Oct. 2001	"Assault of 15-year-old male Matthew Meagher who was waiting for a bus outside Wortman's denture clinic in Dartmouth, NS. Suddenly Matt hears a man yelling 'you're too close to my door' and scared, he starts walking to the next bus stop a long way away. Bang, a fist hits the back of his head, *hard*. Stunned, the child turns around and the man, reeking of alcohol, grabs his shirt and begins whaling at his face, Matt cries out in pain time and again. Suddenly another man arrives from out of nowhere and hits Matt on the back of his head with what feels like a crowbar. Now he's on the ground, thoroughly stunned and the men together begin kicking him into the dark street and its oncoming traffic. Wortman changed plea to guilty October 7, 2002 and received 9 months' probation with conditions, including no contact with the victim, no firearms or any prohibited weapon, and to 'attend for assessment, counselling and programs for anger management,' as directed by his probation officer. A spokesperson with Nova Scotia's Department of Justice would not confirm whether the probation officer directed Wortman to take any such programs and if so, whether he completed them. The department also wouldn't provide any details about the probation officer" (Global News, April 2020).
May 2004	In 2004, Wortman took a dispute with his tenant, Stephen Zinck, at a Mineville, NS, property to the province's residential tenancies board. Wortman said the tenant was restricting him from cleaning up and making repairs to the property, while the tenant argued he still owned it, according to court documents. A residential tenancies officer ruled in favour of Wortman, terminating the tenancy and ordering that he "be given vacant possession" of the property.
~2005?	Lisa Banfield reports IPV to Brenda Forbes.
"Years earlier," < 2007	On a family vacation in Cuba, a vacation paid for by Wortman, he beat his father, Paul Wortman, unconscious. Paul claims that the assault was unprovoked but fueled by alcohol.
2007	Wortman told his uncle Glynn that he was going to Moncton to "shoot" and "kill" his parents. Paul Wortman reported the incident to the RCMP in Bible Hill, NS, and, apparently, an officer interviewed Gabriel Wortman who denied his father's claims. Alcohol may have been a factor.
~ 2010	Portapique neighbour John Hudson told Canadian Press the gunman was extremely jealous about Lisa Banfield, whom he locked out of the house about 10 years ago after an argument and, at one point, took the tires off her car so she couldn't leave.

(continued)

Table 10.3. Timeline of Wortman's conflicts and criminal activities (*continued*)

DATE	INCIDENT
June–July 2010	Small Claims Court: Lisa Banfield v. Gerry Blackwood & Park Jewellery Limited – dispute over diamond ring (allegedly purchased by Gabriel Wortman for $9,000 in February 2010 but may have been bequeathed to Wortman by Tom Evans) and allegedly damaged by jeweller; claim dismissed.
May 2011	Police agencies across Nova Scotia were warned that Wortman had a stash of guns and had said he wanted "to kill a cop." An unnamed source had approached Truro police with detailed information about where Wortman kept his guns, including that he may have been transporting a handgun between his home in Dartmouth and his cottage in Portapique (Donkin & McMillan, 2020).
2013	Brenda Forbes reports to RCMP an incident of IPV that she heard about from Glynn Wortman; Forbes tell RCMP about Wortman's history of IPV and cache of weapons; IPV witnessed (and recently confirmed) by Glynn Wortman; he and two other men saw Wortman hold his girlfriend down on the ground, screaming at her as he choked her. Glynn Wortman did not want to get involved, claiming, "No way, because (the gunman) already told me that he's killed somebody in the United States. He'll kill me if I say anything."
2015	Property/financial dispute with Glynn Wortman, Gabriel Wortman's uncle. Glynn took him to the Nova Scotia Supreme Court over a dispute involving a Portapique property (135 Orchid Drive) that he bought with the help of bridge financing from Gabriel. A judge ordered that all proceeds from the sale of the property should be the sole property of Glynn Wortman.
12 Feb. 2020	Wortman had an unusual interaction with two Dartmouth police officers whereby he confronted them about their illegal parking in his denture clinic lot and refused them access to their undercover police car. The matter was resolved peacefully, but Wortman later bragged about the incident to *Frank Magazine* and provided photographs. Later that day, he was caught speeding in Portapique.
18–19 April 2020	Spree killing.
Date unknown	In Portapique, he burned down a building with a neighbour's property in it, threatened another neighbour with his guns if he dared step on his property, and raged against a neighbour with similar stonework to his.

indications that Wortman was plotting an attack, but he had liquidated his assets and was stockpiling food and gas: "We do know that the gunman was very paranoid. We also know some would describe him as a survivalist." It seems "he wanted to be prepared in the event of things not working in the way they normally would." Apparently, Wortman didn't think it was safe to leave savings in the bank.

According to Campbell, witnesses described Wortman as "hardworking" with "many holdings" (approximately $700,000 in six properties and $500,000 in personal investments). Apparently, no evidence confirmed that Wortman was linked to organized crime or worked as a confidential informant for police.

Paul Wortman has claimed in interviews that his son never had friends. Candy Palmater's testimony about Wortman's time at UNB would seem to support that supposition. One notable exception seems to have been his relationship with Tom R. Evans. Evans was a disgraced Fredericton criminal lawyer, 19 years Wortman's senior. Wortman claimed they had been friends "since childhood." While the exact nature of their relationship has garnered speculation, Evans seems to have been a mentor to Wortman. Before his death in November 2009, Evans made Wortman the executor of his estate and left him all his possessions, including two properties and a semiautomatic rifle that Wortman used in the killing spree. Evans's will and other documents released after his death detailed a long and complicated business relationship between Wortman and Evans that, apparently, explained some of Wortman's wealth. It seems the two often travelled to the United States together and smuggled cigarettes, alcohol, and maybe other illegal items across the border using a sailboat Evans owned and that Wortman inherited. Evans was forced to relinquish his right to practise law following a string of criminal offences (sexual assault of a minor, firearms), liquor control convictions, and an alleged association with a Colombian cartel in the late 1980s and early 1990s (see Richie et al., 2021).

Possible Pathway to a Spree Killing

In June 2020, the RCMP revealed the initial findings of a psychological autopsy on Wortman. The report characterized him as being an "injustice collector," someone inclined to hold on to conflicts until they boil over with rage or violence. The term was coined by Mary Ellen O'Toole (2014), a former FBI profiler, and is commonly used by police and criminologists. Tracy Vaillancourt, Canada Research Chair in Children's Mental Health and Violence Prevention at the University of Ottawa, explains: "It's a way of seeing the world" (MacDonald, 2020a, 2020b). Criminologist Michael Arntfield says injustice collectors are disproportionately middle-aged males who have tabulated an inventory of every perceived slight over the course of their lives, nurturing grudges for years. Vaillancourt prefers the term "anger rumination," which is sometimes linked to growing up in a hostile environment and suggests that it can result in a "threat-sensitive brain that is always looking for evidence to confirm the world is against them" (Canadian Press, 2020). Arntfield, who works with the Canadian Association of Threat Assessment Professionals, claims that obsessions with police or the military and access to firearms can be risk factors for violence and intimate partner violence.

Evidence indicates that Gabriel Wortman would fit the labels of "injustice collector" or "grievance collector." While these are catchy terms, such labels are more tautological than explanatory. What do they really tell us about the 51-year-old denturist who wreaked so much havoc and horror? On the other hand, many witnesses, including Lisa Banfield, talked about Wortman's mounting paranoia in the days leading up to the spree, and the role of paranoia as a factor in violence is supported by a substantive body of clinical research.

Paranoia literally means "beside self" and, in ancient times, referred to insanity, madness, and delirium (Lewis, 1970). In the 19th century it came to refer to psychiatric disorders characterized by persistent delusions. Delusions are unshakeable beliefs that are not amenable to change, preoccupying and distressing, and not shared by other people (Freeman, 2007). Individuals with persecutory or paranoid delusions believe that harm is going to occur due to someone else's bad intentions. The two distinguishing features of paranoia are the anticipation of a potential threat and the intentionality attributed to the "other," which distinguishes paranoia from nonpersecutory anxiety. Although delusions are commonly associated with psychosis, increasingly such beliefs are recognized as being on a continuum with normal experiences (see Freeman, 2007; Martinelli et al., 2013).

From a cognitive perspective, Beck and Rector (2002) proposed that delusional thinking is characterized by three cognitive biases: *egocentric* (irrelevant events construed as personally meaningful; a feature of narcissism), *externalizing* (internal sensations or symptoms attributed to external agents), and *intentionalizing* (attributing malevolent intentions to other people's behaviours; a feature of holding grudges). Compounding the problem is defective reality testing, which prevents the individual from reevaluating and rejecting erroneous conclusions. As a result, the individual is vulnerable to cognitive distortions, such as *selective abstraction* (i.e., focusing on a detail taken out of context), *overgeneralization* (i.e., drawing grand conclusions from limited data), and *arbitrary inferences* (i.e., drawing a conclusion without sufficient evidence). Such distortions tend to fuel negative affect (anxiety, depression, anger).

Cognitive-behavioural models of persecutory delusions have been linked to certain coping strategies, such as catastrophic worry and rumination, in maintaining paranoid beliefs. Rumination is characterized by repetitive and perseverative thinking about the causes, consequences, and symptoms of one's negative affect. Research shows that rumination is associated with the onset and severity of depression, exacerbation of anxious mood following anxiety induction, and the maintenance of intrusive memories posttrauma, anger following provocation, and paranoid ideation (see Martinelli et al., 2013).

According to Beck and Rector (2002), most persecutory delusions arise from a fear of being observed or harmed in some way. Recent findings from the attachment literature support this view. A meta-analysis conducted by Lavin et al. (2019) found that paranoia was significantly related to anxious attachment in 11 of 12 studies. A similar review by Murphy et al. (2020) of 26 studies found paranoia to be significantly associated with both attachment anxiety and attachment avoidance.

Insecure attachment has been linked to intimate partner violence (Dutton et al., 2013), childhood and adolescent aggression (Fearon et al., 2010), and mediation of the link between childhood adversity and paranoia (Sitko et al., 2014). Attachment theory (Bowlby, 1988) posits that early in life we develop enduring expectancies about how others will respond when we are in distress based on our experiences with primary caregivers. Consistent and responsive care fosters secure attachment; less responsive and/or rejecting behaviour fosters internalized negative views of self and others. The ways in which emotions are shared, communicated, and regulated in the context of the attachment relationship contribute to individual differences in attachment security (Cassidy, 2008). Individuals high in attachment avoidance use *deactivating* strategies (e.g., overregulating or suppressing emotional displays) in an effort to reduce their need for proximity, avoid intimacy, and ensure their emotional independence, while individuals high in attachment anxiety use *hyperactivating* strategies (e.g., exaggerating their emotional displays) in an effort to have their attachment needs met (i.e., keep a partner close; Mikulincer & Shaver, 2018). Individuals exposed to interpersonal abuse in childhood may show disorganized or dual attachment, meaning they could present the conflicting characteristics of both anxious and avoidant attachment together with an inconsistent pattern of responses to attachment-related stimuli (see Paetzold et al., 2015).

About 10–15 per cent of the population might exhibit features of disorganized attachment. These features can develop in situations where the behaviour of the primary caretaker is extreme, erratic, frightening, intrusive, or perhaps passive (e.g., postpartum depression). This results in a child having no effective strategy for getting their needs met. This can lead to features in childhood such as limited sense of safety in relationships; inability to self-regulate emotion; or seeming dazed, dissociated, and confused. In adulthood, it might be revealed by fears of intimacy, proximity, showing vulnerability; extreme rage or anger response to confrontation or threat; little or no empathy for others (including children); limited understanding of personal boundaries; and a tendency to respond in contradictory ways (see Paetzold et al., 2015). Personality traits associated with disorganized attachment include *negative affectivity* (i.e., prone to a wide range of intense negative emotions), *detachment* (i.e., avoidance of socioemotional experience, restricted affect, anhedonia), *antagonism* (i.e., anger, aggression, callousness, grandiosity), and *psychoticism* (i.e., odd and eccentric cognitions and behaviours). These personality traits commonly comprise personality disorders, such as borderline, antisocial, narcissistic, and paranoid (American Psychiatric Association, 2013, p. 779).

Paranoia has long been recognized as a feature in mass killings. According to Dietz (1986), "paranoid symptoms of some kind have been evidenced by all men who have killed ten or more people in a single incident in the United States" (p. 480). More recently, Knoll and Meloy (2014, p. 237) proposed a four-stage model of cognitive progression in paranoid thinking among mass murderers: (a) *Perception* of threat, expectation of persecution, and inadequacy of self; (b) *Contemplation* that threat is strong and self is unlikely to prevail; (c) *Decision* – inability to accept, compromise, or seek assistance, abandonment of hope, and increased reliance on revenge fantasy; and (d) *Resolution*, which involves retreat to omnipotent fantasy and/or obliteration of reality, to plan and execute targeted murders.

Substantive evidence gleaned from media reports, as well as witness testimony included in RCMP search warrants (see Tutton & McKenzie-Sutter, 2020), supports the role of paranoid thinking in Wortman's case. It seems Wortman perceived many threats in the days leading up to 18 April 2020. Numerous people attested to his mounting anxiety and paranoia about the COVID-19 pandemic. Apparently, he was "consumed" by the pandemic, increasingly paranoid about the virus and potential financial collapse. Not trusting that the social structure could withstand the pandemic, he started liquidating his assets and withdrew $475,000 in cash. Lisa Banfield told police it was like he was "preparing for the end of the world" (Doucette, 2021). In the weeks leading up to the spree killing, Wortman had been stockpiling gas and food. As someone inclined to "survivalist" tendencies, Wortman had long stockpiled weapons (including assault rifles) and equipped his various properties with elaborate security systems, secret rooms, false walls, and hiding places.

Wortman also stockpiled perceived insults and injuries. His many territorial disputes with family, neighbours, and even strangers (see the incident with Matthew Meagher in 2001) centred around a need to own, control, and fend off threat – a siege or fortress mentality. His paranoia pervaded his relationships and fueled his perpetration of extreme violence against his partner, father, and others. Clearly, Wortman viewed the world as a dangerous place, rendered more so by a potentially deadly virus. Consistent with the four-stage model of cognitive progression in paranoid thinking, Wortman's paranoia in the weeks leading up to the spree killing was increasing, while his confidence in being able to meet the threat was decreasing. This would have activated omnipotent fantasies of how to regain control and/or obliterate reality, while exacting revenge for perceived wrongs – the narcissistic wounds that fuel narcissistic rage (Krizan & Johar, 2015).

Wortman thought it fitting that he execute his plan while fully attired in a fake RCMP uniform and driving a replica RCMP car, one of four such vehicles he owned. In high school, he had aspired to become a police officer (two of his paternal uncles were RCMP members). As an adult, he acquired a habit of collecting police memorabilia even though, as his partner claimed, he disliked law enforcement (perhaps because the RCMP declined his application to join); he "thought he was better than them." He may have anticipated that one of his victims would be an RCMP officer.

SUMMARY AND CONCLUSIONS

As this chapter was being written, an independent public enquiry – the Mass Casualty Commission (MCC) – was convening in Halifax, NS, to examine what happened on 18–19 April 2020. The commission released its findings and recommendations on the 31 March 2023. While serving to address many questions surrounding this tragedy, other questions remain. Could this tragedy have been predicted? Was it planned? At what point could it have been averted? Certainly, our best chance of preventing future tragedies of this kind is to learn from this one. (For more information on the MCC's final report see https://masscasualtycommission.ca/final-report/.)

Gabriel Wortman appears to have been moving toward a catastrophe for a long time, perhaps all his life. He grew up as an only child in a home that seems to have been marked by dysfunction, turmoil, abuse, and secrets (e.g., that he had a brother). His formative years left their imprint in a disorganized attachment style, meaning that he would have lacked strategies for establishing and maintaining healthy relationships. Attachment styles feed into our developing personality (i.e., enduring ways of perceiving self, others, and the world) and, in Wortman's case, fed the development of prominent paranoid, narcissistic, antisocial, and psychopathic traits. Each trait, in its own way, would serve to protect his fragile self-esteem. Each trait would be maintained and cultivated by a closed cognitive system characterized by biased ways of thinking (e.g., overpersonalizing, overgeneralizing) and faulty attributions (e.g., perceiving ill intentions where none existed). Wortman would have lacked an effective mechanism for reality testing.

Throughout his life, Wortman struggled to fit in (earning monikers like "UNB's asshole loser of the year award"), struggled to be liked (see Candy Palmater's comment), and struggled to succeed (denied the family tradition of being an RCMP member). No doubt he struggled with mental health issues (e.g., depression, substance abuse, paranoia, hopelessness). Despite these challenges, Wortman seems to have prospered financially and professionally, all the while dabbling in criminal activities and straddling the line between prosocial and antisocial activities. No matter what he achieved or acquired, however, it never seemed to be enough to assuage his need for esteem nor his resentment of others. With the COVID-19 pandemic came new challenges – shuttered businesses, financial concerns, more idle time, more use of alcohol, all fertile ground for mounting paranoia.

Moving toward a catastrophe is different than premeditating a catastrophe. In the words of *Professor T* (Season 1, Episode 2), "The mind of the murderer is formed in increments." As Schmidt et al. (1977) suggested, it is a chain of events leading to a moment in time when a "homicidal paroxysm" is unleashed and, once unleashed, is impossible to stop. (See the description of the Malaysian phenomenon *amok* in the note below.) Gabriel Wortman, like other spree killers, was alienated from his society. Motivated by revenge for injuries and insults, perceived or real, he sought to make his transgressors suffer; to show them what a force he is to be reckoned with. Better to be reviled than ignored or humiliated. Marauder spree killings tend to end in suicide or suicide by cop because the spree is the end game. By embarking on the spree, the killer has effectively abandoned his connection to life. He expects to die, to "slip the surly bonds of earth," as it were.

Wortman must have felt a sense of a relief on 18 April to finally unleash all the anger, frustration, and rage that he had accumulated over time. It must have been cathartic to finally give full vent to his spleen. The expression "to vent one's spleen" derives from the ancient Greeks' theory of humoural medicine whereby the spleen's black bile was linked to melancholy (pervasive sadness) and believed to be the cause of foul moods. To be splenetic means to be bad-tempered or spiteful (an injustice collector). In *Julius Caesar,* Brutus cautions Cassius that "you shall digest the venom of your spleen, though it do split you." Ultimately, Wortman was consumed by the venom of his own spleen.

The reference to venting one's spleen was, perhaps, never so well-articulated than by Polish author Zygmunt Miloszewski. In *A Grain of Truth* (2013), Miloszewski distinguishes between so-called crimes of passion and crimes of spleen:

> [S]pleen reflects a certain mental and psychological state.... Embitterment, frustration, sneering underlined with negative energy and a sense of one's own lack of fulfillment, being on the "No" side, and constant dissatisfaction.... Spleen builds up slowly, in small droplets. At first it just makes itself felt occasionally, then it changes into an unpleasant ache, it starts getting in the way of life, becoming an ever more irritating noise in the background.... except that we cannot remove the causes of spleen in a single procedure. Few people know how to deal with it, and meanwhile each moment adds another droplet of vexing emotion.... Finally, we feel nothing but bile, there is nothing else inside us, we would do anything to get rid of it, not to feel that bitterness any more, that humiliation. This is the moment when the sufferer casts everything to the Devil. Some cast themselves off – a bridge or the top of a tall building. Others cast themselves at someone – a wife, a father, a brother.... His actions appear to be the fulfillment of a plan and of course revenge is the motive that suggests itself. (pp. 196–201)

Miloszewski could have been describing Gabriel Wortman.

CRITICAL THINKING QUESTIONS

1. What is it about April that makes it the "cruelest month"? Are there specific social and psychological factors that coalesce during this transitional season that may have been particularly influential in Wortman's deadly spree?
2. How big a factor did COVID-19 play in Wortman's psychopathology? Would we have otherwise seen his psychopathology manifest in such a deadly way? Put differently, was it only a matter of time before he "snapped"?

3. The idea of someone perpetrating violence while impersonating a police officer is particularly unsettling. Do you think there should be stricter laws around procuring police memorabilia, police cars, and police uniforms?

NOTE

In the Malay world, a spree killing phenomenon known as *amok* (i.e., uncontrolled outburst of murderous aggression; see Schmidt et al., 1977) has been documented since the middle of the 16th century. The amok has four stages: (a) brooding and withdrawal; (b) homicidal paroxysm; (c) continuation of homicidal behaviour until killed, restrained, or falling into a stupor of exhaustion; and (d) complete or partial amnesia. It has evolved from a culturally sanctioned means of self-expression to an indictable offence in the 19th century, to an indication of psychopathology in the 20th century, with motives including infidelity by spouse, loss of money in gambling, and an injury or insult (real or fancied). "The wounding of an inflated self-esteem is over compensated for by the amok's need to rehabilitate himself in the eyes of his fellow men" (Schmidt et al., 1977, p. 266). Van Brero (1897) explains that the Malay is hypersensitive to minor sufferings or humiliations, "has little self-control, attaches small value to human life and is always armed" (p. 266). Schmidt et al. (1977) examined 24 cases of amok and confirmed insult, jealousy, and paranoid ideation as factors in almost half.

REFERENCES

American Psychiatric Association. (2013). *Diagnostic and statistical manual of mental disorders* (5th ed.).

Beck, A. T., & Rector, N. A. (2002). Delusions: A cognitive perspective. *Journal of Cognitive Psychotherapy*, *16*(4), 455–68. https://doi.org/10.1891/jcop.16.4.455.52522

Bowlby, J. (1988). *A secure base.* Basic Books.

Braid, T. (2020). Nova Scotia shooting rampage by 'quiet man,' Gabriel Wortman, now worst one in Canadian history. *Todayville Edmonton.* https://www.todayville.com/edmonton/173324-2/

Canadian Press. (2020a, April 20). Who was Gabriel Wortman, the denturist behind the Nova Scotia mass shooting? *National Post.* https://nationalpost.com/news/who-was-gabriel-wortman-the-denturist-behind-the-nova-scotia-mass-shooting

Canadian Press. (2020b, June 8). Seeking to explain Nova Scotia shootings: Inside the "threat-sensitive brain." *Rocky Mountain Outlook.* https://www.rmoutlook.com/national-news/seeking-to-explain-nova-scotia-shootings-inside-the-threat-sensitive-brain-2416755

Capellan, J. A. (2016). *Looking upstream: A sociological investigation of mass public shootings* (Publication No. 9-2016) [Doctoral dissertation, City University of New York]. ProQuest Dissertations Publishing.

Cassidy, J. (2008). The nature of the child's ties. In J. Cassidy & P. R. Shaver (Eds.), *Handbook of attachment: Theory, research, and clinical applications* (pp. 3–22). Guilford Press.

Dietz, P. (1986). Mass, serial and sensational homicides. *Bulletin of the New York Academy of Medicine*, *62*(5), 477–91. https://pubmed.ncbi.nlm.nih.gov/3461857/

Donkin, K., & McMillan, E. (2020, May 29). 2011 tip that warned N.S. gunman wanted to "kill a cop" was purged from RCMP records. *CBC News*. https://www.cbc.ca/news/canada/nova-scotia/ns-gunman-2011-warning-1.5589277

Doucette, K. (2021, February 20). Nova Scotia mass shooter's spouse worried he was looking for her when killings began. *CTV News*. https://atlantic.ctvnews.ca/nova-scotia-mass-shooter-s-spouse-worried-he-was-looking-for-her-when-killings-began-1.5317367?cache=tzbrsjtr%3FautoPlay%3Dtrue

Dutton, D. G., White, K. R., & Fogarty, D. (2013). Paranoid thinking in mass shooters. *Aggression and Violent Behaviour*, *18*(5), 548–53. https://doi.org/10.1016/j.avb.2013.07.012

Duwe, G. (2004). The patterns and prevalence of mass murder in twentieth-century America. *Justice Quarterly*, *21*(4), 729–61. https://doi.org/10.1080/07418820400095971

Duwe, G. (2009). Sliding down the slippery slope of multiple murder: Examining offending specialization in a sample of male multiple homicide offenders. *Homicide Studies*, *13*(2), 189–92. https://doi.org/10.1177/1088767909334760

Edelstein, A. (2014). Re-thinking typologies of multiple murders: The missing category of serial-mass murder and its theoretical and practical implications. *International Journal of Emergency Mental Health and Human Resilience*, *16*(2), 350–3. https://www.academia.edu/21087051/Re_Thinking_Typologies_of_multiple_murder

Fearon, R. P., Bakermans-Kranenburg, M. J., van IJzendoorn, M. H., Lapsley, A.-M., & Roisman, G. I. (2010). The significance of insecure attachment and disorganization in the development of children's externalizing behavior: A meta-analytic study. *Child Development*, *81*(2), 435–56. https://doi.org/10.1111/j.1467-8624.2009.01405.x

40 Gallons and a Mule. (2020, June 20). *Laurie Cuvelier came within a penstroke of preventing Wortman killings*. https://40gallonsandamule.blogspot.com/2020/06/laurie-cuvelier-came-within-penstroke.html

Franco, T. A. (2010, April 9). Dreams do come true. *Spencer New Leader*, *34*(15), A1–A9. https://linpub.blob.core.windows.net/pdf/2/SPE.2010.04.09.pdf

Freeman, D. (2007). Suspicious minds: The psychology of persecutory delusions. *Clinical Psychology Review*, *27*(4), 425–57. https://doi.org/10.1016/j.cpr.2006.10.004

Global News. (2020, April 21). Nova Scotia gunman charged with assaulting a 15-year-old boy in 2001. https://globalnews.ca/news/6848816/nova-scotia-shooting-gunman-assault-2001/

Knoll, J. L., & Meloy, J. R. (2014). Mass murder and the violent paranoid spectrum. *Psychiatric Annals*, *44*(5), 236–43. https://doi.org/10.3928/00485713-20140502-07

Krizan, Z., & Johar, O. (2015). Narcissistic rage revisited. *Journal of Personality and Social Psychology*, *108*(5), 784–801. https://doi.org/10.1037/pspp0000013

Lankford, A. (2015). Mass murderers in the United States: Predictors of offender deaths. *Journal of Forensic Psychiatry & Psychology*, *26*(5), 586–600. https://doi.org/10.1080/14789949.2015.1054858

Lavin, R., Bucci, S., Varese, F., & Berry, K. (2019). The relationship between insecure attachment and paranoia in psychosis: A systematic literature review. *British Journal of Clinical Psychology*, *59*(1), 39–65. https://doi.org/10.1111/bjc.12231

Lewis, A. (1970). Paranoia and paranoid: A historical perspective. *Psychological Medicine*, *1*(1), 2–12. https://doi.org/10.1017/S0033291700039969

MacDonald, M. (2020a, June 8). Nova Scotia shootings: The psychology of an "injustice collector." *Global News*. https://globalnews.ca/news/7038278/ns-shootings-injustice-collecter/

MacDonald, M. (2020b, June 8). Seeking to explain Nova Scotia mass shootings: Inside the "threat-sensitive brain." *Globe and Mail*. https://www.theglobeandmail.com/canada/article-seeking-to-explain-nova-scotia-mass-shootings-inside-the-threat/

Martinelli, C., Cavanagh, K., & Dudley, R. E. J. (2013). The impact of rumination on State Paranoid Ideation in a nonclinical sample. *Behavior Therapy*, *44*(3), 385–94. https://doi.org/10.1016/j.beth.2013.02.002

McMillan, E. (2020, June 29). N.S. gunman liquidated assets, stockpiled gas and food due to COVID-19 fears, RCMP say. *CBC News*. https://www.cbc.ca/news/canada/nova-scotia/mass-shooting-rcmp-investigation-gunman-covid-paranoia-1.5628184

Mellor, L. (2013). *Rampage: Canadian mass murder and spree killing*. Dundurn Press.

Mikulincer, M., & Shaver, P. R. (2018). Attachment theory as a framework for studying relationship dynamics and functioning. In A. L. Vangelisti & D. Perlman (Eds.), *The Cambridge handbook of personal relationships* (pp. 175–85). Cambridge University Press. https://doi.org/10.1017/9781316417867.015

Miloszewski, Z. (2013). *A grain of truth*. Bitter Lemon Press.

Morton, R. J. (Ed.). (2005). *Serial murder: Multi-disciplinary perspectives for investigators*. Behavioral Analysis Unit-2, National Center for the Analysis of Violent Crime. https://www.ojp.gov/ncjrs/virtual-library/abstracts/serial-murder-multi-disciplinary-perspectives-investigators

Murphy, R., Goodall, K., & Woodrow, A. (2020). The relationship between attachment insecurity and experiences on the paranoia continuum: A meta-analysis. *British Journal of Clinical Psychology, 59*(3), 290–318. https://doi.org/10.1111/bjc.12247

O'Toole, M. E. (2014). The dangerous injustice collector: Behaviors of someone who never forgets, never forgives, never lets go, and strikes back! *Violence and Gender, 1*, 97–9. https://www.doi.org/10.1089/vio.2014.1509

Paetzold, R. L., Rholes, W. S., & Kohn, J. L. (2015). Disorganized attachment in adulthood: Theory, measurement, and implications for romantic relationships. *Review of General Psychology, 19*(2), 146–56. https://doi.org/10.1037/gpr0000042

Podolsky, E. (1954). Mind of the murderer. *Journal of Criminal Law & Criminology, 45*(1), 48–50. https://doi.org/10.2307/1139303

Rad-X Pictures. (n.d.-a). *Jeff Samuelson, a New Hope* [Video]. YouTube. https://youtu.be/oBMA-brxNXQ

Rad-X Pictures. (n.d.-b). *Jeff Samuelson, a Second Chapter* [Video]. YouTube. https://www.youtube.com/watch?v=e5RTHvCA_jM

Raquel, S. (2021, March 30). The killing season: Why is April full of mass murder? https://www.shaylaraquel.com/blog/thekillingseason

Richie, S., Kress, A., & Hill, B. (2021, January 18). Episode 7: "To my dear friend Gabriel Wortman" – How the Nova Scotia killer got his guns and wealth. *13 Hours Podcast*. https://globalnews.ca/news/7578586/to-my-dear-friend-gabriel-wortman-how-the-nova-scotia-killer-got-his-guns-and-wealth/

Safaric, M., & Ramsland, K. (2020). *Spree killers: Practical classifications for law enforcement and criminology*. Taylor & Francis.

Schmidt, K., Hill, L., & Guthrie, G. (1977). Running amok. *International Journal of Social Psychiatry, 23*(4), 263–74. https://doi.org/10.1177/002076407702300405

Sitko, K., Bentall, R. P., Shevlin, M., O'Sullivan, N., & Sellwood, W. (2014). Associations between specific psychotic symptoms and specific childhood adversities are mediated by attachment styles: An analysis of the national comorbidity survey. *Psychiatry Research, 217*(3), 202–9. https://doi.org/10.1016/j.psychres.2014.03.019

Tutton, M., & McKenzie-Sutter, H. (2020, May 20). Warning of N.S. mass shooter's paranoia, guns, prior abuse in warrant. *Canada's National Observer*. https://www.nationalobserver.com/2020/05/20/news/warning-ns-mass-shooters-paranoia-guns-prior-abuse-warrant

Van Brero, P. C. J. (1897). Einiges uber die Geisteskrankenheiten der Bevolkerung des Malayschen Archipels [Some information about the mental illnesses of the population of the Malayan archipelago]. *Allgemeine Zeitschrift Fur Psychiatrie, 53*, 25–78.

Index

Page numbers in **bold** denote illustrations, figures, and tables.

www.ingramcontent.com/pod-product-compliance
Lightning Source LLC
Chambersburg PA
CBHW062115040426
42336CB00041B/1070
* 9 7 8 1 4 8 7 5 4 2 7 8 8 *